Higher Education by

Faculty in higher education are disciplinary experts, but they seldom receive formal training in teaching. *Higher Education by Design* uses the principles of design thinking to bridge this gap through practical examples and step-by-step instructions based on educational theory and best practices in pedagogical and curricular development. This book offers practical advice for effective teaching and instruction, interdisciplinary curricular collaborations, writing course syllabi, creating course outcomes and objectives, planning assessments, and building curricular content. Whether you are a seasoned professor or new instructor, the strategies in this book can improve your practice as an educator.

Bruce M. Mackh is Chair of Liberal Arts and Sciences at Rocky Mountain College of Art + Design, USA.

Higher Education by Design

Best Practices for Curricular Planning and Instruction

Bruce M. Mackh

Routledge
Taylor & Francis Group

NEW YORK AND LONDON

First published 2018
by Routledge
711 Third Avenue, New York, NY 10017

and by Routledge
2 Park Square, Milton Park, Abingdon, Oxon, OX14 4RN

Routledge is an imprint of the Taylor & Francis Group, an informa business

Library of Congress Cataloging-in-Publication Data
A catalog record for this book has been requested

ISBN: 978-0-8153-5416-1 (hbk)
ISBN: 978-0-8153-5418-5 (pbk)
ISBN: 978-1-351-13371-5 (ebk)

Typeset in Perpetua
by Apex CoVantage, LLC

Visit the eResources: www.routledge.com/9780815354185

Contents

Figures

Preface

We human beings possess a marked tendency to divide ourselves into groups. In academia, these distinctions frequently involve our professional output, such as whether we consider ourselves to be researchers or creative practitioners. However, we could accurately claim that all of us who teach in higher education share both traits since we utilize both research and creativity in the ways we develop and teach our courses.

Creativity is, in fact, a trait shared by all human beings, sometimes manifested in how we respond to problems. Psychological researchers Jacob Getzels and Mihaly Csikszentmihalyi[1] conducted an experiment in which they asked a group of students to create an artwork using a number of objects displayed on a table. They observed that these artists approached their task in two ways. The "problem solvers" spent a few minutes examining the objects, using the remainder of the allotted time to build and refine their artworks. The "problem finders," on the other hand, spent much more time rearranging and selecting the objects, often rejecting initial efforts and returning to the collection of objects to begin again. Once they arrived at a decision, however, they required only a few minutes to build their artworks. At the end of the session, the problem finders' works were judged to be more creative than those produced by their problem-solving peers. Furthermore, the longitudinal study of these students revealed that the problem-finding approach to the experiment's task strongly correlated with students' eventual career success.

Realistically, everyone is a problem solver because we solve problems every day. However, this is usually reactive—we encounter a problem and take steps to find a solution. Problem *finding*, though, is proactive—action originates with the problem finder, who initiates a process of change. Innovators and visionaries like Henry Ford or Steve Jobs exemplify this trait. Each identified a need and took steps to build a solution before anyone knew a problem even existed. Henry Ford didn't invent the automobile—he found a way to produce them faster and more affordably, consequently solving many longstanding urban problems related to equine transportation. Likewise, Steve Jobs didn't invent the computer—he and Steve Wozniak invented a computer that an average person could both use and afford.

Both problem finding and problem solving require an aptitude for analytical thought. Problem solvers analyze the problem at hand and apply this analysis to a proposed solution. Problem finders, however, constantly see the world through an analytical lens, thinking critically about everything they encounter. They often envision a better way to do things expressed through phrases like, "What if we . . ." or "Let's try . . ." They constantly ask themselves *why* something they observe might be so, to try to find the underlying causes of observed phenomena.

MY QUALIFICATIONS

This book arose from the fact that I am a problem finder. Even before I embarked upon a career in higher education, my previous employment demanded a highly analytical approach to handling complex policy documents in order to identify and address problems. This skill set followed me into my studies, causing me to analyze my own academic experiences, the instruction I received, and the systems in which it took place.

While I was the Director of the Mellon Research Project at the University of Michigan, I examined educational programs and policies at more than 40 different institutions of higher learning. Beyond the research I conducted, I gathered a vast store of observations about best practices in curriculum development and instruction, drawing upon examples of excellence as well as noting that most institutions maintain a conventional approach to this task. As the result of my consultancies and research, I have enjoyed the rare opportunity to speak to, observe, and study the work of more than 1,000 individuals in higher education, providing me with a body of experiential knowledge shared by few others. Therefore, I am a scholar of teaching and learning by training, through my professional research, and as the result of being a problem finder, all of which combined have prepared me to author this book, albeit through an admittedly nontraditional path.

PEDAGOGY AND TRADITION

Disciplinary contexts and course content drive most educators' decisions about instructional delivery. For example, philosophy, religious studies, and English often utilize discussion as their primary classroom activity. The sciences alternate between large-group lecture and small-group laboratory experiences. The arts generally involve hands-on learning, instructor demonstrations, and independent student work time. In every discipline, longstanding traditions and practices have shaped the classroom experience for decades, if not centuries. However, just because an instructional practice has existed for a very long time does not mean that it continues to be a *best* practice in higher education. I believe that we must continuously evaluate whether our instructional habits remain effective, moving beyond our acquired expertise within our subject to develop a better understanding of effective teaching.

Our colleges and universities appear to be timeless, yet this not true elsewhere. An axiom known as Moore's Law states that the processing speed of computers doubles every 2 years. We could make a parallel observation about business and industry, where rapid growth is the norm rather than the exception. These shifting realities should inform our curricular and pedagogical practices, yet higher education as a whole has changed little since the mid-20th century, despite the fact that the world surrounding us is dramatically different than it was in the era when our present systems were established.

I have observed that most faculty members (except for those who work in colleges of education) tend to be unaware of trends in educational theory and philosophy. Instead, we teach as we were taught, spending our professional development time on disciplinary pursuits rather than improvement to our pedagogical practice. This is normal and not at all surprising—it's what we've always done and what many of us expect to continue. Nevertheless, we should consider whether this is sufficient. Might there be a higher standard to which we can aspire? I believe there is, as I'll explain in the chapters that follow.

My sincere wish is that you will approach this book as you would a friendly conversation between colleagues. Through these pages, I address you—the reader—directly, sharing what I've learned about best practices in planning curriculum and delivering instruction in higher education. Rest assured that this is not at all an attempt to standardize faculty activities. You are most certainly free to use this information or not, or to make whatever changes you feel are appropriate to your individual teaching.

Please note that this book is in no way intended as a substitute for the excellent resources that university Centers for Teaching and Learning regularly provide for faculty, nor does it discount professional development opportunities within specific academic disciplines. However, I'd like to suggest that all of us working in academia can benefit by considering how we can grow as curriculum developers and educators, while also continuing to adhere to the norms and practices expected of us as disciplinarians.

I hope that you find this to be an informative and enjoyable journey.

A NOTE ABOUT STRUCTURE

Throughout this book, I'll provide concrete examples from a course I created called Design Thinking for Entrepreneurs, a general education course that employs an instructional model combining lecture, discussion, and collaborative projects. Readers will have an opportunity to create their own course components by using specific templates located throughout the chapters. A collection of resources is provided at www.routledge.com/9780815354185.

Each chapter includes a Design Connection that brings us back to the principles of design undergirding our preparation for teaching. Here, we'll pause for a moment of reflection, asking key questions about our purpose and motivation (identify/why are we doing this?), processes and ideas (ideate/how should we do this?) and plans for employing these ideas in our classrooms (implement/what will we actually do?), along with a reminder to continuously monitor our courses as we teach, gathering data about what works, what doesn't, and how we'll make changes the next time (iterate).

Finally, each chapter ends with a brief summary of the most important ideas we've covered, using a few concise bullet points for your continued reference.

Creating sound curriculum depends on our ability to connect the dots between theory, examples, and practical application. Undoubtedly, no single source could address the variety of disciplinary content or instructional models present across the entire university, but by following the sequence of explanation, examples, and application in this book, we should be able to navigate successfully through the process of course development and the improvement of our pedagogical practices regardless of the readers' particular disciplinary perspectives.

Note

[1] Getzels, J.W., and Csikszentmihalyi, M. *The Creative Vision: A Longitudinal Study of Problem Finding in Art*. (1976). New York, NY: John Wiley & Sons. Although this book is now more than four decades old, the findings it contains remain highly relevant to the discussion at hand and to understandings of creativity in general.

Design Connection

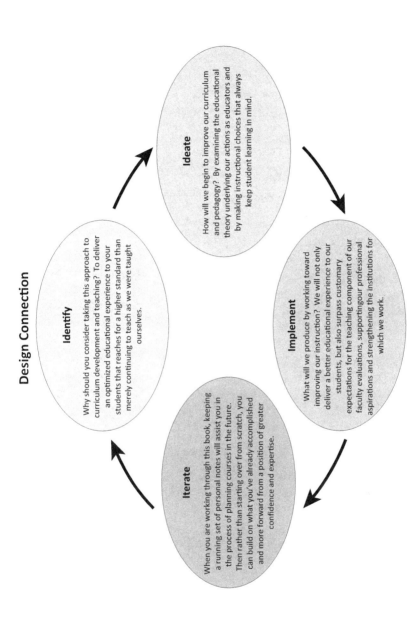

Identify

Why should you consider taking this approach to curriculum development and teaching? To deliver an optimized educational experience to your students that reaches for a higher standard than merely continuing to teach as we were taught ourselves.

Ideate

How will we begin to improve our curriculum and pedagogy? By examining the educational theory underlying our actions as educators and by making instructional choices that always keep student learning in mind.

Implement

What will we produce by working toward improving our instruction? We will not only deliver a better educational experience to our students, but also surpass customary expectations for the teaching component of our faculty evaluations, supporting our professional aspirations and strengthening the institutions for which we work.

Iterate

When you are working through this book, keeping a running set of personal notes will assist you in the process of planning courses in the future. Then rather than starting over from scratch, you can build on what you've already accomplished and more forward from a position of greater confidence and expertise.

FIGURE 0.1 Design Connection

eResources

There are eResources for this book that can be downloaded, printed, used to copy/paste text, and/or manipulated to suit your individualized use. You can access these downloads by visiting the book product page on our website, www.routledge.com/9780815354185, and clicking on the eResources tab.

ERESOURCES

- Figure 3.5 Learning Outcomes—Research and Planning Notes
- Figure 3.7 Outcomes and Objectives Planning Chart
- Figure 5.1 Semester Planning Grid
- Figure 7.1 Peer Evaluation of Project Group
- Figure 7.4 Job Shadow Experience Reflective Report
- Figure 7.5 Volunteer Experience Reflective Report
- Grade Calculation
- Rubric Template
- Pre-course Survey
- Post-course Survey
- Dimensions of Diversity Self-Assessment
- Pre-collaboration Interview Questionnaire
- Environmental Analysis
- Syllabus Build Tool

Chapter 1

Beginning With the End in Mind

CHAPTER SUMMARY

- Educational Philosophy
- Backwards Design: Beginning With the End in Mind
- Learning-Centric Teaching and Instructional Design
- Empathy, Definition, Ideation, and Iteration
- Where Next?
- The Design Process

Higher education is populated by dedicated professional educators who deliver a high-quality academic experience to their students. However, professional development activities related to teaching are usually limited to occasional workshops featuring a single skill, such as creating a syllabus, techniques for assessment, or new instructional technologies. Many of us attended required onboarding seminars for new faculty members that provided basic instruction in the teaching component of our jobs. Nevertheless, no matter how many workshops or seminars we attend, or how experienced we may be, it is not the same as undergoing a formal program of study into the art, science, practice, and skill of teaching.

Faculty members come to their positions as subject-matter experts, having earned the highest degrees available in their respective fields and achieving recognition as producers of new knowledge through research or contributors to culture through creative practice. In fact, these are standard criteria for virtually all faculty job postings. Members of the professorate continue their disciplinary activity throughout their professional lives, with an expectation that each person will make ongoing contributions to knowledge or culture.

Furthermore, all faculty members are educators because we teach students the essential skills and knowledge of our academic disciplines. Our achievements in research or creative activity strengthen this expertise, which we then bring to our classrooms. Professional service further supports our disciplines and our college or university, consequently enriching our teaching as well.

Traditional evaluative criteria for promotion and tenure generally split faculty activities into 40% for research, 40% for teaching, and 20% for professional service, but in actual practice, we often spend the majority of our time teaching or on related tasks such as course development, grading, and meeting with students. According to the National Study of Postsecondary Faculty (2003),[1] teaching and related tasks account for 62% of faculty members' time, with 18% spent on research and 20% on administrative or other tasks. All of these activities ought to work in concert, and all of them ultimately support the success of our alumni as well as contributing to knowledge and culture. Even when research is valued above all other faculty pursuits (which is especially evident at top-tier research universities), it also contributes to our graduates' success across disciplines, as shown in Figure 1.1.[2]

Research, teaching, and service each contribute to student learning and our graduates' eventual success, either directly or indirectly.

1. Research builds upon existing knowledge to create new learning.
2. Teaching improves and expands student learning.
3. Service translates learning into action that improves communities and citizens.

Isn't it curious, then, that we seldom undergo formal training in educational theory or in curricular and pedagogical development, despite the demonstrable importance of our responsibility to teach? Yet instead of the prerequisite study and certification required of many other educators, faculty members typically learn to teach by teaching, sometimes assisted by colleagues and mentors in our academic disciplines.

Speaking from my own experience, the only preparation I received for the first course I taught as a graduate instructor occurred when my academic advisor handed me a copy of the former instructor's syllabus. He answered my questions and dropped by my classroom on occasion, but for the most part, I was on my own. At the institution I attended for my doctoral studies, graduate instructors were first required to serve as teaching assistants, a task mainly involving taking attendance and grading papers for the instructor of

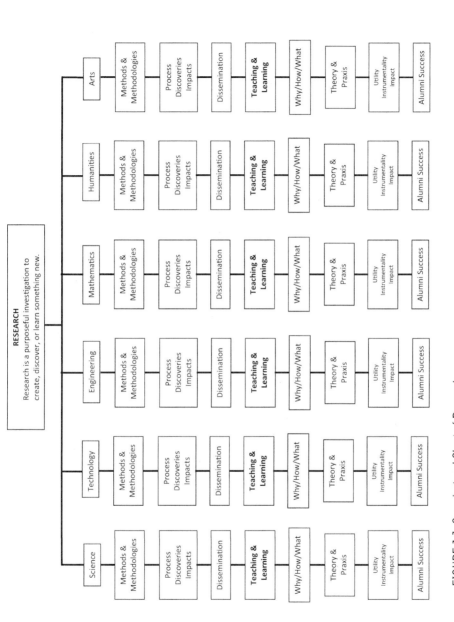

FIGURE 1.1 Organizatonal Chart of Research

record. Once we were given a teaching assignment of our own, a copy of the previous instructor's syllabus and perhaps some verbal advice were treated as sufficient preparation for independent teaching. I opted to take my training a step further by participating in a TEACH Fellowship, a competitive program offered through the university's Teaching, Learning, & Professional Development Center.[3] This yearlong experience included 18 hours of workshops, videotaped consultations, two midterm evaluations of teaching performance, completion of a teaching portfolio and curriculum design project. None of the other graduate instructors in my program chose to take this step, but I found it to be a valuable asset to my subsequent teaching both then and in my later faculty positions.

This book was written as a way to bridge the gap that I observed between the actual practice of teaching and the knowledge that can be gained through focused formal study. As a comparison, consumer electronics have advanced to such high levels that we can use them intuitively right out of the package. Even so, many of us have experienced moments of frustration where we can't make a device do what we want it to do, wishing it had come with a detailed user's manual. Author David Pogue and O'Reilly Media produce a series of publications in response to this need—the "Missing Manuals"—beginning with *Windows 2000 Pro: The Missing Manual* and most currently *Switching to the Mac: The Missing Manual, El Capitan Edition* (2016).[4] I'd like you to consider this book in the same spirit—to be the guide for teaching in higher education that most educators never received when we were given our first teaching assignments. The chapters that follow will help those at all levels of experience to design, develop, and deliver excellent educational content to their students.

EDUCATIONAL PHILOSOPHY

Much of what we do in our classrooms depends on how we view our role as instructors. You're probably familiar with the debate between an instructor's role as "a sage on the stage" or "a guide on the side." Some instructors remain firmly in the sage-on-the-stage camp, lecturing through every class period, while students listen attentively and take copious notes. Conversely, other instructors rarely lecture at all, allowing students to construct knowledge independently, intervening only when the student requests assistance.

This need not be an either/or proposition. Most courses utilize a variety of instructional strategies, including lecture, project-based learning, discussion, group activities, and more. We might visualize this as a dual continuum as illustrated by Figure 1.2: the more active the instructor, the less active the student; the more active the student, the less active the instructor.

Another common debate involves the philosophical orientation of the classroom toward an instructor-centered or student-centered model. An

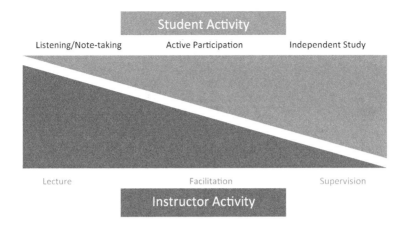

FIGURE 1.2 Student–Instructor Continuum

instructor-centered classroom operates under the assumption that the instructor possesses knowledge that she transmits to the students through a one-way communication. The instructor is responsible for his or her teaching, and students are responsible for their own learning. In contrast, a student-centered classroom places the student at the forefront of this equation, but this might raise troubling issues such as whether the student is a consumer of education and what responsibility the instructor shares in the student's acquisition of knowledge. For example, under a completely instructor-centered model, a student who fails a course is wholly responsible for his own failure. However, under a completely student-centered model, the instructor might be deemed to have failed to provide adequate instruction rather than the student failing to learn.

Taking a *learning-centered* approach avoids the problems of these extremes. In this model, students are neither passive recipients of transmitted knowledge, nor are they demanding clients. Likewise, the instructor is neither the font of all knowledge nor the students' servant. The focus of a learning-centered classroom is the subject matter of the course as it occurs within a specific disciplinary context, engaging both the student and the instructor as active participants. We might frame learning-centered education as a pedagogical triangle (see Figure 1.3), in which the student, instructor, and subject matter exist within a balanced yet dynamic relationship occurring in the context of a given academic discipline.

Therefore, this book adopts a learning-centered educational philosophy. The instructor's primary responsibility is to create and deliver a learning experience in which the student is an active participant, aligned with a particular academic discipline's norms and practices and shaped by the instructor's application of skill and knowledge in teaching.

5

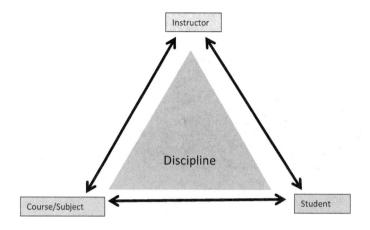

FIGURE 1.3 Pedagogical Triangle

BACKWARDS DESIGN: BEGINNING WITH THE END IN MIND

In his bestseller *Seven Habits of Highly Effective People*, author Stephen Covey recommends "Habit 2: Begin with the End in Mind."[5] Even though it's become somewhat cliché, this isn't just good advice for life—it's the first step toward planning and designing effective curriculum. Beginning with the end in mind is like planning an expedition: First, you choose the destination, then you plan how you'll get there.

In curriculum design, our destination depends on this question: What skills and knowledge should our students acquire by the time they graduate? Just as we can't take a road trip without first planning our route, we can't achieve the goal of producing well-educated graduates unless each course deliberately aligns with that goal, leading students step by step toward the excellence we want them to achieve. When applied to higher education, this is called *backwards design*.[6]

Before we go further, let's stop and consider *why* we're talking about this. In higher education, where colleges and universities have clearly defined educational missions, we want our students to do more than just memorize facts—we want them to become accomplished disciplinary practitioners who contribute to our areas of expertise and go on to lead successful, productive lives. We also want to enhance our institution's reputation for excellence in education and raise the profile of our college and its programs and departments. Therefore, the end we should keep in mind exists on multiple levels: in the outcomes we write that explain what our students must know and be able to do by the time they graduate; in the learning experiences we design that facilitate our students' successful attainment of these outcomes; and in the deepening of our knowledge of educational theory and philosophy that will allow us to improve in our instructional delivery and better fulfill our duty as educators.

Understandably, research and creative practice receive a great deal of emphasis as major contributors to our professional reputations and the status of the institutions where we teach, whereas excellence in teaching lacks comparable prestige. Nevertheless, the impact of our teaching extends far beyond the final exam, shaping our students' academic experience for good or ill. No matter how renowned we may be in our chosen fields, these accomplishments cannot benefit our students at all if we lack the ability to translate our disciplinary expertise into relevant and impactful instruction. Shouldn't we, therefore, devote at least as much passion, energy, and curiosity to our teaching as we do to our other disciplinary engagements?

Nothing prohibits us from continuing to teach as usual. Attempting to change our professorial habits is a far greater challenge, yet there is much to be gained in the attempt. Certainly, it can be awkward and frustrating to change longstanding habits, but by choosing to reach beyond what's comfortable to what's possible, we will benefit our students, our institutions, and ourselves as well.

LEARNING-CENTRIC TEACHING AND INSTRUCTIONAL DESIGN

Traditional approaches to teaching and learning focus on the subject-matter knowledge and expertise that an instructor conveys to his or her students. When we shift the emphasis to our students' learning, we must also enter into a mindset of innovation since we are diverging from long-established procedures and habits of mind in higher education.

Innovation exists within a three-part framework, represented in Figure 1.4.

Desirability is the human factor in innovation. The outcomes we seek through our teaching and curriculum design must be attractive and beneficial to our students and to the institution for which we work, but they must also be of personal benefit at some level. In other words, our efforts must lead to a course that students want to take, that our institution wants to offer, and that we want to teach.

Viability refers to the institutional framework within which our efforts occur. Our plans and goals must be compatible with the mission, vision, and values of our institutions. They must also align with existing policies, procedures, and administrative requirements in our departments, colleges, schools, and the institution at large. For example, a planned course relying on co-teaching will not be viable if one of the cooperating faculty member's home departments cannot

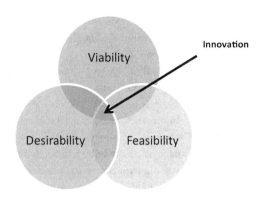

FIGURE 1.4 Design Venn—Innovation Is Here

provide a way for the instructor to receive credit for a course taught outside normal channels.

Feasibility is the third side of our triangle. Even when we can clearly envision what we hope to achieve and can prove it fits within our given institutional context, we must also be able to bring our vision to life. This involves financial resources, administrative support, faculty participation, availability of facilities, as well as things like scheduling and registration. For instance, if an elective course designed for students majoring in a particular discipline is scheduled at the same time as a course required for the major, students cannot enroll regardless of the careful planning and preparation that went into the course's creation.

EMPATHY, DEFINITION, IDEATION, AND ITERATION

Empathy is the cornerstone of innovation and the main component in the desirability of a product. Just think: Why do people stand in line for days before a new Apple product's launch? Because Apple has mastered the art of empathy. The company's focus on desirability leads to products that people are passionate about owning. This is atypical in most commercial ventures. For instance, I used to own a sedan that looked great on the outside, but it was so poorly designed internally that it took my mechanic 14 hours to dismantle the vehicle just to change a leaking $5 transmission gasket. He was so frustrated by the attempted repair that he refused to work on the car again. Apple's focus on customer experience translates into huge sales, whereas the automotive manufacturer's focus on making a visually attractive yet internally flawed product was ultimately self-destructive— production on that model ceased after just a few years.

Higher education, of course, doesn't operate under the same parameters as companies that produce telephones and automobiles, yet empathy-driven innovation occurs across a broad range of contexts. Service-based settings like health care, social services, and government agencies' attempts to envision the client's needs or wants result in a better user experience. Hospitals, for example, now allow patients to preregister for medical procedures, handling paperwork over the phone or online rather than making patients wait in line and then sit at a registrar's desk for an hour or more on the day of their procedure. Attention to the human element of a bureaucratic process increased efficiency and reduced stress for all concerned.

In this same way, higher education benefits from an empathy-driven perspective. Curriculum designed with the student in mind more fully aligns with a learning-centered model of education. In the field of design, this is known as user experience—a process built on empathy.

Learning-centered course design requires that we know our students as fully as possible. Those of us who have been teaching for many years know that students today are much different than we were ourselves, and they also differ from the students we may have taught early in our careers. Higher education itself has also changed, especially in terms of public perception, which directly impacts how our students view their educational experience.

In the not-so-distant past, a bachelor's degree in virtually any field offered sufficient proof that someone was well-equipped for professional-level employment because this credential was comparatively rare: Just 25% of the US population completed high school in 1940, and only 5% of the US population held a bachelor's degree or higher,[7] giving a college graduate a distinct edge in the job market. By 2015, however, 88% of the US population attained a high school diploma, and 33% earned a bachelor's degree or higher.[8] In other words, it's more common to hold a bachelor's degree today than it was to graduate from high school in 1940.

The increasing ubiquity of a college degree is exacerbated by the rising cost of higher education and by changing attitudes of parents, students, and legislators. Many students and their parents incur significant debt to finance the cost of a degree, all in the hope that the student will exit college with the ability to secure a well-paying job. Whether or not we educators know that the educational experiences our courses offer are intrinsically valuable, it is difficult for others to understand how they can be worth the expense when they can't see how the course will equip students with the means to earn a living.

We now face a much different set of cultural expectations for higher education than were prevalent when many current faculty members began their careers, and they differ greatly from the norms under which our present system of higher education arose during the last century. Not only has the perception of a college education as valuable for its own sake shifted to an expectation that earning a degree will prepare a student for a career, but our students themselves place less value on educational experiences when they cannot see how they might be personally relevant.

Educators, however, continue to believe that students should accept our disciplinary expertise as sufficient reason to trust that what we teach is important and expect students to make their own connections between classroom learning and their eventual careers. Empathy exercised within a learning-centered model of education challenges this traditional stance. For just a moment, let's put ourselves in the place of our students. Imagine you were told that you had to undertake mandatory professional development by completing a 3-credit hour course. Because you will not be reimbursed for tuition, you enroll in an online course through a public university, at a cost of $1,000. This is a significant expense, not to mention that you'll have to pay for books and materials on top of the tuition, increasing your cost by an additional $200. Now imagine that the course instructor never explains why this course is required and makes no connection to your professional development. Would you be frustrated and annoyed? Perhaps even resentful? I know I would.

When we imagine ourselves in a scenario such as the prior example, we can experience empathy for our students and, consequently, begin to approach our teaching from a more learning-centric model. If we were to benefit from the mandatory training in the previous example, we would need to know *why* it's important, *how* we could apply the course content to our professional lives, and *what* we were actually supposed to learn. This why, how, and what of instruction is essential. Should it be any different for our own students?

On a macro level, our course planning must consider why our students need to know the concepts we intend to teach, how we will convey this information to them, and what learning experiences and assessments will allow them to learn what we're teaching and let us measure their learning. This process encompasses all of the components we associate with course design: writing outcomes and objectives, textbook selection, creating assignments and assessments, and so on. As we work through these steps, we repeatedly engage empathy and definition on a micro level with each decision we make about the course. Why will this particular textbook best help my students to learn? How should I create this rubric to evaluate their group presentations? What should students be able to do by the time they take the final exam?

The first time we teach the course that we planned can serve as a prototype, allowing us to test our instructional strategies to determine whether students successfully acquired the skills and knowledge we intended to convey. Each time we teach the course thereafter is a new opportunity to refine our instructional methods. These iterations allow us to engage in a process of continuous growth, responding to developments in our disciplines, to shifts in culture, and to the fluctuations common to university life.

Our pursuit of pedagogical and curricular innovation also allows us to incorporate new best practices in teaching and instruction that we may not have attempted before. Cooperative learning, teamwork, student choice, engaged learning, experiential education, and many other strategies are possible beyond standard approaches such as lecture and discussion.

WHERE NEXT?

In the chapters that follow, we'll look at how to achieve this goal. Along the way, we must think through the steps that will allow our students to achieve the results we seek. How do we plan learning experiences? How should we design our instruction to help our students achieve these outcomes? How do we know if the students have actually learned anything in our classrooms? How can we use what we already do to create more effective curricula that also meet institutional and professional expectations?

First, we consider the norms and expectations of our disciplines at the programmatic level, writing outcomes that explain what we intend our students to know and be able to do upon graduation. Second, we create specific, measurable objectives for our courses, clearly defining what students must achieve by the course's completion. Third, we create tools to measure students' mastery of these objectives, designing assessment mechanisms aligned with our objectives and outcomes. Fourth, we create a plan of instruction, mapping out a week-by-week sequence ensuring that appropriate and effective student learning opportunities precede and support our assessments. Last, we select or develop instructional materials to use as we deliver instruction according to the course plan. This sequence is shown in Figure 1.5.

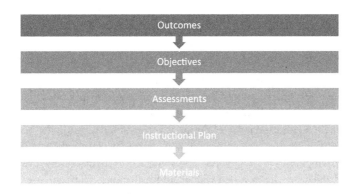

FIGURE 1.5 Course-Planning Flow Chart

This process reverses the way faculty usually plan a course. Many of us begin by selecting a good textbook. Then we map out a weekly schedule, writing quizzes and tests based on the readings and lectures we've planned. Once we've planned the bulk of the course, we look at the body of knowledge we intend to cover and write objectives based this plan. Only after everything else about the course has been set in place do we think about what students should have learned by the final exam.

However, if we begin with the end in mind, or design a course "backwards," we remain mindful of what students should learn in our course as well as what they must know and be able to do once they graduate. This not only allows us to create curriculum aligned from the first day of class to the last, but also from students' first day on campus to the moment they proudly walk across the stage to receive their diplomas.

THE DESIGN PROCESS

Our planning efforts align with the design process, but definitions of this activity are nearly as numerous as designers. Here we'll take a four-part approach to this important task and touch back to this model throughout the book.

1. *Identify:* Under a learning-centered philosophy of education, all of our decisions as educators must first consider our students' needs as learners, driven by the particular outcomes and objectives of our course. There-fore, everything we do must meet this crucial criterion: *How does this serve my students' learning needs in order for them to meet my course objectives and program outcomes?* Empathy must drive all of our decisions, considering our curriculum and teaching from our students' perspective. In product development, this is called User Experience Design (sometimes abbrevi-ated as UX)—the process of enhancing user satisfaction with a product by improving its usability or accessibility to provide a positive interaction with the product. In other words, it's about placing the user's needs first to make sure that their experience is the best it can be. We might also call this user-centric or human-centric design. In education, therefore, it comes down to empathizing with our students to identify their specif-ic needs for instruction, which then informs and shapes our choices in designing curriculum and delivering instruction.

2. *Ideate:* The ideation stage of design involves brainstorming the best way to meet the needs we've identified. This can be an extended cyclical process involving developing possible solutions, prototyping, testing, evaluation, and redevelopment until a viable and feasible possibility emerges.

3. *Implement:* Once we have developed a possible solution, we implement it in our classrooms and observe its results.

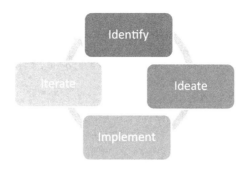

FIGURE 1.6 Design Cycle

4. *Iterate:* Each time we teach a course, we have the opportunity to begin again, to revisit the design process, and to make refinements and improvements that will further support student learning.

Although the design process has four parts, as seen in Figure 1.6, we'll primarily focus on identification and ideation because our goal is to create a course and be prepared to teach it successfully. Implementation occurs when you actually teach the course, and iteration doesn't happen until after you've taught the course for the first time and are ready to make changes based on your first attempt to improve it for the next time you teach.

Remember:

WHY: We want to design curriculum that fulfills our program goals, supports our university's mission, and produces graduates who are excellent in their academic fields.
HOW: By working step by step, beginning with the results we seek, and continuing through the construction of a fully developed, well-designed course.
WHAT: We will plan a course aligned with disciplinary norms and university requirements, and we will be prepared to improve our pedagogical practice.

Notes

[1] Flaherty, C. (April 9, 2014). So much to do, so little time. *Inside Higher Ed.* www.insidehighered.com/news/2014/04/09/research-shows-professors-work-long-hours-and-spend-much-day-meetings

[2] This chart is based on a synthesis of ideas found in:

Sinek, S. (2009). *Start With Why: How Great Leaders Inspire Everyone to Take Action.* New York: Portfolio/Penguin; and Walton, K. (1970). Categories of art. *Philosophical Review*, 79(3), 334–367.

[3] Texas Tech University. (n.d.). *Applying to TEACH*. Teaching, Learning, & Professional Development. www.depts.ttu.edu/tlpdc/Teach_Program/applytoteach.php

[4] O'Reilly. (n.d.). *Missing manuals*. O'Reilly Media Corporate Website. https://ssearch.oreilly.com/?i=1;q=missing+manual;q1=David+Pogue;q2=Books;x1=author;x-2=t1&act=fc_contenttype_Books

[5] Covey, S. (1989, 2016). *The seven habits of highly effective people, habit 2: Begin with the end in mind*. Franklin Covey. www.stephencovey.com/7habits/7habits-habit2.php

[6] McTighe, J., and Thomas, R. S. (2003). Backward design for forward action. *Educational Leadership*, 60(5), 52–55.

McTighe, J., and Wiggins, G. (2004). Understanding by Design: Professional Development Workbook. Alexandria, VA: ASCD.

[7] Ryan, C.L., and Siebens, J. (February 2012). *Educational Attainment in the United States: 2009*. United States Census Bureau. https://www.census.gov/prod/2012pubs/p20-566.pdf

[8] Ryan, C.L., and Bauman, K. (March 2016). *Educational Attainment in the United States: 2015*. United States Census Bureau. https://www.census.gov/content/dam/Census/library/publications/2016/demo/p20-578.pdf

Chapter 2

Understanding Educational Theory

CHAPTER SUMMARY

- Student Development Theory
- Related Theories
- Theories and Practices of Teaching and Learning
- Theories and Practices of Diversity, Equity, and Inclusion
- Rationale

As we discussed in Chapter 1, all faculty members, regardless of our primary academic discipline, are educators. However, few of us have specifically studied the ontologies and epistemologies of education, including study of educational or developmental psychology. These concepts are fundamental to understanding how our students think and learn. This chapter provides a basic overview, particularly with regard to young adults. Some of these theories are decades old, yet they remain staples of textbooks used in current educational psychology courses, such as the widely used Essentials of Educational Psychology (Ormond, 2014), among many other mainstays of teacher-training programs. We need not become experts on educational theory or developmental psychology, but gaining a working familiarity with these concepts can facilitate our understanding of why we should implement the approaches to teaching and learning presented in subsequent chapters.

Nearly everything we human beings do is supported by theory and philosophy, although many of us remain unaware of it. In higher education, our actions are particularly influenced by two branches of philosophy: ontology and epistemology.

To keep things simple, we'll define ontology as the study of the nature of being, which involves attempting to categorize and understand the kinds of things that exist. Epistemology is the study of knowledge, or as a professor under whom I studied for my PhD explained, it's "how we know what we know and why we know it."

Scholars are concerned with both of these philosophical concepts, but their applications across academic disciplines vary widely. Moreover, the more deeply we study any given discipline, the narrower our focus becomes. Once we reach the "terminal degree" stage, we've become super-specialists in just one knowledge area, understanding what exists within it and why this knowledge is important. In other words, we've mastered the ontology and epistemology of our disciplines. Therein lies our claim to disciplinary expertise. At this level of super-specialization, the ontologies and epistemologies of quantum physics would be self-evident to a quantum physicist, but they would be largely opaque to a political historian of Renaissance Italy. Likewise, the quantum physicist would lack sufficient understanding of the ontologies and epistemologies of historical study of the Italian Renaissance. We know what we know, but we don't know what other scholars know. Therefore, we gather together in colleges and universities so that collectively, we form a comprehensive assemblage of knowledge.

To better understand the ideas that support all of our work as educators, we'll take a brief look at a selection of relevant theories of education. Since our design process begins with understanding our students, we'll first consider some theories of student development.

STUDENT DEVELOPMENT THEORY

From approximately ages 18 to 26, college students undergo a period of intense intellectual, social, and emotional growth. They enter college as teenagers, but they leave as adults who are presumably ready to find their own way in the world. Theories related to human development occurring during this age range include student development theory, developmental psychology, and educational psychology.

Jean Piaget

Jean Piaget (1936) was the first psychologist to make a systematic study of cognitive development. His work disrupted longstanding beliefs that children were unable to answer questions correctly only because they lacked proper training. Piaget revealed that development progresses in discrete stages, influenced both by the growing maturity of children's brains and through environmental input. He proposed that human beings acquire and use knowledge according to "schemas," or mental maps about the world. For example, an adult would possess a schema for a basic task such as going to a movie: arrive at the theater, decide which movie to see, purchase a ticket, enter the theater, find a seat, wait for the lighting to dim, watch the coming attractions, and finally watch the movie. The environment of the theater, the progression of actions, and the experience as a whole would each be part of this schema. Young children have few schemas to explain the world around them, but these form as the child progresses toward adulthood.

Intellectual growth is a process of adapting to the world around us, and according to Piaget, it progresses through four distinct stages. First, infants begin life in the sensorimotor stage, marking a major developmental milestone when they are able to understand than an object hidden from view still exists (object permanence). Toddlers and very young children enter the preoperational stage, where they are able to think about things symbolically—a word or other symbol is understood to stand for the object itself. Older school-age children are in the concrete operational stage. They can think logically and work out problems mentally instead of having to solve them manually. For example, a child in the preoperational stage might not be able to associate the symbol "5" without counting the number on the fingers of her hand, but a child in the concrete operational stage can use the logical idea of "5" to perform mathematical calculations mentally. Piaget's last developmental stage is formal operations, lasting into adulthood. During this time, human beings can develop abstract concepts and logically test hypotheses (Piaget, 1936, 1957).[1]

Although we in higher education might presume that all of our students have achieved the "formal operations" stage of development, this may not actually be the case. Keating (1979)[2] found that between 40% and 60% of college-age students failed when attempting formal operation tasks. Dasen (1994)[3] found that only one-third of adults ever reached the formal operational stage. For those of us working in higher education, this means we would be wise to implement some of Piaget's recommendations for teaching an audience of learners in the concrete operations stage. Interestingly, these continue to exist among best practices in teaching and learning today. Figure 2.1 matches Piaget's recommendations in the left column with some higher educational applications on the right.

Piaget's theories remain a cornerstone of developmental psychology, although not uncontested. For example, Vygotsky (1934)[4] and Bruner (1957)[5] preferred to think of development as a continuous process and linked more closely with social interaction and language development. Nevertheless, Piaget's theories remain influential to the present day.

Psychosocial Theories

Psychosocial theories, such as the foundational ideas promoted by scholars such as Erik Erikson (1959)[6] view human development as a series of stages through which individuals experience changes in their thought processes, feelings,

17

Piaget	Higher Education
Focus on the process of learning, not only the end result.	Instruction in strategies for ideation (e.g., critical thinking, design thinking, lateral thinking); institution-wide emphasis on teaching students to become "lifelong learners" and to acquire critical thinking skills
Use active methods that allow students to discover or reconstruct knowledge.	Discussion groups (humanities); studio-based learning (the arts); laboratory requirements (the sciences)
Use both collaborative and individual activities.	Project-based learning; collaborative learning; independent research
Match tasks to the student's level of development.	Scaled courses of instruction with simpler content or tasks for freshmen, progressing in complexity to upper-class or graduate-level students
The role of the teacher should be that of a facilitator.	Student-centered pedagogies; flipped classrooms; online learning; independent study
Learning should be active, not passive.	Internships, co-op and practicum experiences; project-based and/or collaborative learning
Problem-solving skills must be discovered—they cannot be taught.	Hands-on, practical learning, including all of the above

FIGURE 2.1 Piaget and Higher Education

behavior, values, and the ways in which they relate to themselves and others. Erikson proposed that we can identify eight developmental stages, of which many undergraduates may still be in late adolescence and moving into early adulthood or beyond. Adolescence is marked by establishing one's identity, setting goals and finding one's purpose. Young adulthood involves developing lifelong relationships such as finding a life partner and making lasting adult friendships. These developmental stages also include the development of fidelity, which Erikson defines as the ability to accept and make commitments to others even when differences are recognized.

Arthur Chickering (1969)[7] built upon Erikson's theories, proposing seven "vectors" or non-sequential developmental tasks that all individuals work through in their journey toward adulthood. These include developing competence, managing emotions, moving through autonomy to independence, increasingly mature interpersonal relationships, establishing identity, establishing purpose, and emerging integrity.

Student development theories are evident in our everyday observations of our students, whom we know to be highly relational and intensely focused on interactions with their peers. The communities in which students choose to associate shape their collegiate experience significantly, such as co-curricular groups, roommates or housemates, romantic partners, or membership in athletic teams or performing arts organizations. This relational focus affects their performance in our classrooms. Knowing it's normal for our students to be preoccupied by human relationships, we can plan learning experiences that tap into this powerful motivator, such as collaborative learning and group projects. This knowledge also prepares us to exercise understanding and empathy when these relationships impinge on what we expect our students to accomplish. Mature adults learn how to manage their personal relationships and still perform their jobs adequately, but this is a developmental task most college-age students have not yet mastered.

Cognitive and Moral Development Theories

Cognitive and moral development theories focus on the ways people think. Lawrence Kohlberg's Theory of Moral Development[8] explained that human beings progress through six stages occurring at three levels. Elementary school students move through the preconventional level, characterized by obedience to rules set forth by authority figures. In the second stage, conventional morality, individuals follow social norms, first because they seek the approval of others and later because they accept the existence of law and order. The third stage involves learning that morality is a social contract and developing a genuine interest in the welfare of others, leading to an understanding of ethics as a set of universal principles such as justice, equality, and respect for human dignity.[9]

Perry's Theory of Intellectual and Ethical Development[10] also posits that individuals move through stages, beginning with Dualism, an interpretation of the world as governed by unqualified absolutes of right/wrong or good/bad. This is followed by Relativism, in which the individual recognizes multiplicity in the world and understands that all knowledge is contextual and relative, developing analytical thinking skills and the ability to evaluate different perspectives. Authority is seen as open to question, and individuals are able to evaluate their own thinking and to assess their own ideas and the ideas of others. Perry's model is widely accepted among student development professionals, who regularly see the important transition between Dualism and Relativism occurring among the college students with whom they work.

Students who are still in the dualism phase of their development are generally willing to accept whatever their professor has to say as unmitigated truth, since they retain a belief in authority figures. Students who have entered the phase of relativism, however, are more likely to evaluate an instructor's statements critically and to seek additional corroboration, input, or verification before accepting information as fact. They are more likely to question course content, to disagree with assigned readings, or fail to view the instructor as a source of consistently reliable information.

Instructors and university administrators often say they want to teach students how to think critically, which is the fundamental skill of relativism. Therefore, we cannot simultaneously become offended when we find ourselves on the receiving end of our students' questions. Our best course of action in those situations is to provide cogent, thorough, and convincing explanations, just as we would if we were challenged by a colleague or by one of our administrators.

Typology Theories

Typology theories focus on individual differences in how people view and relate to the world. These include, or are based on, Carl Jung's theory of psychological types.[11] Jung proposed that human beings primarily receive information through either their senses or through intuition. They make decisions based on either objective knowledge or subjective feelings. They also tend to be either introverted or extroverted. Based on these categories, Jung identified eight personality types, which were further developed by Katherine and Isabel Briggs who proposed that humans have four primary operational modes that govern their flow of energy, how they receive information, how they make decisions, and the everyday lifestyle they prefer (extravert/introvert, sensing/intuitive, thinking/feeling, judging/perceiving). These theories of personality types remain prevalent, often implemented through assessments such as the Myers–Briggs Type Indicator, a self-assessment tool that leads individuals to identify their dominant personality characteristics.[12]

Several other typology theories pertain directly to college-age individuals. For instance, Astin's Theory of Involvement states that the greater a student's involvement on campus, the more they will persist in their pursuit of academic success, influenced by their satisfaction with the campus environment: in other words, student involvement is directly linked to learning.[13] Typology theories and their applications can be useful, especially when advising students about their choice of major or career, but assessments such as the Myers–Briggs Type Indicator, although popular, might not be generally applicable to a classroom setting. Rather, it's wise for instructors to understand the following:

1. Students have many different personality types, which subsequently affect their learning in our classrooms.

2. Students' involvement on campus can help them to be more successful in their educational journey.
3. Students bring a number of preexisting cognitive and experiential conditions with them when they come to our classrooms, all of which affect their learning: past academic experience, family dynamics, personal preferences, and much more.
4. The institutional environment, the frequency and quality of our interactions with our students, and the character of students' individual effort will all affect their performance in our classrooms.

To be even more concise: These theories tell us that treating all students as though they were the same is mistaken. Just as you and I are different from one another, and both of us are different from our colleagues, our students come to us as individuals, not as a group. High-quality teaching and learning require that we offer the same kind of individual consideration to our students that we would wish for ourselves. Sometimes this includes offering the student additional help or tutoring when course content proves difficult, sometimes we need to exercise leniency and compassion, and sometimes the best choice is to stand firm on course policies. Speaking from my own experience, I've discovered that erring on the side of empathy is seldom wrong.

Person-Environment Theories

Person-environment theories consider the relationships that can be identified between the individual and the environment. John Dewey's *Education and Experience* (1938)[14] remains a seminal work in this field. Dewey proposed that the environment holds a profound and usually unacknowledged influence on the individual, leading to formation of habits that control our behavior and our thinking. Educators who shape the learning environment to encourage student participation increase engagement in the task of learning. Social environments shape human behavior by involving people in purposeful activities that entail specific consequences. Students must learn introspection and self-awareness to recognize the impact of the environment on their thinking and behavior, to evaluate this influence, and then to gain a measure of control over their thoughts and actions. Dewey was a strong supporter of experiential education, emphasizing the importance of learning by doing rather than by passive listening. He also proposed that educators must take into account the individual differences between their students, opposing traditional approaches to education in which a defined body of preordained knowledge was conveyed uniformly to all students. Sandeen (1991)[15] built upon Dewey's work, studying the environment of higher education, identifying the sources of influence on college students as including clarity and consistency of objectives; institutional size; curriculum, teaching, and evaluation; residence halls; faculty and administration; and friends, groups, and student culture.

The structures of higher education continue to operate on a model befitting the Industrial Age rather than the Information Age in which we now live, eloquently explained by Sir Ken Robinson.[16] Consider any large lecture section of a general education course, no matter what academic field: Students sit in an auditorium-style room, all facing a stage with a lectern, where the instructor stands and delivers course content by talking, sometimes assisted by visual aids. Students take notes as quickly as possible, and interaction between students and the instructor is minimal, perhaps limited to 5 minutes at the end of the class period where the instructor acknowledges a few students' questions. All students complete the same assigned readings, take the same standardized exams, and write the same papers. The traditional classroom is effectively a factory designed to convey knowledge provided by the instructor, ensuring uniformity. Dewey, among theorists for the past 80 years, says that we should question this model of instructional delivery. As Graham Gibbs (2013) reported,

> More than 700 studies confirmed that lectures are less effective than a wide range of methods for achieving almost every educational goal you can think of. Even for the straightforward objective of transmitting factual information, they are no better than a host of alternatives, including private reading. Moreover, lectures inspire students less than other methods, and lead to less study afterwards.[17]

We should question, then, why we continue to rely on a method of instruction that has soundly been proven to be less effective than other tools at our disposal. The work of Dewey, Robinson, and Sandeen, among many others, asks us to consider our practices as educators more thoughtfully.

RELATED THEORIES

Two further theoretical models factor significantly into discussions of educational theory.

Maslow's Hierarchy of Needs

Psychologist Abraham Maslow's "Hierarchy of Needs" (1954)[18] remains an influential explanation of human motivation. Maslow proposed that an individual's needs exist in two categories. Deficiency needs must be satisfied in order of importance, beginning with the most basic physiological needs: hunger, thirst, or other bodily comforts. Next, the need for safety and security must be met, followed by the need to belong and to be loved. Finally, an individual must meet their need for esteem: to achieve, to be competent, and to find approval and recognition. Once these deficiencies have been addressed, an individual can act upon growth needs. These include cognitive needs to know, understand, and explore, followed by an aesthetic need for symmetry, order, and beauty. An individual can then move toward self-actualization, or realizing one's potential, and finally to self-transcendence where the individual is able to connect to something beyond the self and help others to find self-fulfillment. These highest levels result in wisdom, or the ability to know what to do in virtually any situation.

Maslow's ideas have had a lasting impact on educational theory because they align with universal experiences and common sense, which is why we can easily see their impact on what we do in our classrooms. We know from our own experiences that being physically distressed—hungry, thirsty, exhausted, too hot or too cold, among other things—prevents us from learning or from doing our jobs well. We know that students who don't feel safe are too anxious to learn. We know that a sense of belonging and the presence of strong caring relationships in our lives help us to be more successful in whatever we choose to do. Every one of the levels of the hierarchy conveys something we've experienced ourselves. We should note that Maslow's work has been criticized as being too simplistic and subjective, with some theorists making a point that a person can become self-actualized even in poverty, danger, or in other conditions that prevent basic needs to be met prior to moving up through the hierarchy. Nevertheless, it is helpful to understand Maslow's concept in order to think about our students' needs from a more comprehensive and holistic perspective.

Bloom's Taxonomy

Next, Benjamin Bloom was an educational psychologist who created a well-known and widely accepted structure for classifying levels of knowledge in higher education, partially in response to his observation that university educators relied much more heavily on lecture and student memorization of information than on higher-order cognitive activities.

The taxonomy, originally produced in 1956, organized the goals of learning, ranging from the most basic to the most complex: Knowledge, Comprehension, Application, Analysis, Synthesis, and Evaluation. This structure has been widely used in education for decades, undergoing revision by Lorin Anderson and David Krathwohl[19] that changed the nouns to verbs, renamed Synthesis as Creating, and reordered the categories slightly.

Figure 2.2 shows the current form of the taxonomy.

Bloom observed that the majority of university courses featured the lower levels such as recalling facts, while students had fewer opportunities to demonstrate higher-order thinking found in the upper levels of this taxonomy. The lowest levels of knowledge exist at the base of the pyramid, ascending to the highest

23

FIGURE 2.2 Bloom's Taxonomy

LOWEST

- ▶ Remembering: define, duplicate, list, memorize, recall, repeat, reproduce, state
- ▶ Understanding: classify, describe, discuss, explain, identify, locate, recognize, report, select, translate, paraphrase
- ▶ Applying: choose, demonstrate, dramatize, employ, illustrate, interpret, operate, schedule, sketch, solve, use, write
- ▶ Analyzing: compare, contrast, criticize, differentiate, discriminate, distinguish, examine, experiment, question, test
- ▶ Evaluating: appraise, argue, defend, judge, select, support, value, evaluate
- ▶ Creating: assemble, compose, construct, create, design, develop, express, formulate

HIGHEST

FIGURE 2.3 Bloom's Verbs Hierarchy

levels at the top. Figure 2.3 organizes these terms in the opposite order, with the lowest stages of learning appearing first, then building to the highest levels at the opposite end of the continuum.

Bloom's taxonomy is foundational to the task of writing outcomes and objectives for student learning in higher education, so we'll revisit this topic in the chapters that follow.

When taken together, these educational theories help us to form a deeper understanding of the students we teach and the ways in which they learn. We enter into teaching with the presumption that students are adults such as ourselves, but in actuality, many of our students more closely fit the profile of a late adolescent, seeking to form their own identities and set individual goals. Now that we've prepared our thinking with this basic knowledge, let's consider some further theories of teaching and learning that are relevant to higher education.

THEORIES AND PRACTICES OF TEACHING AND LEARNING

Although there are far more theories of teaching and learning than a single chapter can contain, the following overview allows us to gain an appreciation for some of the theoretical basis for what we do, or can aspire to, as educators. These theories and practices are organized alphabetically, not chronologically or hierarchically.

Traditional approaches to education might be termed *instructivism,* rooted in John Locke's *Essay Concerning Human Understanding* (1689) in which Locke proposes that the human mind is a blank slate at birth, filled by accumulated experience. Education has, therefore, historically been predicated on the belief that students' minds are empty until filled by the instructor, who carefully plans and organizes a program of study on behalf of the learner. Learners must first become literate and gain a measure of self-discipline to pay attention to the information presented by the instructor and to remember concepts they do not understand, including rote memorization of information.[20] Clearly this is an instructor-centered model of learning, with the student remaining a passive recipient of transmitted knowledge. It's also the predominant model in settings from lecture halls to K–12 classrooms where students sit at individual desks facing the teacher and listen attentively to verbal instruction. Many other educational models have followed this longstanding norm, yet it remains preeminent nevertheless.

Andragogy

We usually refer to the work of teaching as *pedagogy*, a term derived from two Greek words: paîs, which means "child," and agōgós, which means "guide." However, in common usage, all teaching is included in the term *pedagogy,* regardless of the age of the student. In the 1980s, Malcolm Knowles[21] proposed that teaching adults was different than teaching children, an idea that lead to his theory of andragogy (andra- from the Greek word for man, $\dot{\alpha}\nu\delta\rho$-).

According to Knowles, adults are self-directed, and they expect to take responsibility for their own learning, which impacts four key considerations in the design of learning experiences for adults.

1. They want to know the rationale behind what they are asked to learn.
2. They learn best through experience.
3. They approach learning as problem solving.
4. They need to recognize the topic's immediate value.

Andragogy is a much different approach to teaching than traditional lecture-based college courses, where we presume the audience will accept any statement at face value as the wisdom of a qualified expert. Nevertheless, adult learners have moved beyond Perry's dualism phase to a position of relativism, able to think about their own thinking (metacognition) and to question statements that they would previously have accepted unthinkingly. Adults can think critically and trust their own judgments. They approach learning skeptically and want to know the reasons why the course content is important, prioritize and weigh the value of the information or skills being imparted through the course, and accept responsibility for their own learning.

In my experience, most colleagues expect their students to receive instruction at face value, believing that students should simply accept their authority because they are experts in their academic fields. Few faculty members welcome students' questions about why they're being asked to learn something, and they often dislike explaining how the course content will apply to real-world situations. Nevertheless, adult students learn better when they are empowered to understand the instructor's rationale and can see the relevance of what they're asked to learn.

Many faculty members I've encountered believe they need to "prepare students for the real world" by implementing strict classroom policies for missed class periods, late assignments, and so forth. Most adults, however, already know that punctuality, meeting deadlines, and absenteeism carry intrinsic penalties and rewards. They neither need nor appreciate inflexibility by an instructor who feels it is his or her bounden duty as an educator to teach life lessons on top of the stated curriculum.

A philosophy of andragogy leads instructors to treat their students more like peers than children who need instruction in behavioral standards. It also means understanding that older adult students may have encumbrances and responsibilities uncommon among typical 18- to 22-year-olds. Many adult learners have full-time jobs, young children, or aging parents in need of care. These nontraditional students greatly appreciate an instructor's flexibility, such as allowing additional time to complete assignments or granting an exception to an attendance policy. We will discuss these concepts at greater length in our discussion about classroom policies later in this book, but the philosophical foundation of all of these ideas exists in andragogy—treating our students as though they were responsible adults.

Cognitive Flexibility Theory

Not all knowledge comes neatly packaged into a single discipline or context. Spiro, Feltovich, and Coulson's Cognitive Flexibility Theory (1990)[22] examines the nature of the learning related to students' ability to transfer knowledge and skills beyond the context in which they were initially acquired. To allow students to most effectively acquire transferrable knowledge, instruction must impart information from multiple perspectives, incorporate diverse examples or case studies, and allow learners to develop their own representations of information to maximize their learning.

Our instruction should not only apply within the four walls of a classroom or lecture hall. Students must be able to implement their learning in external contexts or situations. Instructors can incorporate this knowledge into their planned teaching, providing explanations and examples of how course topics exist in external contexts and designing learning experiences that allow students to practice this cognitive flexibility. Perhaps the best demonstration of cognitive flexibility would be the 1980s television program *MacGyver*, in which the protagonist was a secret agent with an uncanny ability to use everyday objects resourcefully based on his advanced scientific knowledge. Instructors concerned with imparting cognitive flexibility to their students will incorporate activities that require students to apply knowledge or skills in unfamiliar or novel contexts. Our students aren't likely to emulate MacGuyver's ingenious uses for paper clips and duct tape, but we do need to prepare them to apply their classroom learning to situations we can't anticipate at the time of our instruction.

Constructivist Theory

Cognitive Flexibility Theory is based on a constructivist theory of learning (Jerome Bruner, 1960),[23] which states that learning is an active process through which learners build new knowledge upon the knowledge they've already acquired, standing in marked contrast to "instructivism." Piaget's idea of "schemas" is applicable in constructivism, as well. A student's schema, or mental model, serves as the basis for acquiring new knowledge. Earlier, we discussed the adult schema for going to a movie. Constructivist theory would explain that this schema could serve as the basis for a person familiar with going to a movie who is attending a live theatrical performance for the first time. Many aspects of the two activities are the same, but the variations found in the live performance would then expand the learner's schema to include greater knowledge of both types of experience.

Constructivism explains many aspects of human development. For instance, when my oldest son was a toddler, every round red object was a "ball," every four-legged creature was a "kitty," and all beverages were "juice." Building on this initial knowledge, he learned the differences between a ball, an apple, an orange, and other round objects. He learned that a horse is not just a really big kitty. And, of course, he learned that there are more things to drink from a cup than just juice and that they all have their own unique names and characteristics. All learning builds upon existing knowledge. Instructors cannot expect their students to retain new content unless they have some kind of existing schema upon which to build. It is up to us as instructors to deliberately make these connections for our students, and to anticipate their learning needs by first building the schemas that allow students to acquire the advanced knowledge we intend to teach. Some of this occurs naturally through the logical progression inherent in education. Other times, though, we must be more intentional and more empathetic than may come naturally. Our own schemas, especially within our academic disciplines, are highly developed and habitual, so we seldom stop to consider that our students do not possess similar mental models. Disciplinary vocabulary, for instance, seems quite obvious to us, but it can be as unfamiliar as a foreign language to our students. If

27

we first take the time to provide instruction in key disciplinary terminology, we help our students to build the basic knowledge upon which they can more successfully acquire the learning we seek to impart.

Criterion-Referenced Instruction

Robert Mager (1961)[24] developed a comprehensive framework for training programs that can serve as a functional model for instructional design. This follows four key steps.

1. Analyze the goal or task to identify specifically what students should learn.
2. Determine performance objectives that specify the outcomes students must demonstrate and criteria by which these will be evaluated.
3. Design evaluation mechanisms for student learning of the knowledge and skills specified in the outcomes and objectives of the course.
4. Develop learning modules aligned with specific outcomes and objectives.

This approach to educational design is fundamental to this book and to achieving excellence in teaching. The four principles seem quite obvious, yet many faculty members do not systematically work through them prior to teaching a course, relying instead on their own expert knowledge and the familiar structures endemic to higher education. Unfortunately, this can result in disorganization, excessive subjectivity in grading, and increased likelihood that important course content might not be presented before the end of the course.

Design-Based Research

The idea of design-based research (DBR)[25] originated as early as 1992 in the work of Brown and Collins, among others, later expanded by the Design-Based Research Collective (2002). As the name suggests, it incorporates key principles of the design process, which involves an ongoing cycle of ideation, implementation, evaluation, and revision.

DBR is more closely aligned with the development of theories and processes for education than specific instructional methods, bridging the gap between theory and practice and attempting to create generalizable principles upon which sound actions may be built. As we work to design our courses, each of us utilizes DBR, although perhaps informally or unintentionally. We have an idea for a new course. We teach the course. As we teach, we notice what works and what should be changed. Then we teach it again, implementing the changes we made, which begins the cycle yet again. Applying DBR means that we not only make observations about our own courses, but we thoughtfully apply educational theory to our actions as instructors, and we also share our own learning about curricular and pedagogical design with others.

Experiential Learning

Carl Rogers (1969, 1994)[26] identified two types of learning: cognitive learning, which he considered to be meaningless, such as rote memorization of vocabulary words or multiplication tables, and experiential learning, which addresses the needs and wants of the learner. Experiential learning is self-initiated, involves the learner personally, is evaluated by the learner (not the instructor), and holds pervasive effects on the learner. The instructor's role is that of a facilitator, which involves five actions.

1. Establish a positive climate for learning.
2. Clarify the purpose for the learner.
3. Organize learning resources and make them available to students.
4. Balance the emotional and intellectual aspects of the learning experience.
5. Share thoughts and feelings with students without dominating their learning experience.

Rogers states that students must participate completely in the learning process and must have control over its nature and direction. Learning is most significant when it directly confronts genuine social, practical, personal, or research problems. Students should be the primary evaluators of their own learning, as well as assessing their own progress and success. Further, they should be assisted in learning how to learn and increasing their openness to change.

Rogers' views align well with the principles of andragogy and other educational theories pertaining to adult learners. By implementing the five instructor actions listed in the preceding paragraph, we can increase student engagement—frequently listed prominently among universities' priorities—which then produces better learning experiences for our students. As with andragogy, however, this runs contrary to standard operating procedures for higher education, which rely on the delivery of instructional content that Rogers identified as "cognitive learning," expecting students to assimilate information disassociated from its application.

Heutagogy and Digigogy

If the term pedagogy is inclusive of all teaching, and andragogy is teaching tailored to the identified needs of adult learners, heutagogy is an instructional methodology for facilitating self-directed learning. This term, coined by Steward Hase and Chris Kenyon (2000),[27] is particularly applicable to 21st century educational trends. Kevin Carey's *The End of College* (2015)[28] describes a future in which traditional collegiate systems will cease to exist, replaced by self-directed, mostly online, learning that Carey terms "The University of Everywhere."

Heutagogy takes andragogy a step further, moving beyond problem solving to proactivity. It also includes an emphasis on capability, active learning, reflection, and experiential learning. Instructors taking a heutagogical approach to teaching provide a selection of tasks and learning materials to their students, with which the students structure their own learning around critical questions or issues, determining what is personally relevant and then working with the instructor to select further readings and appropriate assessments. These assessments are also part of the learning experience, not simply measures of knowledge acquisition. Heutagogy strives to develop the learner's capability and skill to produce graduates who are not only competent, but prepared are to cope with a rapidly changing world.

Digigogy, on the other hand, refers to the methods of instruction employed in online learning environments, including growing emphasis on instructional delivery through cell phones rather than desktop or laptop computers, enabling individuals in remote areas unprecedented access to educational opportunities. Educators can access a wealth of resources for creating engaging online course content; however, just because a course is offered online does not mean that it is actually heutagogical or even truly self-directed. The more structured the course content, the more traditional it is in terms of its approach, even if students have freedom of choice as to when to view the lectures or contribute to online discussions. The model in Carey's *The End of College* relies more on heutagogy than digigogy, in that he envisions students creating their own course of study by choosing among a virtually unlimited selection of online content from many different providers. Heutagogy is necessarily learner driven, whereas digigogy is not.

Employing heutagogy can be unnerving for instructors who are accustomed to retaining full control over their students' learning experiences since it puts students squarely in the driver's seat. Nevertheless, this trend is worth exploring. Universities that offer the option of a self-designed major, for example, tap into this instructional model, such as the University of Alabama's New College. At Canada's Open University, students choose a faculty mentor, and together they design a program of study, including selected readings centered on a student-generated question, followed by a comprehensive project demonstrating the student's learning, presented to the university community at the conclusion of the student's course of study. Although this is a radical departure from the norms and traditions of higher education, it holds great promise for the future, moving well beyond the one-size-fits-all approach to education that has been prevalent for centuries.

Problem-Based Learning

Problem-based learning is both an instructional method and an educational theory, based on creating active, hands-on classroom experiences that promote engaged learning (Woods et al., 2003).[29] As the name suggests, students must work to find a solution to a problem, usually linked to a real-world situation. Problems are either selected by the instructor or discovered by the students, depending on the course. They can be well-defined, especially in courses offered at the freshman or sophomore levels, but they can range up to "messy" or very complex issues. The instructor is a guide, mentor, and facilitator. Students may work alone or in collaborative groups, varied by course or subject area.

Problem-based learning presents natural opportunities to form partnerships with local organizations, allowing students to gain firsthand experience in the world outside of the classroom as they attempt to address genuine problems. It is a relatively uncomplicated first step into student-directed learning, making it a good choice for instructors who heretofore have not ventured beyond lectures. As an example, in my Marketing and Promotions course, students were partnered with a local arts organization and given the task of designing its new social media campaign. By the end of the course, they acquired real-world hands-on experience in the professional sector, and the organization had a successful marketing strategy that proved to be quite beneficial. I monitored the students' activities, communicating frequently with the organization's director to make sure that things were progressing smoothly. Our class periods included direct instruction, but they also allowed time to discuss the students' work with the organization and the progress they were making with the campaign. Facilitating this process required as much of my energies as planning and delivering lengthy lectures, but the results were much more satisfying to everyone involved.

Situated Learning

Jean Lave and Etienne Wenger (1991)[30] argue that learning is a process of participation situated in communities of practitioners. New learners engage in "legitimate peripheral participation" until they become assimilated into the community, with mastery of knowledge occurring when an individual achieves full participation in the socio-cultural practices of the community. Educational organizations are also social institutions, within which students must learn to participate according to specific norms befitting this society. This becomes evident when we consider the structure of higher education itself: New students are outsiders who must learn the social norms and practices of the educational community. Professors are those who have mastered the knowledge of the community and have achieved full participation.

Although we can see how situated learning functions, traditional educational practices tend to decontextualize knowledge, presenting it apart from its legitimate situations. We learn about the ecosystem of a rainforest in a lecture hall, not an Amazonian village. We learn about systems of government in a classroom, not in the halls of Congress. In contrast, situated learning takes place in the same context in which it is applied. According to Lave and Wenger, learning should not simply entail the transmission of abstract and decontextualized knowledge from the instructor to the student, but should be a social process through which knowledge is co-constructed, embedded in a specific context and within a unique social and physical environment. Field-based learning, apprenticeships, co-op, practicum, and internship experiences all offer opportunities for situated learning.

As with constructivist theory, andragogy, and other learning theories we've examined thus far, situated learning involves a move away from the lecture hall and toward more engaging methods of instructional delivery that allow students to make knowledge explicit and concrete rather than remaining in the abstract. The problem-based learning in my Marketing and Promotions course could also be identified as situated learning, since students actively engaged in a real-world workplace and participated in the same type of task they would be expected to do as employees of the organization.

Systems Thinking

Based on the recognition that the world itself is a complex system, systems thinking promotes understanding of the interconnected nature of a whole rather than examination of its diverse parts (Meadows, 2009).[31] For example, instead of taking separate courses in urban architecture, city planning, urban sociology, municipal water systems, and so on, a systems-thinking approach would combine all of these subsystems into a larger and more comprehensive study of a city. Natural phenomena, too, can be seen as complex systems such as climate change or the human circulatory system. Study of interconnected components and the relationships between them is the heart of a systems-thinking approach to education.

Systems thinking is included in this list of theories because it is the approach applied to the design of this book itself. To a lesser extent, all instructors should be cognizant of how a given course fits into the overall system of their students' educational experience as well as its relevance to their eventual professional careers. This information should be communicated to students from the first day of class, explaining why the course is of value, how it will apply to further study or professional engagement, and what connections and relationships the course bears to other courses or contexts.

THEORIES AND PRACTICES OF DIVERSITY, EQUITY, AND INCLUSION

The movement beyond oppressive socio-political systems and practices in the United States ranks high among the most significant developments of the past 100 years. Cultural shifts including women's suffrage in the early 1900s and the changing role of women in the workforce during and after World War II, the civil rights movement of the 1960s, and activism by the LGBTQQIP2SAA[32] community up to and including the US Supreme Court's 2015 decision in favor of marriage equality have fundamentally changed the character of our society. This is most certainly not to say that we no longer experience problems with sexism, racism, homophobia, or a plethora of other forms of prejudice and hate. Rather, our society has become increasing aware of the destructive influence of systematic exclusion and oppression, and we have begun to reject the notion that prejudice is inevitable or acceptable. By no means have we arrived at a truly equitable, just, or inclusive civilization. But many of those who work in higher education embrace this goal as a driving force behind organizational, programmatic, and individual choices as educators.

Critical Theory

These sweeping social changes were fueled, at least in part, by the growth of critical theory. Beginning with the Frankfurt School in the 1930s, theorists such as Max Horkheimer, Herbert Marcuse, Theodor Adorno, Water Benjamin, Erich Fromm, and Jurgen Habermas challenged Enlightenment-era beliefs that knowledge is objective and discoverable, existing apart from an individual knower. Instead, we now view knowledge as contingent upon specific socio-historical contexts and further influenced by individuals' values and beliefs. We have begun to accept that many views can coexist simultaneously rather than insisting that our particular viewpoint is the only "right" way to interpret information. Textbooks, for example, were once widely accepted as neutral, objective, and reliable tools for educating students because they convey provable facts. Critical theory revealed that the authors' and publishers' decisions of *which* facts to include and exclude from the text, and the manner in which the book's content is presented, implicitly communicate attitudes and ideals about what is important and what is not, all conducted under the guise of factual objectivity.

Bias and Privilege

No social institution is immune from intrinsic bias, either in its history or its present practices. Privilege—the unearned, unasked for, often invisible benefits given to some—and oppression—discrimination of one social group by another backed by institutional policy—continue to be widespread. Our colleges and universities work to promote diversity, equity, and inclusion, employing comprehensive efforts to identify, overcome, and eliminate exclusionary systems and practices. Yet thus far, the results fail to reach our aspirations.

Perhaps nowhere is this more evident than in the demographic composition of our faculties and student bodies. Data from the National Center for Education Statistics (www.nces.ed.gov) and the US Census Bureau (www.census.gov) illustrate differences in representation among four demographic categories (White, Black, Hispanic, and Asian—the descriptors used by the two government agencies)[33] for full-time faculty, undergraduate students, and the US population as a whole. Of course, race is only one analytical dimension among many that could be considered, yet the findings of this cursory investigation are enlightening nonetheless. Whites comprise 62% of the general population, but 78% of the faculty, whereas 18% of the general population identifies as Hispanic but hold only 4% of faculty positions. Blacks exemplify similarly unfavorable disparities, at 13% of the general population and only 6% of the faculty. We could make similarly startling representations of other demographic categories such as religion, gender and sexual orientation, ethnicity, or socio-economic factors, all leading to the conclusion that White, Christian,[34] heterosexual, relatively affluent individuals of European descent represent the majority of persons involved in US higher educational institutions. Admittedly, I fall into this category myself, as do most of my colleagues.

Despite ongoing efforts to promote diversity among faculty and students, including increasing scrutiny for hidden bias in our institutional policies and practices for hiring and admissions, many of our systems remain inequitable. Much remains to be done before higher education can live up to its potential as a positive force for promoting diversity, increasing equity, and truly helping all persons to achieve their potential. Our examination of educational theory, therefore, should also be informed by the present reality in which we attempt to recognize the inherent bias of the systems in which we live and work as well as the influence of our own attitudes and assumptions.

The climate for diversity varies greatly between our higher educational institutions, influenced by four key factors. Our institutions' historical track record of inclusion or exclusion of racial or ethnic groups, their present levels of representation of diverse groups, faculty and student attitudes, perceptions, and beliefs about diversity, and the patterns of interaction between racial and ethnic groups on campus each have an impact on an institution's diversity climate, as shown in Figure 2.4.[35] We cannot control our histories or legacies, but we can work toward increasing our demographic range, working to change our value structures, and promoting positive interactions among campus groups.

FIGURE 2.4 Diversity Climate

Individual Attitudes

Since the emphasis of this book is on the choices we make as individual instructors with regard to our curriculum and instruction, we will shift our focus from the inequities that are still present in society and in our higher educational institutions to steps we can take as educators. Each of us has considerable power to make a positive difference in the lives of others through our personal and professional actions, but to do so, we must first become aware of our own hidden biases through reflective self-analysis.

Most conscientious educators strive to be open-minded, inclusive, and supportive of diversity, yet each of us harbors hidden preferences and biases of which we may not be aware. We humans are especially good at passing judgment on one another, most of which occurs below the level of consciousness. This ability had survival value for early humans, where instantly distinguishing between friend and foe, or telling the difference between members of one's own group and "outsiders" was sometimes a matter of life and death. Daniel Kahneman, author of *Thinking, Fast and Slow* (2011), explains that our brains have two systems for cognitive functioning. System 1 operates automatically and extremely quickly, capable of processing about 11 million bits of information per second, nearly all of which occurs outside of conscious awareness.[36] We rely on our System 1 responses for driving a car, for example, a task that demands we make up to 200 decisions per mile,[37] nearly all of which depend on our unconscious, automatic capabilities. We fluently receive, process, categorize, and act upon incoming sensory information, handled with ease by our brains' powerful System 1. Conscious processing, on the other hand, occurs in System 2, which works at a much slower rate. We depend on System 2 for tasks that require concentration such as conducting research, assembling a newly purchased piece of furniture, or preparing a tax return. Active learning engages System 2, whereas prior knowledge occupies

System 1. I know that the product of 4 and 6 is 24 without engaging in conscious thought because this knowledge is instantly available via my brain's System 1, but if I were to attempt to convert US dollars to British pounds at the present rate of exchange rate, I would need to engage System 2 and actively concentrate on finding an answer.

We continuously acquire information about the world through multiple channels: our personal experiences, our family and upbringing, the kind and quality of our education, our existence with in a particular socio-cultural context, environmental factors, and our lifelong exposure to media, among others. Each of these causes us to form implicit associations occurring below the level of conscious thought, which instantly transpire through System 1. Such associations are helpful when they tell us to step on our car's brakes when the stop light turns red, but when they create unconscious bias, our implicit knowledge doesn't serve us as well. Furthermore, we tend to create broad categories and generalizations out of this information. If someone was bitten by a Cocker Spaniel as a child, she may well develop a lifelong aversion to all dogs of this breed. Likewise, the identities we perceive in others, including ethnicity, gender, race, age, and any number of other factors will necessarily affect our attitudes toward the people we encounter, but because they are deeply embedded in System 1, we usually remain unaware of their existence or influence. Even those of us who genuinely strive to value inclusivity, open-mindedness, and diversity cannot help but harbor these invisible biases.

Our work toward a more just and equitable world must, therefore, begin with ourselves, attempting to recognize and change our implicit biases. Each time we successfully question our underlying assumptions or work to alter an ingrained behavior, we remove an invisible bar in the cage that imprisons us, preventing us from truly living our conscious values. Harvard University's "Project Implicit" offers a series of free online Implicit Associations Tests that can reveal hidden bias related to sexuality (gay/straight), disability, gender and career, gender and science, age, weight, skin tone, Arab/Muslim, Asian, Native American, and race (Black/White).[38] If you've never completed one of these surveys, I recommend the experience, even though it's disturbing or disappointing to learn that we're not as open-minded as we'd formerly believed ourselves to be.

Implicit preferences are not harmful in their own right, as long as we do not act negatively upon them. They can also change over time. We might compare this to our aesthetic preferences. Most of us naturally prefer or dislike certain types of music, genres of literature, or foods and beverages. However, these preferences can change when we learn more about something that we formerly disliked. For example, most of us can remember a time when we didn't enjoy something like jazz music, or mystery novels, or coffee. As we experience something repeatedly over time or learn more about them, such as taking a college course about jazz, our affinity grows. We might still like Led Zeppelin better than Wynton

Marsalis, but we can understand and appreciate a greater variety of musical forms by becoming more familiar with them. Similarly, our political views or religious beliefs may change over time as the result of our experiences, education, and relationships. No one is predestined to hold one set of beliefs, tastes, or preferences forever, which (in my opinion) is a very good thing. I can only speak for myself, but I know that I am not the same person I was 20 years ago. I'd like to think that the transformations I've undergone have caused me to be more ethical, compassionate, open-minded, and receptive to new experiences and ideas. The same can be true of us all.

Dimensions of Diversity

Since understanding is the foundation of empathy and compassion, achieving greater knowledge of others hinges upon getting to know them as whole human beings rather than only by name and appearance. When we speak of diversity, equity, and inclusion, the conversation generally relates to groups or individuals who have experienced negative treatment based on one or more identifying characteristics. Yet each of our identities is comprised of multiple factors, not only our race, gender, sexual orientation, or ethnicity, but characteristics such as income level, occupation, marital status, and others. We might organize these identities in four dimensions: personality, internal, external, and institutional.

A model of diversity in higher education based on these four dimensions, adapted from Gardenswartz and Rowe (2003, partially based on Loden and Rosener, 1991) appears in Figure 2.5.

Any one of these dimensions can place an individual into a minority group or among a population that is subject to prejudice or condemnation by others who hold membership in a more dominant group. We tend to equate "diversity" with internal factors such as race, ethnicity, physical ability, age, gender, and/or sexual orientation. However, external factors can also exert significant influence on an individual's life. These 24 dimensions affect everyone to varying degrees, depending on a complex array of circumstantial, environmental, and associative factors.

Discrimination, just like diversity, takes many guises, both covert and overt. Nearly everyone has been on the receiving end of another person's unfair judgment based on generalizations, prejudice, or preconceptions. This can even involve judgments based on our disciplinary affiliation, academic rank, or others' opinion of the institution where we work. By no means should this imply that all forms of discrimination are equally harmful—we cannot draw a parallel between disciplinary stereotypes and systematic racism, for example—but it's unproductive to create a rank order of the ways in which we humans hurt one another based on prejudicial perceptions of our identities. Our emphasis should not be to say, "My suffering is worse than your suffering," but to engage in empathy, saying, "I can understand something of how you're feeling because I have

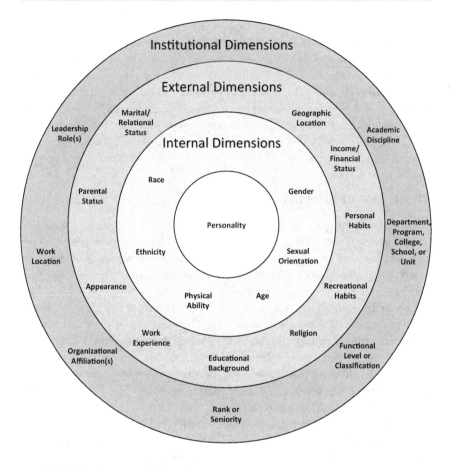

FIGURE 2.5 Dimensions of Diversity

also suffered discrimination, even though it was different from the situation you face." The points that divide us can also be points of connection, depending on the worldview we choose to employ. I cannot truly know what it is to be Black, or female, or transgender, or Muslim, or Hispanic. Nevertheless, I can draw upon my own experiences as the recipient of other forms of prejudice to empathize with those who have undergone discrimination, to advocate for diversity, equity, and inclusion, and to practice these core values in my classroom.

It's easy to make a philosophical argument that all discrimination is wrong. It's much more difficult when we're faced with so many different manifestations of discrimination, or when individuals exhibit multiple dimensions of diversity that combine to make their lives extraordinarily difficult. Experiencing discrimination based on things we can change, such as the place where we live, is quite different than the impact of factors that are beyond our control such as race, age, or ethnicity. However, no matter why it occurs, how it is exhibited, or what has happened, discrimination is always wrong. We will not eradicate this evil until we have achieved its complete absence—becoming fully diverse, equitable, and inclusive.

Heightened awareness of the incredible complexity of diversity should inform our decisions as educators, causing us to be sensitive to our students' multifaceted identities and to maintain awareness of how our own implicit and explicit biases affect our actions. Designing curriculum with diversity, equity, and inclusion in mind takes this personal awareness a step further, providing opportunities to engage in critical thinking about how our disciplines intersect with these values. We must move beyond longstanding "stale, pale, male"[39] disciplinary perspectives by implementing purposefully designed, aesthetic, creative communication in/through/with/about our academic disciplines that motivates students to develop critical consciousness, builds community, and inspires them to work toward a more just society and a better world for future generations.

RATIONALE

The purpose of presenting all of this background information is to provide the readers of this book with a means of learning more about how our student learn and to increase their awareness of how institutional climate and personal attitudes toward dimensions of identity can influence our decisions as educators. Then we will be better able to subsequently utilize this information to become more skillful in the execution of the teaching components of our professional lives.

The overview provided in this chapter is but the tip of a very large iceberg. Many more theories, philosophies, and practices exist, and each one is sufficient to fill numerous books on its own, from both supporters and critics. Those interested in exploring such theories further can easily find many intriguing resources.[40]

Developmental psychology, educational theory, and even the philosophical domains of ontology and epistemology are always in flux, with each new theory or emerging philosophy altering the conversation. Even though most educational theory focuses on children, this does not prohibit its applicability to our purposes in higher education. This field is constantly expanding, especially through cognitive neuroscience and its revelations about how the human brain functions. Despite the fact that we cannot possibly pin down a comprehensive theory of education that will serve to inform all we do as educators, acquiring working knowledge of these ideas is the first step toward improving our pedagogical practice and to subsequently creating optimal learning experiences and environments for our students. The same is true for recognizing our own biases and the inequities that

Identify ➡	Ideate
Why should we acquire a working knowledge of the theories and philosophies behind our teaching? We should understand the impact of our choices as educators and the effect of these practices on student learning.	How can we implement this knowledge in our teaching? Our new awareness of the theoretical basis for educational practices can shape our choices as instructors, allowing us to teach more mindfully and less reflexively.
Iterate ⬅	Implement
When you teach, take note of the educational theories you're employing, especially if you find yourself reverting to an instructivist position. We don't need to remain under the influence of educational theory from the 17th century when more effective models exist.	What should we do with this information? If you've recognized your prior teaching practice in any of the theories presented in this chapter, you can build upon this to improve your approach to curriculum development and instruction. You can also begin to incorporate models or ideas that you might not have known about before, which can significantly improve your students' learning.

FIGURE 2.6 Chapter 2 Design Connection

are present in higher education. The more aware we become of these attitudes, the better prepared we are to work for positive change in the world, beginning in our own classrooms.

Remember:

- Although we cannot identify a single, unifying educational theory that will serve all of higher education, numerous theories can inform and guide our practice as educators.
- Curriculum should be designed with educational theory in mind to deliver the best possible learning experience to our students.
- When we grow in our knowledge of these theories, we are better able to enact pedagogical and curricular practices that serve our students' learning needs.

Notes

[1] Piaget, J. (1936). *Origins of Intelligence in the Child*. London: Routledge & Kegan Paul; Piaget, J. (1957). *Construction of Reality in the Child*. London: Routledge & Kegan Paul; Piaget, J. (1958). The growth of logical thinking from childhood to adolescence. *AMC*, 10, 12.

[2] Keating, D. (1979). Adolescent thinking. In J. Adelson (Ed.), *Handbook of Adolescent Psychology*. New York: Wiley, 211–246.

[3] Dasen, P. (1994). Culture and cognitive development from a Piagetian perspective. In W. J. Lonner and R. S. Malpass (Eds.), *Psychology and Culture*. Boston, MA: Allyn and Bacon.

[4] Vygotsky, L. S. (1978). *Mind in Society: The Development of Higher Psychological Processes*. Cambridge, MA: Harvard University Press.

[5] Bruner, J. (1957). On perceptual readiness. *Psychological Review*, 64(2). http://dx.doi.org/10.1037/h0043805

[6] Erikson, E. (1959). *Identity and the Life Cycle*. New York: W.W. Norton & Company.

[7] Chickering, A. (1969). *Education and Identity*. San Francisco, CA: Jossey-Bass.

[8] Kohlberg, L., and Hersh, R. (April 1977). Moral development: A review of the theory. *Theory into Practice*, XVI(2).

[9] Barger, R. (2000). *A summary of Lawrence Kohlberg's states of moral development*. University of Notre Dame. www.csudh.edu/dearhabermas/kohlberg01bk.htm

[10] Perry, W. G., Jr. (1981). Cognitive and ethical growth: The making of meaning. In A. W. Chickering and Associates, *The Modern American College*. San Francisco, CA: Jossey-Bass, 76–116.

[11] Jung, C. (1921; translated by H. G. Baynes, 1923). *Psychological Types*. Classics in the History of Psychology. http://psychclassics.yorku.ca/Jung/types.htm

[12] *MBTI basics*. (2017). The Myers & Briggs Foundation. www.myersbriggs.org/my-mbti-personality-type/mbti-basics/

[13] Astin, A. (1999). Student involvement: A developmental theory for higher education. *Journal of College Student Development*, 40(5).

[14] Dewey, J. (1938). *Experience and Education*. Indianapolis, IN: Kappa Delta Pi.

[15] Sandeen, A. (1991). *The Professional Student Affairs Administrator*. San Francisco, CA: Jossey-Bass.

[16] For an excellent explanation of changing educational paradigms, see Sir Ken Robinson's influential TED Talk at www.ted.com/talks/ken_robinson_changing_education_paradigms. Robinson's remarks are directed at K–12 education, but those working in higher education can also learn from this message.

[17] Gibbs, G. (November 21, 2013). Lectures don't work, but we keep using them. *Times Higher Education*. www.timeshighereducation.com/news/lectures-dont-work-but-we-keep-using-them/2009141.article

[18] McLeod, S. (2016). Maslow's hierarchy of needs. *Simply Psychology.org*. www.simplypsychology.org/maslow.html

[19] Anderson, L., and Kranthwohl, D. (2000). *A Taxonomy for Learning, Teaching and Assessing: A Revision of Bloom's Taxonomy and Educational Objectives, Complete Edition*. Boston, MA: Pearson.

[20] Hase, S., and Kenyon, C. (2001). *From andragogy to heutagogy*. http://pandora.nla.gov.au/nph-wb/20010220130000/http://ultibase.rmit.edu.au/Articles/dec00/hase2.htm

[21] Knowles, M. S. (1980). *The Modern Practice of Adult Education: From Pedagogy to Andragogy*. Englewood Cliffs, NJ: Prentice Hall/Cambridge.

[22] Spiro, R. J., Coulson, R. L., Feltovich, P. J., and Anderson, D. (1988). Cognitive flexibility theory: Advanced knowledge acquisition in ill-structured domains. In V. Patel (ed.), *Proceedings of the 10th Annual Conference of the Cognitive Science Society*. Hillsdale, NJ: Erlbaum.

[23] Bruner, J. (1966). *Toward a Theory of Instruction*. Cambridge, MA: Harvard University Press.

[24] Mager, R. F. (1961). On the sequencing of instructional content. *Psychological Reports*, Southern Universities Press, 9, 405–413. doi:10.2466/pr0.1961.9.2.405

[25] Design-Based Research Collective. (2003). Design-based research: An emerging paradigm for educational inquiry. *Educational Researcher*, 32(1), 5–8.

[26] Rogers, C. R. (1969). *Freedom to Learn*. Columbus, OH: Merrill; Rogers, C. R., and Freiberg, H. J. (1994). *Freedom to Learn* (3rd ed.). Columbus, OH: Merrill/Macmillan.

[27] Hase, S., and Kenyon, C. (2000). From andragogy to heutagogy. *Ultibase Articles*, 5(3), 1–10.

[28] Carey, K. (2016). *The End of College: Creating the Future of Learning and the University of Everywhere*. New York: Riverhead Books.

[29] Wood, D. (2003). ABC of learning and teaching in medicine. *British Medical Journal*, 326, 328–330. doi:10.1136/bmj.326.7384.328

[30] Lave, J., and Wenger, E. (1991). *Situated Learning: Legitimate Peripheral Participation*. Cambridge: University of Cambridge Press.

[31] Meadows, D. H. (2009). *Thinking in Systems—a Primer*. London: Earthscan.

[32] This acronym has undergone rapid change in recent years, expanding from LGBTQ to include additional identities and designations. At present, LGBTQQIP2SAA is among the more inclusive forms in use, which encompasses Lesbian, Gay, Bisexual, Transsexual, Queer, Questioning, Intersex, Pansexual, 2S (a Native American identifier), Asexual, and Ally. From: Urban Dictionary, www.urbandictionary.com/define.php?term=LGBTQQIP2SAA

[33] Demographic categories representing less than 5% have been omitted simply for the sake of brevity.

[34] This designation does not refer to an individual's personal belief, but to the overarching influence of Christianity on US culture, history, and government. An individual may ascribe to Christian values apart from personal acceptance of Christian doctrine or theology.

[35] Based on Hurtad, S., Milem, J. F., Clayton-Pedersen, A. R., and Allen, W. (1998). Enhancing campus climates for racial/ethnic diversity: Educational policy and practice. *The Review of Higher Education*, 21(3), 279–302.

[36] Nørretranders, T. (1999). *The User Illusion: Cutting Consciousness Down to Size* (New York: Penguin) and Kahneman, D. (2011). *Thinking, Fast and Slow* (New York: Farrar, Straus and Giroux). See more at: www.aft.org/ae/winter2015-2016/staats#sthash.b58KyinW.dpuf

[37] United States Department of Labor. (n.d.). *Guidelines for Employers to Reduce Motor Vehicle Crashes*. www.osha.gov/Publications/motor_vehicle_guide.html

[38] Harvard University. (2017). *Project Implicit: Test Selection*. https://implicit.harvard.edu/implicit/selectatest.html

[39] See the Yale School of Management. (November 2, 2013). *Getting conscious about unconscious bias* (by Anees Chagpar). http://som.yale.edu/getting-conscious-about-unconscious-bias

[40] For a very comprehensive interactive map of learning theories and theorists, visit http://cmapspublic3.ihmc.us/rid=1LNV3H2J9-HWSVMQ-13LH/Learning%20Theory.cmap, created by Richard Millwood (2013).

Chapter 3

Creating Course Outcomes and Objectives

CHAPTER SUMMARY

- Course Context
- Outcomes and Objectives
- Writing Objectives

University syllabi typically include a set of statements called "Outcomes" and "Objectives" that describe what students should know and be able to do by the end of a course or at the conclusion of a degree program. Outcomes broadly align curriculum with departmental, institutional, and external standards. Objectives define measurable and observable benchmarks for student learning.

Now that we've become familiar with the theoretical basis of our work as educators, the next step in the curriculum planning process is to write outcomes and objectives for our courses. Conventional wisdom suggests that we save this task for last, writing these statements only after we've determined what we'll teach throughout the course, much like a summary at the end of a textbook chapter. Instead, this is the best place to *begin* when planning a course, asking ourselves, "When the students leave my classroom for the last time, what should they have learned, and how will I know that they've learned it?" The answer to this crucial question drives everything we do in planning instruction, learning experiences, and assessments. Our goal is to create curriculum that supports disciplinary norms and is aligned with university requirements, both of which determine what our students must learn during our courses.

COURSE CONTEXT

The first step in formulating our outcomes and objectives is to understand the context in which they exist. What is the course's underlying purpose, and how is it situated within the program, department, college, school, and university? This is true whether we're designing a new course or simply preparing to teach a course that other instructors have taught previously. The answers to the following questions will help to contextualize the course you'll plan.

1. Why would students take this course?
   a. General education requirement
   b. Major/minor requirement
   c. General elective
   d. Major/minor elective
2. How does this course fit into students' educational experiences?
   a. Prerequisites
   b. Level: beginning, intermediate, advanced, graduate
   c. Primary purpose
      i. General knowledge
      ii. Disciplinary-specific knowledge
      iii. General skills
      iv. Disciplinary-specific skills
      v. Professional preparation/experience
3. What do I want the students to learn in this course?

The order of these questions is intentional. If students will fulfill a general education requirement through the course, it shapes their attitude toward their collegiate experience. If it's a departmental requirement, the course could hold greater importance in their degree progression, especially if the course is a prerequisite for more advanced study. On the other hand, if the course is an elective, this will also influence students' attitudes regarding the course's importance and allows the instructor a bit more creative freedom in the course's design since it need not lead sequentially to other courses.

In every case, the bottom line that the instructor must always keep in mind is just this: What do I want students to learn? The point of every course is student learning, which seems terribly obvious, yet it is something we may forget in our day-to-day activities. Every action we take in planning the course, in delivering instruction, and in assessing our students' work must always lead back to this one fundamental question and its corollaries: What should students learn? How will their learning fit into their educational experience overall? Why should students learn it?

Sometimes, these answers are very simple. Let's consider a basic general education course like History 101.

- *Why should students take this course?* Because it is among the core of courses that the university has determined will provide all students with a high-quality liberal arts foundation for their studies.
- *How does the course fit into students' educational experience?* It is the first step in the study of history at the undergraduate level. Students must take this course before they can enroll in other history courses, should they wish to do so. This course is generally completed within a student's first 2 years of study.
- *What should students learn in this course?* Students will acquire a broad knowledge of the history of human civilization, including both Western and non-Western perspectives.

If you were charged with the task of planning this course, you might be tempted to begin with the last statement, deciding what students should learn. The other two steps seem obvious, but deliberately acknowledging their existence gives us a more grounded perspective in our later actions. We know that the students enrolled in this course are most likely to be motivated by checking a requirement off of their list, which means that the instructor will have to work harder to get and keep their attention. We know that not all students will move onto other history courses, but for those who do, it's important to provide the foundational information they will need. All students should walk away from the course with a better understanding of the history of human civilization than they possessed prior to taking the course, which should build on and expand their prior knowledge from high school history courses rather than repeating what they already know.

The practice of repeatedly asking *why, how,* and *what* proves useful when planning curriculum. In the example of the introductory history course, we might decide that students should learn about ancient Chinese culture, but then we should ask ourselves why they should learn this, how it will be of value to them, and what they could do to demonstrate their learning.

For the remainder of this book, we will presume that the reader has a particular course in mind and is going to apply the steps that follow to the planning process. If you're teaching a course that's been taught at your institution in the past, a previous syllabus for the course will be helpful in our work together, whether it's your own or a syllabus that you've received from a colleague. If you're creating an entirely new course, it's helpful if you've at least worked through some preliminary planning: developing a working title, creating a basic course description, and identifying the level of the course along with any prerequisites that might be appropriate. This allows us to consider each step of the planning process specifically rather than discussing them only as abstract generalizations.

OUTCOMES AND OBJECTIVES

Outcomes and objectives exist at both the programmatic and course levels. These statements are similar, but not synonymous. Outcomes broadly describe the learning students should have achieved by the end of the course or program. Objectives, on the other hand, designate specific goals of the program, course, or even an individual lesson or activity, defined in terms of the skills or knowledge that students will acquire or demonstrate as the result of instruction. To paraphrase an instructor resource published by Iowa State University's Center for Excellence in Teaching and Learning, "[O]utcomes are where we want to be. Objectives are the steps needed to get there."[1] Outcomes must align with objectives, and they must both remain consistent with the actual instruction, activities, and assessment that take place within a course. Further, all instructional activities should be reflected in the course's outcomes and objectives: Whatever we teach must align with these statements. We might see this as a progression from the most general learning goals to the most specific instructor actions. We plan from the top to the bottom of this continuum, but we implement from the bottom to the top—delivering instruction then assessing student learning to see if our students have met the specific objectives for our course and accomplished the broad learning outcomes we hoped to achieve (see Figure 3.1).

One of the best resources for planning outcomes and objectives for our courses is the *Quality Matters Program* employed by many universities.[2] Even though this program is specific to online curricula, it's very helpful in designing courses to be held on campus as well. Briefly, this specifies "Eight General Standards" that should be present:

1. Course Overview and Introduction
2. Learning Objectives (Competencies)
3. Assessment and Measurement
4. Instructional Materials
5. Course Activities and Learner Interaction
6. Course Technology
7. Learner Support
8. Accessibility and Usability

FIGURE 3.1 From Outcomes to Instruction

In particular, Standard 2, "Learning Objectives," and Standard 3, "Assessment and Measurement" are the primary determinants of how we will plan and organize our course development activities. (We will revisit the Quality Matters Standards later in this book as well.)

Developing Outcomes

The process of creating course outcomes varies between disciplines, depending in part on the uniformity of knowledge and practice present in each. Ideally, the outcomes for each course should align with outcomes that have already been developed for an entire program or specific degree progressions within it, maximizing the potential for consistency across all courses. Where robust program-level outcomes exist, instructors of individual courses build on those pertaining to the particular course they will teach to formulate the course's outcomes. This supports alignment between each course and the program in which it exists.

The task of creating outcomes and objectives for both programs and the courses that are offered within them involves consideration of information from any or all of the following sources to compose statements that define the distinctive, specific, and measurable body of skills and knowledge that we want our students to learn. This list provides a short overview of these information sources, which will be discussed in greater detail in the next sections. Not all of these sources will apply to the planning of every course, depending on the norms of the discipline, department, or program in which the course will occur, but they provide us with some structure for the task ahead.

- Examine the *accreditation standards* for your particular academic discipline. What should the graduates of an accredited program know and be able to do to be considered to have achieved adequate professional-level preparation?
- Consult *professional organizations* in your discipline, considering their published guidelines, goals, mission statement, or professional standards. What unifying ideas are present at the professional level?
- Evaluate *syllabi* for all the courses you've taught or syllabi from your colleague's courses (when available). Where do you see common themes and ideas?
- Investigate your *department, college, or school*'s published goals, objectives, values, mission statements, by-laws, or similar statements. What important ideas or themes emerge?
- Assess *degree program requirements* relevant to the course you're planning. What courses must all students take to earn this degree? What ideas or themes carry across those courses?

■ Determine which *institutional policies, initiatives, or goals* apply to your program and your course. These might exist at any level, whether the department, college, school, or university as a whole.

To understand the process of writing outcomes and objectives more concretely, we'll apply these general practices to the design of an interdisciplinary undergraduate course, Design Thinking for Entrepreneurs.[3]

Accreditation Standards

In some academic fields, we need look no further than our discipline's accrediting body. These usually provide standards and guidelines that are useful in shaping our learning outcomes, whether or not our academic unit has earned (or is seeking) accreditation. Countless such organizations exist. For example, schools of engineering typically align their programs and courses with the standards set forth by the Accreditation Board for Engineering and Technology (ABET).[4] Similarly, the National Office for Arts Accreditation (NOAA) includes four accrediting organizations: the National Association of Schools of Art and Design (NASAD), the National Association of Schools of Dance (NASD), the National Association of Schools of Music (NASM), and the National Association of Schools of Theatre (NAST).[5] Such organizations exist for most academic disciplines, typically publishing a handbook or guide to the standards that institutions must meet in order to earn accreditation. Some of these organizations define a common body of knowledge and skills that clearly explains what students must know and be able to do by the time they graduate from an accredited program.

Professional Organizations

The next place to look for information when writing learning outcomes are professional organizations related to your discipline. Fortunately, you're probably already familiar with the relevant professional organizations in your field of expertise, so looking into these groups' published guidelines isn't likely to require extensive research. Professional organizations don't usually issue "standards" unless they also serve as accrediting bodies. However, they often give a cogent overview of the skills and competencies that their members should possess. For instance, I taught in and directed a program in Arts and Cultural Management, which is related to the field of arts administration. One of the professional organizations related to this field is AAAE—the Association of Arts Administration Educators. AAAE provides a very detailed narrative explanation of program expectations, listing student competencies for each area of professional practice. This document was very useful to me when planning courses and student degree progressions in the Arts and Cultural Management program I formerly directed.

49

Course Syllabi and Degree Program Requirements

Your own syllabi from past courses and those of your departmental colleagues can also yield important information about the outcomes and objectives you might want to write for your course. For example, if you're planning a course that falls in sequence between one colleague's introductory-level course and another's course for juniors or seniors, you can plan learning experiences that build on the prerequisite knowledge of the introductory course and also prepare students for the advanced learning in the upper-level course—this is called vertical differentiation. If both of those other instructors have written high-quality outcomes and objectives, your task is all the easier—you can use their outcomes as a model when creating your own course. Even when courses are non-sequential, it's very helpful to know what your colleagues are teaching so as not to duplicate their course content and also to ensure that all relevant professional skills and knowledge appear at some point along students' progress toward their degrees.

During my work as a consultant, I often recommend that programs and departments undertake a process of curriculum mapping, in which the content of all departmental courses is made explicit and aligned with accreditation standards and professional guidelines. Admittedly, this is rather time consuming and painstaking, but it can be a tremendous tool for identifying curricular redundancies that should be eliminated and knowledge gaps that should be filled. The result is a stronger program that provides students with an optimized educational experience.

Institutional Information, Requirements, or Recommendations

We should also investigate the information that already exists within our institutions, including the mission, vision, or values statements at all organizational levels. Many universities also publish lists of standards, guidelines, goals, or recommendations that provide actionable information for writing program outcomes and course objectives. For example, Michigan State University's Undergraduate Learning Goals[6] should be reflected in course outcomes at this institution. The institution for which you work undoubtedly will have its own set of statements, which you should access during your course-planning efforts.

- *Analytical thinking*: Students will use ways of knowing from mathematics, natural sciences, social sciences, humanities and arts to access information and critically analyze complex material in order to evaluate evidence, construct reasoned arguments, and communicate inferences and conclusions.
- *Cultural understanding*: Students will comprehend global and cultural diversity within historical, artistic, and societal contexts.

- *Effective citizenship*: Students will participate as members of local, national, and global communities and will possess the capacity to lead in an increasingly interdependent world.
- *Effective communication*: Students will use a variety of media to communicate effectively with diverse audiences.
- *Integrated reasoning*: Students will integrate discipline-based knowledge to make informed decisions that reflect human social, ethical, and aesthetic values.

Additional Research

If you've considered all of the preceding resources and still haven't found enough information to write your course outcomes, you can conduct additional research by examining published information from the following sources. The intent is not to replicate other courses or programs, but to gather information such as models of overall goals, outcomes, missions, or ideas. These can provide you with helpful insights or lead you to additional resources.

- Published information about programs similar to the one in which you teach, including their goals, values, mission, vision, outcomes, and objectives
- Information about courses offered at other institutions such as course catalog descriptions or departmental websites
- Syllabi for courses like the one you're planning, found on databases such as Academia.edu or the OpenSyllabusProject.org.

Searches such as this can also offer insights about how the course we're planning compares to others offered elsewhere. For example, if your course will include content not included at similar programs, you should carefully consider whether this would give you a competitive edge or be a signal that your course might diverge too far from the norm.

Expectations for Outcomes Statements

Before we begin to work with the information we've gathered, let's look at the particular type of format used when writing course outcomes. These statements should be:

- Reflective of disciplinary norms
- Aligned with institutional standards and expectations
- Limited in number (no less than three, no more than ten)
- Frame student learning broadly rather than being specific to an individual course or student
- Distinctive, specific, and simple
- Measurable by more than one method of assessment

- Written to clearly indicate
  - Fields that are the focus of the outcome
  - Knowledge, skills, and abilities students in the program must demonstrate
  - Depth of knowledge and ability students must achieve

Let's take a look at Figure 3.2 and a few hypothetical examples of outcomes, comparing some that are too generic with others that are more specific and measurable.

Both outcomes and objectives should use active verbs aligned with Bloom's Taxonomy. You might find Figure 3.3 helpful in completing this task. Please note that this list is not all-inclusive. It merely serves as a place to begin your course development process. The important point is to avoid vague terminology and employ more specific and measurable verbs. Some terms may appear in more than one column.

Synthesis

Finally, we must synthesize all of the information we've gathered into a concise set of outcomes written in accordance with the guidelines and requirements stated in the previous section. At first, this might be cumbersome, since you'll

Discipline	Too Generic	More Specific
Biology	Students will learn fundamental theories of biology.	Students will write knowledgeably about theoretical aspects of biology, using appropriate scientific references and examples.
Philosophy	Students will understand a variety of philosophical positions.	Students will develop relevant arguments and examples in order to discuss a variety of philosophical positions.
History	Students will know the difference between primary and secondary sources.	Students will appropriately utilize primary and secondary sources in their written work, demonstrating knowledge of sound disciplinary practices in historical scholarship.

FIGURE 3.2 Generic and Specific Outcomes

Remembering	Understanding	Applying	Analyzing	Evaluating	Creating
collect	associate	apply	analyze	appraise	adapt
define	cite	articulate	categorize	assess	build
describe	compare	complete	classify	convince	compose
enumerate	contrast	construct	connect	criticize	construct
examine	discuss	demonstrate	correlate	defend	create
identify	distinguish	discover	diagram	discriminate	design
label	estimate	experiment	formulate	explain	develop
list	explain	illustrate	generalize	judge	devise
match	extend	modify	infer	justify	formulate
quote	interpret	prepare	integrate	measure	generate
record	paraphrase	report	prioritize	persuade	invent
select	predict	show	speculate	rank	negotiate
tabulate	summarize	solve	validate	support	produce

FIGURE 3.3 Bloom's Verbs

likely find far more source information than can comfortably fit into a mere hand-ful of course outcomes.

My personal preference is to begin by organizing the information I've gathered into a table (see Figure 3.4) so that I can make a column-by-column comparison between these sources. For the Design Thinking for Entrepreneurs course, I aligned two documents from the Entrepreneurship & Innovation program (E&I) with the university's Undergraduate Learning Goals, combining them into a set of outcomes. To show the process of synthesis, bold typeface indicates key ideas from E&I, while italic typeface indicates key ideas from the Undergraduate Learning Goals.

The outcomes for the course essentially reduce 3 pages of text to 3 sentences. They include active verbs from Bloom's Taxonomy and create a broad picture of what students in the course should know and be able to do.[7]

Your Turn: Writing Your Outcomes
1. Create a chart similar to Figure 3.5, including notes based on informa-tion you gather from any or all of the listed sources. Look for keywords,

Students will **investigate the principles and practices underlying innovation and entrepreneurship** through *critical analysis* of ideas and information, *synthesizing* this knowledge with increased understanding of the *social and cultural* contexts in which innovations occur and *their impact on diverse populations*.

Students will **develop the** *knowledge and skills* **necessary to create, launch, or sustain a business venture** *or community organization*, including ideation, vision, prototyping, modeling, financial management, strategic planning, *knowledge of applicable governance systems*, effective business *communications*, promotions and marketing, branding and identity, social engagement, and other factors.

Students will *integrate their learning* **in the course by** *critically applying* **acquired skills and knowledge within an entrepreneurial context**, using a *variety of strategies for inquiry and ideation in order to make value judgments, solve problems, respond to challenges, and generate new understanding*.

FIGURE 3.4 Design Thinking for Entrepreneurs—Outcomes

Standards published by disciplinary accrediting organizations	
Professional organizations' published mission, standards, or guidelines	
Syllabi from other courses you've taught. If available, syllabi from your departmental colleagues' courses.	
Departmental goals, objectives, values, and mission statements	
Degree program requirements (program, department, college, school, and/or university levels)	
Other sources as appropriate	

FIGURE 3.5 Learning Outcomes—Research and Planning Notes

important ideas, or themes that appear in more than one of the sources you consult.

2. Analyze the data you gathered in a chart such as the one above. What common themes, ideas, skills, competencies, or data can you observe?

3. Sort these observations into conceptual categories. It might be helpful to use highlighting tools to color-code the areas of commonality you identify.

4. Write outcomes statements for each category you identified. Be sure to use active verbs from Bloom's Taxonomy. *Avoid vague language such as* **know, learn,** *or* **understand.**

WRITING OBJECTIVES

Once you have created your course outcomes, the next step in the curriculum planning process is to consider the specific body of knowledge you will cover in the course you're planning. Think through the disciplinary content you want to present, informed by your own expert knowledge, in order to decide what your students should know and be able to do by the time they exit your classroom. As with the outcomes you've written, your course objectives should align with but not duplicate those of other courses offered in your program.

If you're writing a new course instead of revising a course that's been taught in your program before, you might want to review syllabi from similar courses, either those at your own institution or published online by peer institutions, professional organizations, or on databases such as Academia.edu or the Open-SyllabusProject.org. Just as researchers stand on the shoulders of scholars who have come before, instructors can examine and analyze our peers' courses to inspire our own curriculum development, informed by the practices of good scholarship. Sometimes it's difficult to know just where to begin, so finding some comparable examples might spark your creative process or provide inspiration. Again, the intent is not to replicate other courses or programs, but to gather information.

Activity

If you already have a previous syllabus for the course you're planning to instruct, either your own or from a colleague, it's helpful to compare the course's prior content to the outcomes you just created in order to identify the objectives you'll use for the new course. If you don't have an existing syllabus to use as a starting point in your planning process, please skip to Step 3.

Step 1: Compare and Contrast

First, we'll compare the outcomes you've just created to the syllabus you're using as a starting point for the course you're developing. You'll need printed copies of (1) the syllabus and (2) the outcomes you created, plus two highlighters (say, yellow and blue).

1. Read both documents.
2. Mark the places where they are similar in yellow.
3. Mark the places where they are different in blue.

Look for corresponding keywords or similar ideas, not a word-for-word match. Depending on how the syllabus was originally written, you might find everything you need in the course overview. Remember, we're looking for big ideas, not fine details.

Step 2: Analyze Your Findings

After you finish highlighting your two documents, examine the areas of similarity and important differences you identified.

1. Start with your outcomes document:
   a. What did you highlight in blue? This shows you the requirements that are missing from your syllabus.
   b. What should you add to your syllabus in order to align your course with your outcomes?
2. Now look at your syllabus. If you have a lot of blue highlighting here, it indicates that you're teaching things that are not mentioned in your outcomes. That's not necessarily a problem: We can always teach *more* than is required *if* it aligns with our broad outcomes.
3. What did you highlight in yellow on both documents? This shows you where you are on track to writing strong course objectives.

Step 3: Determine Specific Content Within the Course Context

1. Next, think about the level of your course (beginner or intermediate/advanced) and apply your knowledge of your discipline to determine if your intended objectives are appropriate to students' educational progression. Consider the following:
   a. What should be taught at the introductory level?
      i. General disciplinary knowledge such as relevant history and theory
      ii. Direct instruction in disciplinary methods, procedures, and terminology
      iii. Basic technical skills where appropriate
   b. What should be taught at the intermediate and advanced levels?
      i. Increasingly complex disciplinary knowledge

      ii. Increasing proficiency in communication, critical thinking, and problem solving in disciplinary contexts

      iii. Focused study within the disciplinary context

  c. What should students already have learned in prior courses (if anything)?

  d. How must a student demonstrate acquisition of skills and knowledge required for graduation?

      i. Disciplinary knowledge and/or skill sufficient to qualify for admission to graduate study or entry-level professional employment in the field

      ii. Proficiency in communication, critical thinking, and problem solving within disciplinary contexts

Course objectives must encompass *all* of the content of your course and each action for which students could gain or lose points from their grade. This includes consequences tied to your classroom policies. For example, most instructors have a policy regarding submission of late assignments, deducting points for each day the work is late. The rationale behind such policies is usually that "in the real world" students must meet their professional obligations in a timely manner. If so, then one of the course objectives should address the acquisition of professional competencies, including an expectation for punctuality and responsibility.

Step 4: Write Your Objectives

1. Using a chart similar to the one provided in Figure 3.6, write objectives for your course that
   a. Align with your outcomes
   b. Address the specific content of your course
   c. Use active verbs from Bloom's Taxonomy
2. Outcomes and objectives do not necessarily require a 1:1 correspondence:
   a. One objective can address more than one outcome if they are essentially similar.
   b. One outcome can be broken down into several objectives if greater detail is beneficial to your course's plans.
3. Make sure you include institutional requirements such as writing, collaborative work, service learning, and so on.
4. Every action tied to students' course grades should be linked to an objective, including those related to instructor policies.

Example

Here's a copy of the outcomes and objectives developed for Design Thinking for Entrepreneurs. Please note that each descriptor begins with an active verb from Bloom's Taxonomy. Remember, everything in our outcomes and objectives should be measurable, so we want to avoid vague terms like *learn, understand,* or *know.*

OUTCOMES	OBJECTIVES
Students will investigate the principles and practices underlying innovation and entrepreneurship through critical analysis of ideas and information, synthesizing this knowledge with increased understanding of the social and cultural contexts in which innovations occur and their impact on diverse populations.	Students will explore the intersection of ethics, social responsibility, cultural contexts, multiple ideation strategies, and entrepreneurial skills and knowledge as they identify problems to address through the development of a project addressing a "wicked problem" by engaging in instrumental research, synthesizing their findings, and articulating possible solutions. Students' participation in course discussion and activities will reflect their knowledge of entrepreneurial strategies and their ability to identify opportunity, demonstrate empathy, assess and mitigate risk, create value, and to understand the social contexts and issues surrounding innovative solutions to wicked problems.
Students will develop the knowledge and skills necessary to create, launch, or sustain a business venture or community organization, including ideation, vision, prototyping, modeling, financial management, strategic planning, knowledge of applicable governance systems, effective business communications, promotions and marketing, branding and identity, social engagement, and other factors.	Students will examine practices and principles of social and ethical responsibility as they solve problems by using multiple ideation strategies in the service of pursuing a solution to a "wicked problem" through an innovative and entrepreneurial process. They will utilize and refine their communications skills as they interact with potential clients or customers, compose documents related to their project, and build professional relationships. They will develop awareness of applicable governance systems and strengthen their ability to ethically solve societal problems through empathetic understanding of the target population's needs and wants.

FIGURE 3.6 Design Thinking for Entrepreneurs—Outcomes and Objectives

OUTCOMES	OBJECTIVES
Students will integrate their learning in the course by critically applying acquired skills and knowledge within an entrepreneurial context, using a variety of strategies for inquiry and ideation to make value judgments, solve problems, respond to challenges, and generate new understanding.	Students will formulate a business model for a venture intended to create a product, service, or organization that allows them to begin building professional networks, to attempt multiple strategies for inquiry incorporating differing points of view, to define and solve problems, to conduct field research, and to experience the full spectrum of the entrepreneurial process from inspiration through ideation, innovation, implementation, and evaluation of their completed projects. Project evaluation will be based on the business model's • Creativity or innovation • Strategy toward a solution • Identification of opportunity • Understanding of and empathy for customer's needs • Recognition and mitigation of risk • Creation of value for the target constituency • Social engagement • Self-evaluation of the proposed solution

FIGURE 3.6 Continued

Your Turn: Writing Your Objectives

Create a chart similar to the one presented in Figure 3.7 and enter the outcomes you developed in the first part of the chapter. Then write your specific course objectives, ensuring that each outcome links to an objective and each objective proceeds from an outcome. You may wish to look back at the chart of active verbs from the higher levels of Bloom's Taxonomy.

Remember:

• Outcomes are where we want to be. Objectives are the steps needed to get there.[8]
• Course objectives and outcomes must align with one another, and they must also support institutional requirements.
• The process of composing outcomes and objectives involves analyzing information gathered from multiple sources, linked to your professional expertise and knowledge of disciplinary norms and practices and meeting relevant institutional requirements.

Outcomes	Objectives

FIGURE 3.7 Outcomes and Objectives Planning Chart

Identify ➡️	Ideate
Why should we create outcomes and objectives before we've decided anything else about the course we're planning? Beginning with the end in mind ensures that our instructional choices throughout the course all support the goals we're trying to achieve: making sure our students meet program-level outcomes and meet our course objectives.	How can we best create strong outcomes and objectives? Writing these statements depends on gathering information from many sources such as disciplinary accreditation standards, university requirements, and disciplinary norms, then synthesizing it into a series of concise, actionable statements.
Iterate ⬅️	Implement
When you teach the course each time, you have an opportunity to revise and refine your outcomes and objectives. As you teach, pay attention to whether these statements align with what you're actually teaching and make changes prior to teaching the course again the next time.	What can we do to make this task more achievable? Your course outcomes and objectives will rely on your own expertise and your knowledge of the course content you intend to deliver. Conducting research into courses and programs offered elsewhere can inspire and inform your work, but be careful to follow the practices of good scholarship in all your investigations.

FIGURE 3.8 Chapter 3 Design Connection

Notes

1 Iowa State University. (2017). *Tips on writing course goals/learning outcomes and measurable learning objectives*. Center for Excellence in Teaching and Learning. www.celt.iastate.edu/teaching/preparing-to-teach/tips-on-writing-course-goalslearning-outcomes-and-measureable-learning-objectives

2 Quality Matters. (2017). *Higher Ed rubrics and standards*. www.qualitymatters.org/

3 I selected this course because I designed and teach it myself. Nothing in this example should indicate that the exact same considerations would apply broadly to all courses everywhere. Rather, this is merely an example of the process I undertook when creating outcomes for this particular course within the specific program and academic discipline in which it exists.

4 ABET. (2017). www.abet.org/. This acronym formerly stood for Accreditation Board for Engineering and Technology, but the organization now accredits computer science, applied science, and engineering technology programs.

5 National Office for Arts Accreditation (NOAA). www.arts-accredit.org/national-office-for-arts-accreditation/

6 Michigan State University. (2016). *Undergraduate learning goals*. http://undergrad.msu.edu/programs/learninggoals

7 We should note that this class was not developed under the umbrella of a specific academic department or program, so its outcomes and objectives are unique to the course itself, not mirroring other programmatic outcomes.

8 Iowa State University. (2017). *Tips on writing course goals/learning outcomes and measurable learning objectives*. Center for Excellence in Teaching and Learning. www.celt.iastate.edu/teaching/preparing-to-teach/tips-on-writing-course-goalslearning-outcomes-and-measureable-learning-objectives.

Chapter 4

Assessing Student Learning

CHAPTER SUMMARY

- Formative and Summative
- Grading
- Written Assessments: Quizzes and Exams
- Weighting Assignments and Assessments
- Calculating Student Grades
- Online Assessment Resources
- Fairness and Objectivity
- Industrial Age Assessment
- Your Turn: Writing Your Assessments

As professional educators, we're expected to evaluate student learning and assign a correct grade. Students deserve accurate evaluation of their work, which helps them to prepare for the rigors of the professional world or for advanced study. Learning how to create and employ a few simple tools can demystify this process for both students and educators.

The outcomes and objectives we write for our courses must be measurable, not vague or overly general. That is, you must have a means of determining whether your students have mastered the skills and knowledge that you intended to deliver during your course. Planning for assessment before determining what to teach seems counterintuitive—after all, assessment comes at the end. Why not decide what to teach and then figure out how to assess it afterwards?

When we "begin with the end in mind," we start with assessment and then plan learning experiences to lead us toward that goal. Returning to our analogy of a road trip, we usually decide on a destination first and then plan our route afterwards. The same is true of instruction. We decide where we want to arrive (students' achievement of our objectives) and then plan how to get from Point A (the first day of class) to Point B (the last day of class, when we've hopefully met our course objectives).

Therefore, your next task is to decide how your students will demonstrate their learning relative to each objective you've written for the course you're planning. Remember: Everything you teach in the course should relate to an objective, and every objective must be assessed. A single assessment may cover more than one objective. For example, a midterm exam might address each of the course objectives presented in the first half of the course.

As you plan your assessments, keep Bloom's Taxonomy in mind. It's true that objective assessment tools like multiple-choice tests are much easier to grade, but these tend to focus on lower-order thinking like memorization of facts and information. Higher-order thinking can be assessed objectively as well, but this requires crafting your test items very thoughtfully.

FORMATIVE AND SUMMATIVE

Assessment isn't difficult in and of itself. After all, most instructors possess an almost intuitive sense of whether or not a student's work meets our expectations. The discussion of assessment theory and practice in higher education, however, is complex, including formative, summative, cumulative, formal, informal, subjective, objective, process, interim, and many other assessment types and approaches.

Assessments usually serve one of two purposes: *Formative* assessments measure learning in progress, providing feedback to students and allowing the instructor and student to make adjustments to both teaching and learning in order to achieve a successful outcome. Examples of formative assessments include quizzes, in-progress critique of student projects, and writing assignments. *Summative* assessments, on the other hand, measure learning at the completion of a course or unit. They might include tests, final exams, performance tasks, or research papers. An easy way to remember the difference comes from Robert Stake:[1] "When the cook tastes the soup, that's formative; when the guests taste the soup, that's summative."

Generally speaking, formative assessments carry a low-point value within the overall grading schema, while summative assessments are weighted more heavily. Most instructors use a combination of both types of assessment throughout their courses.

GRADING

Not all assessment necessarily leads to a grade. When we assess students' performance during a learning experience, the knowledge we gather can guide our subsequent teaching (formative). For example, an instructor might hold a meeting with a student to provide feedback on a writing assignment, which the student would have the opportunity to revise prior to submitting the final version of the paper. Grading occurs at the end of an assessment, serving as the basis upon which we keep our records (summative).

There are primarily two ways to determine student grades: norm-referenced assessment (NR) and criterion-referenced assessment (CR).

To put this in simple terms, instructors using NR assessment compare students to the norm, or the average student's performance in the course. The top-performing students receive A's, and the lowest-performing students receive F's, and everyone else falls somewhere in-between. Professors using this type of model sometimes graph student test scores on a line plot, resulting in the classic bell-shaped curve. Indeed, this is where the phrase *grading on the curve* originated. This approach can produce intense competition among students, since only the top performers can earn the best grades. It also creates a situation where some students must fail simply because their scores are comparatively lower than the rest of the class. When students have highly similar overall scores, the difference between success and failure can be measured in mere fractions of a point.

CR assessment, on the other hand, compares each student's performance to a predetermined standard or set of criteria. Generally speaking, this will be based on a student's percent of correct answers on a test, or the student's relative success in completing a given task. Grading percentages are sometimes (but not always) set by the university or the department (e.g., 90–100=A; 80–89=B; 70–79=C).

An instructor utilizing CR methods should provide students with specific information at the beginning of the course detailing what is necessary to receive a good grade. Commonly, this information is conveyed through a checklist, rubric, or written instructions.

Our system of letter grades is a relic of NR systems that were prevalent a century or more ago. We still *believe* that A means "excellent," B means "above average," and C means "average," which was true according to the NR system used in the past, even though we know quite well that these designations merely apply to percentage-based grading.

On the other hand, CR grading compares students' performance to an established standard rather than to their peers, meaning that, theoretically, every student could achieve an *A* for the course. Under this mindset, an A indicates

Student Name	Final Grade Percentage (Class average = 93.2%)
Albert	99
Barbara	92
Charles	88
Deborah	90
Edward	95
Francesca	87
George	97
Heather	98
Isaac	93
Jill	93

FIGURE 4.1 Sample Class Scores

that students have met the course requirements to a 90% or greater standard of success.

Let's consider a hypothetical class:[2]

As Figure 4.1 demonstrates, under an NR grading strategy, only Albert, with the highest score in the class (the top 10%), would receive an A. Francesca, with the lowest overall score (the bottom 10%), would receive an F. Our "average group" of Barbara, Edward, Isaac, and Jill—the scores clustered in the middle— would receive C's. George and Heather, whose scores are between the "average" group and the top performer, Albert, would get B's, while Charles and Deborah, whose scores fell between the "average" group and the lowest person, Francesca, would receive D's for the course.

Under CR grading, however, everyone would receive an A for the course, except Charles and Francesca, who would each have earned a B. Of course, not all universities use a standard 10% scale, but the point should still be clear. If you're the Albert of the group, you might not care which system your instructor uses because you'll earn an A either way. But if you're Francesca or Charles or Deborah, it makes a very big difference how the instructor chooses to assign a grade to your work (see Figure 4.2).

NORM-REFERENCED GRADES			CRITERION-REFERENCED GRADES		
A	99	Albert	A	99	Albert
B	98	Heather	A	98	Heather
B	97	George	A	97	George
C	95	Edward	A	95	Edward
C	93	Isaac Jill	A	93	Isaac Jill
C	92	Barbara	A	92	Barbara
D	90	Charles	A	90	Deborah
D	88	Deborah	B	88	Charles
F	87	Francesca	B	87	Francesca

FIGURE 4.2 Norm-Referenced and Criterion-Referenced Grades

Looking at the wide variations in student success between these two models, we have to ask ourselves: is NR grading fair? Now consider this: If the class average were 10 points lower (83.2%), students like Deborah, Charles, and Francesca would probably be the A and B students rather than the D and F students, even though their objective performance would be the same. So, does comparing students' performance to one another rather than to a predetermined standard make sense in a 21st century classroom? Do you really want to establish a grading system in which some students are required to fail in order for others to succeed? I'd hope your answer is, "Of course not."

The best approach, therefore, is to formulate clear criteria for student work and to communicate your expectations at the time you assign a project or other academic task. For this reason, the use of grading tools such as checklists and rubrics is highly recommended. Further discussions in this book presumes the use of CR assessment.

Tools for Grading

Generally speaking, the majority of assessment tools tend to fall into four basic categories:

- *Rubrics and Checklists*: Providing students with written criteria for any work they perform during your course is simply good pedagogical practice. We should make our expectations clear at the time we give an assignment, and then follow through to evaluate the assignment according to the criteria we originally presented. The simplest solution is to use a rubric or a checklist. These may be either formative or summative, depending on how you employ them in the course.

- *Written Assessments:* Tests, quizzes, and exams are ubiquitous in higher education, especially in lecture-based courses. But even in performance-dependent settings like lab-based or studio-based courses, students should acquire a body of knowledge as well as increasing their skills, measuring this learning through written assessments.
  - *Quizzes* can assess learning in progress, checking for student understanding of current instruction (formative). They can also measure student learning at the conclusion of a section, unit, or module (summative).
  - A *final exam* is a more comprehensive learning tool, evaluating student understanding of the course's overall content. Since it occurs at the end of the course, when there's no time left for improvement, final exams are always summative.
- *Surveys:* We're interested in knowing how students view their learning experience in our classes. Colleges and universities customarily survey students at the end of a course, but administering your own pre- and post-course surveys and analyzing the results you gather can provide you with important information not encompassed by institutional survey instruments. Conducting your own student surveys can also help to guide your instruction and improve your effectiveness as an educator.
- **Writing Assignments:** Student writing can serve a variety of purposes in a course. It might be an instructional tool, it might be an assessment tool, or it might simply be a means of communication. Because writing is such a complex topic, we'll discuss it at greater depth in Chapter 6.

In the next section, we'll examine each of these types of assessment in greater depth, considering some examples and templates that you might choose to incorporate in the course you're planning.

Rubrics and Checklists

The word *rubric* comes from the Latin word for red, meaning the red ink that teachers tend to use when grading student work.[3] A rubric is basically a table or chart presenting the criteria according to which the assignment will be evaluated and the performance levels students might demonstrate. A checklist is a bit simpler, indicating the student's grade on the project or assignment by means of a list of criteria.

When students have access to written grading criteria before beginning a project, they can easily see what the evaluator expects, allowing them to know how to meet those expectations. This is an advantage to the instructor, because it reduces the likelihood of disputed grades. If you assess work based only on opinion or intuition, it's hard to justify your decision when a student says, "Why did I only get a C on this?" With clearly defined grading criteria, you can point to the specific criteria that the student did not meet: "You earned a C because you didn't format your work according to the instructions and it didn't meet the specific expectations for the sources you chose to use. Therefore, you earned only 75% based on the rubric that you were given on the day the project was assigned."

Rubrics

A rubric can be as complex or simple as you want it to be, but they usually contain between 3 and 6 criteria for evaluation and from 3 to 6 performance levels, arranged in a grid format. Each box of the rubric contains a point value and a short description. The student's grade is based on the number of total points earned.

Let's consider a sample of a simple rubric for an oral report (Figure 4.3).

Report Rubric	Excellent 5 points	Satisfactory 4 points	Poor 3 points	Unsatisfactory 0 points
Content	Student addresses the assigned topic thoroughly, supporting key points with convincing evidence.	Student addresses the assigned topic, providing adequate supporting evidence.	Student strays off topic and/or does not provide evidence for certain points.	Student does not address the assigned topic or fails to provide any evidence at all.
Presentation	Student is an engaging speaker, able to maintain audience interest.	Student speaks adequately and conveys the required information to the class.	Portions of the student's presentation were inaudible, awkward, or incomprehensible.	Student fails to maintain even minimal audience interest and/or is totally inaudible or incomprehensible.
Expectations	The presentation exceeds all specified guidelines for length, content, and quality.	The presentation meets specified guidelines.	The presentation meets most of the specified guidelines with few exceptions.	The presentation fails to meet several guidelines for length, content, and/or quality.

FIGURE 4.3 Sample Rubric—Oral Report

According to this rubric, an excellent oral report could be worth up to 15 points (100%), but a poor report might be worth only 9 points (60%).

The tricky part of creating a rubric isn't deciding what to write in the different fields, but in determining the relationship between point values and the student's potential grade. The best method is to assign point values to each category so that the simple total can be converted directly into an appropriate grade.[4]

- Your first thought might be to give the Excellent rating 5 points, Satisfactory 3 points, and Poor 1 point. But, that means that a student scoring all Satisfactory marks would receive a final score of 9 points out of a possible 15, which is only a 60%. That's too close to a failing grade to be reasonable: After all, the work was judged to be satisfactory, but a 60% is definitely not a satisfactory grade.
- A better approach is to set the value for Excellent at 5 points, Satisfactory at 4, and Poor at 3. Then a student scoring a satisfactory in all three categories would have 12 points out of a possible 15, or 80%.
- Under this same point value system, the poor report would score 9 points, or 60%. This is reasonable, since even the poor example is still a report—it's not a failure, just an unsatisfactory presentation.
- A student should only receive a score of less than 60% (a failing grade) if the assignment was so unacceptable that it could not be evaluated at all or entirely missed the mark. In terms of our oral report example, a failing presentation would involve something that prevented the audience from understanding the speaker or a major disregard for the project's expectations.

You can also *weight the different criteria* to suit your assignment. Using the previous example, let's say that you want Content to be worth more than Presentation or Expectations since your main concern was for the information the student is attempting to convey to her peers. The rubric would then look like Figure 4.4 (showing point values only).

Report Rubric	Excellent	Satisfactory	Poor	Unsatisfactory
Content	10	8	6	0
Presentation	5	4	3	0
Expectations	5	4	3	0

FIGURE 4.4 Sample Rubric—Weighted Scores

It's easiest if the point total you choose is a factor of 100, making it fairly simple to calculate a percent. With a 20-point rubric like this, you can just multiply the student's score by 5 to find the percent instead of having to solve a more complicated math problem.

Checklists

A checklist is a simplified version of a rubric in which the grading criteria are evaluated on a pass/fail basis. If the instructor determines that the work meets the criterion, the student gets credit. If not, the student does not get credit. A checklist typically includes 10 items, making for very easy grading. An example of a checklist addressing criteria for a Group Presentation follows.

Group Presentation Checklist

_____ addresses the assigned topic

_____ provides evidence from 3 to 5 sources

_____ makes cogent, reasoned arguments in support of main points

_____ includes one or more multimedia components

_____ includes a component of audience participation

_____ meets stated guidelines for time

_____ all group members participate in the presentation

_____ all group members acknowledge ownership of presentation components

_____ presenters consistently maintain a professional demeanor and appearance

_____ all aspects of the presentation maintain audience interest

Total Points = _____ x 10 = _____ %

A checklist is easier for the instructor to create and to fill out than a rubric, but it doesn't include much in the way of qualitative assessment. However, if the idea of creating a rubric seems daunting, try a checklist first.

WRITTEN ASSESSMENTS: QUIZZES AND EXAMS

Students may or may not learn course content, especially when it's presented in required readings and lectures, unless we hold them accountable through a grade. One strategy is to require students to write about their readings in a reaction paper, précis, or journal. However, many instructors dislike grading student writing because it can be time consuming or too subjective.[5] A quiz or exam can give the instructor objective knowledge of students' learning much more directly. True, good written assessments take time to create, but once you've invested the effort in developing a quiz or exam, it's ready to go the next time you teach your course. The prevalence of written exams varies by discipline. In some academic fields, these are a baseline expectation for instruction. In other fields, however, written exams are less common, with instructors more often relying on evaluation of performance-based tasks.

- The main differences between a quiz and an exam are length and importance.
  - A quiz is usually short (5 to 10 questions) and checks for understanding of learning in progress or a portion of the course content.
  - An exam is longer (20 questions or more) and measures learning at the end of a course or unit of study.
- Writing questions:
  - *Objective questions* have definite right and wrong answers, making them easier to grade.
    Objective question types include
    - Multiple choice
    - True/false
    - Matching
    - Short answer (fill in the blank; respond with a phrase or sentence)
  - *Subjective questions* require more thoughtful evaluation, usually involving some opinion on the part of both the student and the evaluator.
    - Essay (extended answer—one paragraph or more in length)
    - Performance task (demonstration of learning by completing a short project or solving a problem)

How to Write a Good Quiz

- Quiz questions should measure student learning in progress.
- They should ask about course content or information the instructor wants the student to remember long term—asking questions about big ideas rather than insignificant details.
- Time required to complete a quiz should be approximately 1 or 2 minutes per question.

Example
Let's say a professor in the Department of English teaching Literary Studies 201 required students to read J.R.R. Tolkien's *The Hobbit* and wants to give them a quiz to verify that they've actually read and understood the book rather than simply watching the films by Peter Jackson.

A parallel example of two potential quizzes about this novel appears in Figure 4.5.

Good Quiz	Poor Quiz
Which of the following statements best summarizes Bilbo's decision to accompany the dwarves on their quest? a) He is an agreeable fellow and wants to honor Gandalf's request. b) He is bored with his present life in the Shire and secretly craves adventure. c) He suddenly becomes impoverished and needs the promised share of the dwarves' treasure. d) He is shamed into the trip, not wanting to seem cowardly in front of the dwarves.	What was Bilbo's mother's maiden name? a) Baggins b) Maggot c) Gamgee d) Took
The author fills a great many pages of the book with descriptive passages. Which of these passages could the author have shortened or omitted without significantly affecting the storyline? a) The dwarves' journey through Mirkwood b) Bilbo's experiences while the dwarves were held captive by the goblins c) The trip down the river from the Wood Elves' palace to Laketown d) Gandalf's strategy for introducing the dwarves to Beorn	In what year was the book first published? a) 1937 b) 1945 c) 1956 d) 1962
Why did Tolkien position Bilbo as the hero of the story rather than a more traditionally heroic figure like Gandalf or Thorin? a) Bilbo is an "everyman" and as such is easier for the readers to identify with. b) Bilbo is secretly a wizard and possesses hidden magical powers. c) Bilbo symbolizes every person's capacity to achieve greatness no matter what their upbringing or present circumstances. d) The author's rationale for this choice is not determinable.	What item did Bilbo hand Gandalf at the end of the book? a) The One Ring b) A book c) A tobacco jar d) A glass of wine
Where and when does Thorin's deathbed scene take place? a) In the throne room under the mountain when Thorin is very old b) Near the snowy peak of the mountain during the Battle of Five Armies c) In an encampment in the valley following the Battle of Five Armies d) In the goblin's stronghold under the mountains during the dwarves' journey toward Smaug's lair	Gandalf's Elvish name is a) Radagast b) Mithrandir c) Saruman d) Elrond

FIGURE 4.5 Good Quiz–Poor Quiz

The questions in the good quiz ask the student to evaluate and analyze as well differentiating between the book and the film, whereas questions in the poor quiz simply require recall of insignificant detail. Good questions feature important concepts; poor questions dwell on irrelevant or minor facts.

How to Write a Good Exam

The rules for writing questions for an exam are the same as for a quiz; however, they should assess learning that the instructor hopes the student will remember in the long term, especially concepts that are foundational to later courses.
A final exam can include the following:

- *General questions* about important concepts from assigned readings and class discussion
  Ex: Which philosophical position emphasizes the primacy of objectivity and direct evidence provided by sense data?
  a) Rationalism
  b) Empiricism
  c) Aestheticism
  d) Relativism

- Important *vocabulary*
  Ex: Match the following terms and their definitions:

  _____ *dramaturge*   *a. orchestral opening to the second act of a musical*
  _____ *entr'acte*   *b. wall forming a framing arch between the stage and audience*
  _____ *proscenium*   *c. member of a theater company who acts as a script consultant*

- Questions about *technical processes or materials* might be encountered in a practice situation or professional problem.
  Ex: Explain how technical writing differs from ordinary prose and list at least three strategies a writer could employ to ensure clear communication in a technical text. (Essay)

There's no ideal formula for universal assessment: Each one will be as individual as the person who writes it. If you'd like a technological boost, numerous online test generators are available to assist you in this task. Resources are included at the end of this chapter.

How to Write a Survey

A survey can be a good tool to measure students' progress from the time they begin the class until they complete it. Survey data can also serve as a formative assessment, guiding your instruction. For example, if you administer a survey at the beginning of your course and find that students are already familiar with many of the topics you intend to teach, you can spend less time on that material and focus your instruction on the topics with which students are less skilled. Conversely, if students express doubt about their abilities in areas where you had presumed they were already skilled, you can plan to provide additional instruction to address the gaps in their prior learning.

Surveys, like quizzes and tests, can contain different types of questions. One of the most common is a *Likert* item, in which the respondent marks an answer along a scale, or continuum.

Ex. 1: I'd rate my current knowledge of philosophy as

1. *Novice: I know virtually nothing about philosophy.*
2. *Basic: I can provide a basic definition of philosophy and can name at least three important philosophers.*
3. *Intermediate: I have read some philosophical articles and books and possess a general familiarity with the discipline.*
4. *Advanced: I have taken more than one previous philosophy course.*
5. *Expert: I previously earned a degree in philosophy.*

A survey can assess student attitudes and opinions about topics important to your curriculum, measure prior knowledge, or check for understanding of important concepts that might be difficult to assess on a standard exam.

Ex. 2: What is your opinion of the following statement? "Excellent acting is the most important element in a successful theatrical performance."

1. *Strongly disagree*
2. *Somewhat disagree*
3. *Neither agree nor disagree*
4. *Somewhat agree*
5. *Strongly agree*

Administering the same survey at the beginning and end of the course allows the instructor to examine the difference in students' responses, which is another tool to measure growth and learning. Your survey can be based on the course objectives or outcomes, giving students a range of response options.

Examples:

- *I am familiar with historical achievements in theater.*
  1. *Strongly disagree*
  2. *Somewhat disagree*

3. *Neither agree nor disagree*
4. *Somewhat agree*
5. *Strongly agree*

- *I can identify a novel's historical, cultural, or stylistic context.*
  1. *Strongly disagree*
  2. *Somewhat disagree*
  3. *Neither agree nor disagree*
  4. *Somewhat agree*
  5. *Strongly agree*
- *I would rate my knowledge of film studies as*
  1. *Nonexistent—I've never watched a movie.*
  2. *A little knowledge—I've watched many movies and documentary films.*
  3. *Some knowledge from watching films and reading film criticism*
  4. *Working knowledge gained in previous film courses*
  5. *Advanced knowledge gained through professional experience in the movie industry*

A survey can be administered using pencil and paper, but you'll have to collect the papers and analyze the data you've gathered. If you don't want to bother with this step, using online tools such as SurveyMonkey or SurveyGizmo can make the task of data analysis much easier. You might need to confine your survey to 10 questions unless you purchase a subscription to one of these services, but you'll be able to access graphics, correlations, and other interesting ways to look at the data you've collected.

Using Assessment Tools

For educators in fields that primarily rely on holistic or subjective analysis of student work, beginning to introduce written assessments and objective grading criteria will be a big step. You'll have to approach this task in the way you're most comfortable. After all, a tool you don't use is—by definition—useless. You should try to keep your assessments as simple as possible, but they should be thorough enough to generate the student data you need in order to assign a fair grade. Every assignment you give to students should have a corresponding assessment mechanism, or students will see them as being unimportant and ineffective.

Now that you're familiar with different assessments you might employ, the next step is to look back at your outcomes and objectives and to match each one with the right type of assessment.

Basically, if you teach something, you must assess it somehow. How do you decide which type of assessment to employ?

- If you're evaluating complex or creative work such as a project, performance, or presentation, use a rubric or a checklist.
- If you're assessing factual content covering only a portion of the course, such as technical vocabulary, use a quiz.
- If you're checking for student comprehension of subjective content, assign a précis or response paper.
- If you're determining students' assimilation of knowledge spanning the entire course, use a final exam.

Example

Now let's look at the assessments for Design Thinking for Entrepreneurs in Figure 4.6 to see how they align with the outcomes and objectives we developed in the previous chapter.

In this example, we can see that the outcomes, objectives, and assessments remain in alignment with one another, pairing each objective with an assessment mechanism. This reflects best practice in course development and provides students with an optimal learning experience in which their efforts clearly lead to the program outcomes.

Wait . . . why are there no surveys in the plan for Design Thinking for Entrepreneurs?

- Surveys are not a tool to use in grading so much as they serve to inform your instruction. They don't need to appear on your Outcomes, Objectives, and Assessments chart.
- A pre-course survey gives you an idea of what students already know and believe about your discipline, allowing you to employ that knowledge as you deliver your instruction.
- A post-course survey helps you to determine whether your instruction was successful, and you can also use that knowledge to plan for the next time you teach the course.
- Neither type of survey specifically measures student achievement, so they are not included in the plans for the course.

WEIGHTING ASSIGNMENTS AND ASSESSMENTS

The last task when creating assessments is determining their value as components of your students' final grades. As with many of the things we've discussed, there really isn't a perfect formula for accomplishing this task. The easiest approach is to make sure the maximum number of points a student can earn is equal to 100 or 1,000.

	OUTCOMES	OBJECTIVES	ASSESSMENT
KNOWLEDGE	Students will apply the principles and practices of entrepreneurship through critical analysis of the social and cultural contexts in which innovations occur to effect beneficial change within diverse populations.	Students will examine entrepreneurial principles and practices and their application to improving the quality of human life. Students will develop skill in multiple ideation strategies and adapt them to entrepreneurial opportunities addressing the needs of diverse populations. Students will explore the concepts of ethics and social responsibility within the cultural contexts of wicked problems.	Students' participation in (1) classroom discussions and activities, and (2) their achievement on written assessments will demonstrate • Knowledge of entrepreneurial principles and practices • Understanding of multiple ideation strategies • Ability to apply their learning to the improvement of human life.
SKILL	Students will develop the ability to create, launch, and sustain a business venture or community organization, identifying applicable governance systems and utilizing effective business communications and entrepreneurial practices.	Students will apply the principles and practices of entrepreneurship to the creation of a business model addressing a wicked problem. Students will utilize effective written and verbal communication appropriate for business contexts. Students will create supporting documents and materials demonstrating their knowledge of applicable governance systems and the social context of the problem.	

FIGURE 4.6 Design Thinking for Entrepreneurs—Outcomes, Objectives, and Assessments

	OUTCOMES	OBJECTIVES	ASSESSMENT
INTEGRATION	Students will integrate their skills and knowledge of entrepreneurship with multiple strategies for inquiry as they generate a potential solution to a wicked problem by critically analyzing information, making value judgments, responding to challenges, and demonstrating empathetic understanding of the socio-cultural context of the target population.	Students will employ strategic innovation and entrepreneurial practices in the development of projects addressing wicked problems. Students will investigate the problem's social, cultural, and political context as they conduct field research, interacting with the target population. Students will formulate the business model for an entrepreneurial venture creating a product, service, or organization intended to address a wicked problem.	Students' projects and supporting materials will demonstrate: • Creativity or innovation • Strategy toward a solution • Identification of opportunity • Understanding of and empathy for customer's needs • Recognition and mitigation of risk • Creation of value for the target constituency • Social engagement • Self-evaluation of the proposed solution

FIGURE 4.6 Continued

You can give each assignment or assessment an equal weight, but assessments requiring the most student effort usually carry higher point values.

Our example from Design Thinking for Entrepreneurs in Figure 4.7 uses a 1,000-point scale and distributes these point values across the course components.

CALCULATING STUDENT GRADES

Presuming that we're going to use the point distribution above, how do we turn the percentage score from each assignment or test into a point total?

Brace yourselves: This involves math.

One way of minimizing the number of calculations you have to do is simply to make the graded item (the project, quiz, or paper) worth exactly the number of points as its weight. This doesn't give you many options when grading each individual item, though. For instance, if you ask students to write a précis that's

Assignments & Assessments	Weight
Nine Assignments/5% each	450
Three Quizzes/5% each	150
Project	300
Final Exam	100
Total	1,000

FIGURE 4.7 Design Thinking for Entrepreneurs—Assignments and Assessments

Assignments & Assessments	Weight	Student Score
Nine Assignments/5% each	450	375
Three Quizzes/5% each	150	120
Project	300	275
Final Exam	100	95
Total	1,000	865

FIGURE 4.8 Sample Student Grade

worth just 2 points, it essentially becomes a pass/fail grade with little room for qualitative assessment.

For Design Thinking for Entrepreneurs, the grade calculation is fairly simple (see Figure 4.8). In this case, we would add the student's point totals and divide by 10 to arrive at the final percentage grade. In the following example, the student earned 865 of a possible 1,000 points. 865/10 = 86.5%, or a B for the course grade.

For a bit more challenging example, let's take a look at a page from a hypothetical instructor's gradebook. The content of these assignments is irrelevant to our purposes here. We're only considering the instructor's method of calculating grades.

This example demonstrates a method by which instructors can set whatever point value they think is appropriate for each assignment and determine the *percent* for each. When it comes time to determine final grades, they do a very simple calculation to find the point total for that assignment. Don't worry yet—this isn't all that hard.

Take a look at the shaded row in the sample gradebook in Figure 4.9. Let's say the instructor evaluated a student's work on Assignment 4 using a rubric, based on which the student earned 87%. However, the assignment itself was worth 7 points out of the 100 points possible for the course. To calculate the grade, the instructor would multiply 0.87 (the decimal version of 87%) by the 7 points possible, resulting in 6.09 points for that assignment. Simple! 0.87 x 7 = 6.09 points.

Helpful Hint: If you set up your gradebook in a chart like this, you can get MS Word to add the points for you! Here's how:

1. When you set up the gradebook chart, make sure each point value is in its own cell.
2. Click the bottom cell of the "Points Earned" column (highlighted in yellow on the chart).
3. In the Table Tools menu (located at the top right of the screen—it opens when you click on a cell in the table), there's Layout tab. Click this.

Assessment (100 points possible)	Student's Score	Calculation	Points
Class participation (10)	83%	0.83 x 10	8.3
Quiz 1 (3)	80%	0.80 x 3	2.4
Quiz 2 (3)	95%	0.95 x 3	2.85
Assignment 1 (7)	100%	1.0 x 7	7
Assignment 2 (7)	80%	0.80 x 7	5.6
Assignment 3 (7)	75%	0.75 x 7	5.25
Assignment 4 (7)	87%	0.87 x 7	6.09
Assignment 5 (7)	85%	0.85 x 7	5.95
Assignment 6 (7)	94%	0.94 x 7	6.58
Assignment 7 (7)	100%	1.0 x 7	7
Midterm (15)	85%	0.85 x 15	12.75
Final Project (20)	95%	0.95 x 20	19
FINAL GRADE			88.77

FIGURE 4.9 Sample Gradebook

4. Select Data in the Layout tab.
5. Click on Formula.
6. A window will open on your screen. Don't change anything in this window—the default option is to calculate the sum of the chart cells above the cell you selected. If you click OK—Voilà!—the column is added for you.

ONLINE ASSESSMENT RESOURCES

If you don't like the idea of doing these calculations for yourself, you can use an online grading program. In fact, many helpful teaching resources can be found on the Internet, from grading programs to survey analysis services. Some of these are free, some are free on a limited basis, and some require a fee.

Online Gradebooks

Numerous online gradebooks are available that can simplify the task of grading, organizing your data, and calculating student scores. Many of these are designed for K–12, but that only means they'll have some features you can ignore.

iGradePlus—Free Online Gradebook	www.igradeplus.com/
School Management Software	www.thinkwave.com/
JumpRope	http://jumpro.pe/
Track My Grades.com	www.trackmygrades.com/

Online Surveys

It's possible to administer a survey using pencil and paper, but online survey programs make the job much easier, saving you from tedious tasks like data tabulation and percent calculations.

Survey Monkey	www.surveymonkey.com/
Free Online Surveys	http://freeonlinesurveys.com/
Survey Planet	www.surveyplanet.com/
eSurvey Creator	www.esurveycreator.com/
Google Docs	www.youtube.com/watch?v=5sOFs4ai2oY

Online Rubric Generators

If you're new to using rubrics, these websites can assist you in creating tools that will help you in grading student work.

Rubistar	http://rubistar.4teachers.org/
Teachnology	www.teach-nology.com/web_tools/rubrics/
iRubric	www.rcampus.com/indexrubric.cfm

Quizzes and Exams: Online Generators

Creating tests, quizzes, or exams is easier using an online test generator.

| Easy Test Maker | www.easytestmaker.com/ |
| Testmoz | https://testmoz.com/ |

FAIRNESS AND OBJECTIVITY

Assessment is intrinsically subjective, even when we attempt to maintain an objective position. After all, we create our grading tools according to our own preferences and then evaluate students' work using our personal perception of whether students met the criteria we selected. Nevertheless, we should still strive to a standard of fairness and objectivity.

Some instructors continue to reserve the right to artificially increase or decrease students' grades based on nothing more than their own opinion. The following email was sent to me by a student who was concerned about an instructor's preference for subjectivity in grading:

Given my particular situation in [the course], and the fact that as far as I know no one has received any feedback in this course, do you think the following excerpt from the syllabus could have a potential negative impact on my grade? I have completed and turned in all work on time. I have missed only one class and that was due to my mom's knee surgery.

Syllabus Excerpt:

Discretionary points: At my discretion, I reserve the right to round up or down to the nearest grade per my assessment of your overall performance. Points may be subtracted for talking, texting or web surfing during lecture, poor attendance, habitual and unexcused lateness (more than 4 minutes), or leaving early from class without special permission. They may be given for initiative, collaboration and enthusiasm. There are no extra credit assignments in this class.

Maybe I am reading too much into this, but those of us that she does not care for could potentially be downgraded due to this extremely subjective clause. I don't think this is the same as you making judgment calls to give students a "second chance", but maybe I am wrong?

When you set forth clear criteria, you foster a positive belief in your own trustworthiness as an instructor. The student who sent the email above had clearly lost faith in the instructor, which was detrimental to the learning process occurring in that classroom. We discussed NR and CR grading earlier in this chapter, but this student's email raises another option that many instructors utilize, but which is not at all best practice: grading based on opinion. Academic freedom allows us this option, and you are within your rights as an instructor to decline to provide your students with a rationale for the grades that you assign to their work. We must not forget, however, that students have rights, too. They can and do protest grades that they feel are unfair. It's best not to set up a situation that could lead to an adversarial relationship with a student, especially if you do not have any evidence in support of your grading decisions. Whether or not you value fairness, ensuring that your grading criteria are defensible protects you from unwanted consequences like being called to the dean's office to explain yourself when the student files a complaint.

Likewise, assessment can seem capricious and inconsistent to students if it's not based on written criteria. The following email exchange chronicles a grade dispute between an instructor and a student. The assignment in question had been given twice during the course and was graded using the same rubric each time. The first time, the student had received 100%—25 of the 25 possible points. The second time, however, the instructor deducted points from one of the grading criteria, which caused the student to earn a B instead of an A—a situation she was unused to, being a very driven and high-achieving student. The student's and instructor's names have been redacted to protect their privacy, and their original text has been reproduced verbatim except where noted.

From: Student, To: Instructor, cc to Program Director

The recent grading of my written response 2 has left me with a few questions. I have attached both my written response #1 which got a 100% and my written response #2 which I got an 88%. The reasoning according to the feedback is that I was vague with the demographic section. I am not sure how it is vague? Was I supposed to count the amount of parents, students, non-students, etc. in the theater? Was I supposed to know the exact capacity of the theater? I am confused how this grade is justified when I touched upon what I experienced and I did in fact touch upon the demographic. In my previous written assignment I didn't have to say the exact sizing and such of the demographic and I got a 100% so I am not sure why I lost 3 points in this section for this assignment. Please get back to me as soon as possible after reviewing the screenshots and written assignment 1 and 2 so I can have further clarification of the justification of this grade because as a student I feel as though I am being retaliated against. Thank you.

From: Instructor, To: Student

First off, let me say that you are an excellent student, your grades certainly reflect your commitment. As I've stated before, I want to assure you that all students in my class are marked in the same way within the same context. I am a fair and lenient grader and everyone is treated equally. If one student was marked down for a certain reason, all were marked down for the same.

So why the difference in your grades from the first written response to the second? As you will recall, in class after the 1st papers had been turned in, I discussed with the entire class that I was looking for more emphasis and detail in the administrative portion of the 2nd paper. I graded the first papers more broadly and with less emphasis on this section as we hadn't discussed this prior to them being submitted. I certainly was looking at the second written response in a different way with more emphasis and detail on the administration—which is what this class is about.

[The portion of this response detailing the instructor's comments on the student's paper has been omitted for the sake of brevity.]

I reduced your grade (and other students as well) for vague responses to each portion of the questions. Basically each area of the response (2 as a patron and 3 as an administrator) had 5 points total for a total of 25 points for the entire paper—you received all points for all other questions, but not for this one—while you stated a basic idea, it was not up to the standards of a detailed response and I reduced your grade by 3 points.

I hope that helps you understand the justification for your grade on this assignment.

From: Student. To: Instructor, cc to Program Director

Thank you for your response. However, that response doesn't help me understand the grade justification. Where on the rubric does it give the point valuation for the grade deduction? We didn't get a rubric just a set of what to include. Yes, in class you said you wanted us to go more in depth for the administrative side but you also said you were going to give us new questions so we could go more in depth then you changed it to just go more in depth with the original questions given. So I strongly disagree with the connotation that it was "too vague." I am there for the performance, I did in fact guess estimate like you stated you wanted me to by saying it's a medium sized venue, and stating the types of people I saw there. As a student, to not have a rubric or be given a rubric at all that states the point valuation of each category to then be deducted 3 points for something so minute confuses me greatly. Bruce what is your opinion on this situation? I look forward to both of your responses.

Also just to follow up, to say something is vague is completely different than saying something isn't there or not what I have. Meaning to give a zero in a category for it apparently being "too vague" I can't see how that is justifiable. I look forward to hearing back from both of you. Have a great day.

If this instructor had provided students with written criteria for the work she wanted them to perform, including specific examples of what a good response would look like, the student would have been able to complete the work satisfactorily. Instead, the instructor herself was vague in her expectations and communicated them only verbally during a class period. Furthermore, she used the same evaluation instrument for both assignments (when the student received 100%), but she changed her expectations for student performance without changing the grading criteria. It was not unreasonable for the student to expect a similar grade for a similar effort on the same assignment, graded with the same list of stated criteria as the first time.

The instructor's explanation was too little too late for the student to accept. I met privately with the instructor and asked her to consider the possibility that she had also been vague in communicating her requirements, suggesting that she offer to restore 1 or 2 points to the student's grade. This would have raised the grade to an A− and served as a gesture of good faith. She categorically refused, standing firm on her original evaluation of the student's work. Undoubtedly, she was within her rights to do so. Students often question their grades, so we cannot habitually acquiesce to every demand for higher scores. Nevertheless, we should be courageous enough to admit our errors. The instructor claimed that she explained the new criteria in class, but it is unfair to expect our students to remember every word we say, nor should they have to guess at our expectations or requirements.

This incident illustrates the purpose behind publishing clear criteria for every assignment we expect our students to complete. When we provide written expectations from the onset of a learning task, we maximize our students' chances for success and minimize the likelihood of disputed grades for which we can legitimately be found liable, as was the case in the preceding example.

INDUSTRIAL AGE ASSESSMENT

Before we conclude this chapter, let's briefly revisit the idea of formative and summative assessment. Bestselling author Sir Ken Robinson and educator Salman Khan, founder of Khan Academy, have each spoken frequently about the fact that our present academic system was created to meet the needs of the Industrial Age, when businesses demanded workers who would reliably possess the same skill set and would do the same job for years. Our ideas about grading and assessment also operate under this outdated industrial model. For instance, if we administer an exam and the student answers three-fourths of the questions correctly, she earns a 75%, or a C. That's where we stop. We don't pause to think, "Hmmm, this student still doesn't know 25% of the material we've covered. How can I help her to learn what she's missing?" Our goal is not for our students to attain mastery of the course content, but to present the course content, assess their performance level, and move on. We give little thought to whether or not students have learned what we intended to teach. If they fail our course, they can retake it. We offer no other options, nor are our institutions structured to allow anything else.

When we only determine our students' level of mastery in our courses after the final exam, we've missed crucial opportunities to teach. Genuine formative assessment, on the other hand, should be a tool to guide our instruction. If student learning is truly our goal, then students who perform poorly on a formative assessment should receive additional instruction or be given a second chance to improve their work so that they can prove that they've truly learned what we've taught.

I believe that we should question our underlying assumptions about the relationship between teaching and learning as measured only by summative assessments such as final exams. When the course is over, it's too late to teach students who have not yet achieved mastery of the course content. Effective use of formative assessments such as quizzes or checkpoints gives the instructor a more complete picture of students' learning, but we also have to act upon this information, not just record the students' scores in our gradebook and move on to the next thing in the course. Continued reliance on a traditional, Industrial Age approach to grading keeps the classroom focus on us as instructors—our teaching, our assessments, our assignments of grades. A learning-centered philosophy of education demands more of us. We don't go to the doctor just to find out what's wrong—we also expect that we'll receive treatment that cures our illness. Just so, our students don't sit in our classrooms just to subject themselves to our evaluation—they come to learn. Shouldn't our assessment practices reflect this crucial difference?

YOUR TURN: WRITING YOUR ASSESSMENTS

Unlike the previous chapter, there's no template or formula for creating the assessments you'll need in your course. You must design these according to your particular objectives, driven by the content you plan to teach. Once you've determined which types of assessment you want to use and have completed a chart such as the example provided for Design Thinking for Entrepreneurs, you can defer the task of actually creating your rubrics, quizzes, checklists, or exams until you complete the planning of your entire course, a task we'll tackle in the next chapters.

As you write your assessments, bear in mind that *anything* students might do to raise or lower their grade in your course should be connected to an assessment

Identify	→	Ideate
Why should we first plan our assessments before we decide what we're teaching? By beginning with the assessment, you can decide how best to ensure that your students will successfully acquire the skills and knowledge that you're attempting to deliver through the course.		How do I determine which assessments to use and when to use them? This depends entirely on your preferences as the instructor. Whatever assessment methods you employ, they should measure your students' achievement of your course objectives and program outcomes.
Iterate	←	Implement
When you teach your course, take note of how your students performed on each assessment. For example, if particular test items were missed by a majority of students, you might need to re-write that question or eliminate it from your exam. Or you could take this as an indicator that your instruction had not adequately prepared your students to answer correctly, in which case you'd need to revise your instruction.		What methods can I use to assess my students? This all depends on your course content. Rubrics, checklists, exams, quizzes, performance tasks, peer evaluation, self-evaluation, and many more options are available to you as an instructor.

FIGURE 4.10 Chapter 4 Design Connection

mechanism. For example, if it is your policy to deduct points for late work, the grading rubric you design for each assignment should include criteria regarding submitting the work on time. This makes your expectation crystal clear to students and can help to avoid problems later on.

Remember:

- You must plan an appropriate assessment for each of your course objectives.
- Norm-referenced assessment compares students to one another, while criterion-referenced assessment compares student performance to pre-established performance criteria.
- Formative assessment measures learning in progress, generally having a low-point value. Summative assessment measures learning at the end of a course or unit, generally having a high-point value.
- Rubrics, checklists, surveys, quizzes, exams, and writing assignments can be either formative or summative, depending on how you use them.
- A good quiz or exam should require students to access higher-order thinking skills rather than simple recall of facts or information.

Notes

[1] Quoted in Scriven, M. (1991). Beyond formative and summative evaluation. In M. W. McLaughlin and E. D. C. Phillips (eds.), *Evaluation and Education: A Quarter Century*. Chicago: University of Chicago Press.

[2] Please note that this is just a rough demonstration, not an exercise in statistical analysis.

[3] Just as a side note, the color red is very emotionally powerful. That's why stop signs and fire engines are red, so that we see them quickly and avoid trouble. While red ink is easy for a student to see on a graded paper or test, it also packs a negative subliminal punch. Choosing a different colored grading pen such as green or purple is just as easy for students to see but doesn't carry the same cognitive baggage.

[4] Divide the number of points earned by the total number of points, then multiply by 100 to find the percent. For example, 12 points earned divided by 15 total points = 0.80. Multiplied by 100 = 80%

[5] More information about grading student writing is included in Chapter 6.

Chapter 5

Planning for Effective Instruction

CHAPTER SUMMARY

- Long-Range Planning
- Modules
- Building Your Schedule
- Your Turn: Writing Your Assessments, Revisited
- Lesson Planning
- Scaffolding Instruction
- Your Turn: Planning Your Lessons

Once you've written your outcomes and objectives and planned for the methods you'll use to assess student learning, the next step in course design is to look at the entire body of knowledge you intend to cover over the duration of the class and to break it down into logical units spanning all your class periods. Even though our first inclination might be to let the class evolve organically, disciplining ourselves to make and stick to a schedule ensures that we can achieve all our objectives by the end of the course.

We can break the task of making a plan for our weekly instruction into two basic steps: (1) create a long-range plan and a (2) determine a day-by-day schedule of instruction, readings, assignments, and assessments.

LONG-RANGE PLANNING

Your first job is to map out a master plan of instruction for the entire course. The easiest place to start is to create a chart or calendar broken into the number of weeks of the course. You can divide the week's tasks into specific class periods later on, after you've decided what you'll cover. As you create this master plan of instruction, always keep your outcomes and objectives in mind.

Remember, if you have an instructional unit on your current syllabus that doesn't relate to the objectives you've written, you'll either need to omit it or to revise the objectives to include it. A chart such as the one presented in Figure 5.1 is helpful in working through your plans.

MODULES

One of the best organizational methods involves dividing the course into modules, each ending in an assessment. Minimally, this would include a midterm and a final, as is common across the landscape of higher education. An even better practice would be to create four modules by dividing each half of the semester into two

Week	Date	Topics and Activities	Assignments and Assessments
1			
2			
3			
4			
5			
6			
7			
8			
9			
10			
11			
12			
13			
14			
15			
16			

FIGURE 5.1 Semester Planning Grid

separate modules, each ending in an assessment. For example, you could place an assessment for Module 1 at Week 4, an assessment of the content in Module 2 at Week 8 (midterm), an assessment for Module 3 at Week 12, and a final exam at the end of Module 4 in Week 16. Modules can be of any length, from 1 week to multi-week divisions of study. They can build upon one another or can present discrete topics. The midterm and final assessments need not evaluate student learning of the entire half-term—they can measure only those modules with which they're associated, if that makes the most sense in your particular course. The point is to build periodic assessment into your course by creating conceptual groupings of instructional content.

1. Consider the entirety of your objectives.
2. Determine an appropriate assessment for each objective.
3. Input these assessments into your long-range plan, creating module groupings.

To illustrate this point, let's return to Design Thinking for Entrepreneurs. This course blends lecture, discussion, and project-based learning. Assessments in this course include several assignments, quizzes, an extensive project, and a final exam. Modules were constructed around these course benchmarks, aligning with the steps of the design thinking process:

Module 1: Ideation (Weeks 1–3)

- Introduction to design thinking; Virtual crash course in design thinking
- Why? How? What? Human-centered design and social entrepreneurship
- Wicked problems and systems thinking
- Quiz 1—Design Thinking and Wicked Problems

Module 2: Innovation (Weeks 4–6)

- Problem solving and problem finding
- Lateral thinking
- Critical and computational thinking
- Quiz 2—Strategies for Ideation

Module 3: Implementation (Weeks 7–12)

- Entrepreneurship
- Business modeling
- Failure and risk

- Prototyping and project management
- Information for innovators
- Funding and regulations
- Marketing, branding, and social media
- Quiz 3—Business Basics

Module 4: Evaluation (Weeks 13–16)

- Leadership
- Ethics, histories, and social context
- Project presentations
- Final exam

Modules in this course align with the stages of innovation that students will explore in the course. As an instructor, you need to evaluate your own course content to see what works best for you. No concrete rules govern the creation of modules within a course. Rather, these groupings should align with conceptual divisions in your course content and with your planned assessments. If you're not used to this type of organization, beginning with two modules is a good choice, one ending at midterm and one ending with the final exam. You can always refine your plans later, once you've taught the course and see where the natural stopping points arise.

Materials Selection, Readings, and Assignments

Before you can create a plan of readings and assignments for your students based on the modules and assessments you've created, you must select the print materials you'll use in your course. Textbook publishers abound, and many offer features such as online resources, pre-made quizzes and exams, and student study guides, among others. Your selection of course texts and supplementary materials such as articles from professional journals, multimedia content, guest lecturers, and even field trips should be governed primarily by your outcomes, objectives, and assessments. If the book, item, or experience you'd like to include in your course doesn't align with these overarching concepts, you should carefully consider whether it is beneficial. If so, you must revise your objectives to align the item with your course.

Every course will necessarily utilize different materials, and even parallel sections of the same course at a university may vary in their materials if taught by different instructors. Design Thinking for Entrepreneurs uses excerpts from 10 different texts, published in a course pack. Students are encouraged to read those texts in their entirety, but it would be unfair to burden students with both the reading load and the expense of asking them to read that many books in just one semester when the course project takes up the lion's share of their time. Instructors must approach this topic judiciously, as we'll discuss shortly.

Reading Schedule

When planning readings and assignments based on the materials you've selected, remember to keep student workloads manageable. Consider the number of pages of required reading very carefully. An average adult can read about 300 words per minute, and typical page is about 250–300 words in length, (both of which can vary widely, of course) for a rough calculation of about 1 page per minute. Does this mean if you assign students 50 pages of reading, it will take about 50 minutes to complete it? Unfortunately, that's not actually true because we also have to factor in the difficulty of the reading material. If you ask students to read some thing that's immediately understandable, like a novel or newspaper article, this might be true, but textbooks or dense academic language will require much more intensive cognitive activity, not to mention the time required for note-taking. This increases the expected time for reading, sometimes double or more what you'd expect. In fact, technical reading rates might even be as low as 50 to 75 words per minute.[1] That means 50 pages of technical reading, or 15,000 words (at 300 words per page), could require as much as 5 hours for a struggling student to complete.

Even though it might sound too obvious to mention, it's also a good idea for the instructor to read the same pages as the students each time she teaches the course. A colleague shared a story with me about a summer school literature course she took during her undergraduate studies. As we know, summer school classes generally condense 16 weeks of learning into 8 or fewer weeks of instruction, making for a challenging workload under the best of circumstances. The reading list for this class was quite long, comprised of rather obscure works that were all unfamiliar to the students. At the start of a class period about 2 weeks into the course, the instructor asked the students if they were having trouble keeping up with the readings. Feeling self-conscious, none of them spoke up. The instructor was crestfallen. "Oh," he sighed, "I was hoping that you were, because *I'm* having trouble keeping up with them." With that, all of the students admitted that they, too, found the reading expectations too demanding. This instructor had undoubtedly already read all of these novels when teaching past sections of the course, but by reading along with the students, he shared in his students' experience and kept the novels' content fresh in his mind, allowing him to be well prepared for their class discussions. As the result of this discussion, he cut some of the selections from the syllabus, making the remainder of the class a much better learning experience for the students.

Assignment Schedule

Besides scheduling your assigned readings, it's important to make a reasonable estimate of the amount of time necessary for students to complete each assignment, project, or research paper. As a general rule, it ought to take an average student about an hour to write a page of text. For many students, however, this is only the time involved in the actual *writing* of the page, not in researching source material or creating correct citations or a reference list (if required by the assignment), nor does it include time spend to refine and revise the paper prior to submitting it. Some students write more quickly than others, just as some read more quickly than others. Allowing an hour per page is a reasonable rule of thumb, but you need to bear in mind that individual students may find the task of writing to be much more onerous than others. In fact, some of us (including me) will take 2 or 3 hours per page of text, including research, writing, rewriting, and re-researching until it begins to align with our personal expectations.

We usually presume that our undergraduate students should spend 2 to 3 hours working outside of class for each clock hour in the classroom. For an average 3-hour course, therefore, students should be expected to complete about 9 hours of work outside of class. Empathy dictates that we should remember that ours is not the only course in which our students are enrolled. If the average undergraduate student takes 5 courses for a total of 15 credit hours per semester, and if each of those five instructors assigns 9 hours of outside work per week, this expands the student's workload to 60 hours per week. Furthermore, an optimal collegiate experience encompasses co-curricular involvement such as clubs, teams, performing arts groups, and so forth, each of which makes demands on students' time. Our students can easily face 80-hour workweeks, on top of their social relationships and commitments to paying jobs.

None of this ought to prevent us from expecting our students to complete the work we assign. But it does mean that we should take the time to calculate the total hours it's likely to take our students to read, write, research, or otherwise accomplish the tasks we require each week. If some weeks require more than 9 hours outside of class, trading off with weeks that require less is good practice. It's also a good idea to keep major events in mind when planning students' work. Homecoming, Thanksgiving, Spring Break, and other days off are scheduled years in advance and most of us already work these into our plans. However, major sporting events, national conferences being held on campus, and a host of other campuswide happenings can impact even the most carefully planned schedules. If your institution's most popular sports team is playing a home game against its greatest rival, it's best to expect that your students will be distracted and to adjust your plans accordingly.

We should also be mindful of the monetary costs of projects we ask students to do, if this will require students to acquire supplies off campus, and whether they have the ability to do so. These hidden costs can have a significant impact on students' learning experiences, sometimes even prohibiting them from remaining enrolled in our courses. In *Surveying the Landscape*, a professor of architecture[2] discussed this financial barrier:

> We require these students to go buy and make stuff. We lose a whole percentage of population when we require them to buy materials. Some don't have $50 or $1000! I've seen some projects cost $1000. And this causes problems in assessment—how to compare a $1000 dollar prototype vs a cardboard one that someone couldn't afford. So this is an exclusive club; this is a real problem. It doesn't affect retention, but affects engagement in first place. I've seen students walk in and then leave when seeing what they have to buy. Then we look around and say, 'Oh, our diversity isn't there. How do we become more inclusive?' Well, that cost is a big issue.

Your syllabus should include a reasonable estimate of the cost of required materials and a list of sources where students can obtain them. You should also encourage individuals to meet with you if they have problems meeting these expectations. I formerly taught an online course that asked students to purchase the latest edition of the course textbook. Every time I taught the course, panicked students would email me saying they couldn't afford a $75 book, especially on short notice. The newest version of the book was good, to be sure, but in my opinion as the course instructor, any of the prior editions of the book could suffice if necessary. I directed these students to Amazon, where used copies of older editions were available for less than $5.

I sincerely believe that we should do everything in our power to make our courses accessible and to place the fewest possible burdens on our students. If these costs are unavoidable, we need to make this information known to students well in advance. I know a student who was informed that the cost of tuition and books for the first semester of a community college nursing program would be about $1,900. On the first day of class, however, students were informed that there would be an additional $1,000 program fee and books would cost $500 more than they'd been told to expect. This student was distraught, very nearly having to drop out of the program when faced with nearly double the cost he'd been told to expect. Would we react any differently ourselves? If you wanted to install new carpeting in your home, agreeing to an estimate of $1,900 for the project, but were told on the day of installation that it would actually cost $3,400, you'd be enraged, right? Clearly, education isn't a commodity like carpeting, but unfair or inaccurate representation of costs and expenses are just as unethical, even if they're inadvertent.

Implicit and Explicit Expectations   Every instructor holds a set of expectations for students, which commonly involve things like meeting deadlines, classroom civility, correct formatting of written work, and appropriate use of college-level English. These are sometimes published in the syllabus, but many of us believe them to be self-evident. *Of course*, college students should use college-level English. *Obviously*, an assignment with a stated due date should be completed *by* that due date. Whether or not these expectations are made explicit on a syllabus, many instructors simply assume that their students will understand these as conventions of academic life.

Problems arise when any of these implicit expectations carries a potentially negative impact on students' grades. Therefore, best practice requires us to include these expectations in our course objectives and proactively provide *explicit* classroom instruction in these standards. If a student could be penalized for using an incorrect style guide when writing a research paper, such as formatting the paper in APA when MLA was expected, then the instructor must address this expectation by *overtly teaching a lesson about* MLA formatting. If a student could lose points for submitting a project after the published deadline, then best practice requires the instructor to first clearly and directly address this requirement in class, providing a lesson on why meeting deadlines is an important aspect of professional practice in the given academic discipline. We cannot assume our students will automatically understand *why* we require them to meet our expectations unless we deliberately *teach* them what we want them to do and how to do it. We need to show our students what success looks like and provide them with the tools to actually achieve this success.

Many instructors whom I've met, whether consciously or not, subscribe to the idea of *in loco parentis*. That is, they feel it is their duty to take on the role of parent with their students, guiding them toward correct adult behavior. Statements in defense of late penalties such as, "I need to prepare my students for the real world!" or "In the real world, nobody is going to make exceptions for you," are common. This belief is incorrect on at least two levels. First, our students are generally at least 18 years old, which legally makes them adults. It is not appropriate to treat them as children. Next, the "real world" does provide some exceptions or exemptions for deadlines. Mortgage payments, for example, are due on the first of the month, but most lenders include a 10-day or 15-day grace period before late penalties are assessed. In cases where no such grace period exists, failure to meet institutional or contractual obligations carries an intrinsic consequence. If we fail to renew our drivers' licenses or vehicle registrations, we could receive a costly ticket. If we consistently arrive late for work, we'll receive poor employee reviews or perhaps even face losing our jobs, as is also the case with excessive absenteeism or failure to complete work-related tasks according to schedule. Productivity, punctuality, and professionalism are worthy goals to communicate to our students, but they must also be made explicit in our syllabi, present in our course objectives, and the topic of direct instruction that not only explains our classroom requirements but conceptually links them to the type of workplace most of your students will enter upon graduation.

As you begin planning for instruction, make sure that you schedule class time for these lessons, including every expectation or requirement that holds the potential to significantly alter a student's grade. For example, you might decide to include an objective related to professionalism that covers punctuality, use of appropriate professional language, and strict adherence to published deadlines. These expectations should be supported by explanatory material in the course syllabus *and written* into your grading rubrics, checklists, and assignment directions. We'll revisit this topic in subsequent chapters, but it should be part of your plans from the very beginning of the process.

BUILDING YOUR SCHEDULE

Now that we've established our baseline expectations for what should be included in our courses, we can turn our attention toward mapping the structure of the course itself.

Step 1: The first step in building your schedule is to block out any scheduled time off, such as Thanksgiving or Spring Break. Then input your planned assessments for each of the modules you've created.

Step 2: Next, think back from each assessment to the teaching and instruction that should precede it, filling in the schedule with the specific topics and activities for each week of each module. You'll need to anticipate:

- Lectures, demonstrations, work time, readings, and discussions that must occur before students can complete a project or take a written assessment
- The amount of time you feel is reasonable for students to complete a task, such as a creative project or research paper
- The number of in-class and out-of-class hours available to deliver requisite instruction or complete these tasks
- Instruction in important classroom policies or assignment expectations

This schedule of assignments and assessments is just a skeleton, which you'll flesh out with additional planning later on. Upon further analysis, you might want to re-order assignments or make any number of other changes depending on your previous experience with the course content or teaching in general. Making a plan for instruction doesn't mean that it's set in stone. Every syllabus is a work in progress, subject to continuous development. The point is to exercise your best judgment as you formulate a plan for your instruction, but then to use your professional knowledge and disciplinary expertise to make the plan work, implementing changes as necessary.

PLANNING FOR EFFECTIVE INSTRUCTION

Figure 5.2 shows a partial course schedule for Design Thinking for Entrepreneurs. The grid has been divided into two class periods per week, with the first class of the week designated as a lecture section, and the second class dedicated to discussion and active learning.

Week	Date	Topics	Assignments
		MODULE 1—IDEATION	
1		Course introduction Introduction to design thinking	Read Brown Ch. 2 & 4; Kelly Ch. 4
		Virtual Crash Course in Design Thinking	
2		Why? How? What? Human-centered design and social entrepreneurship	Read Brown Ch. 9; Collins; Liedtka et al. Assignment 1: *30 under 30*
		Discuss relationship between design thinking and social entrepreneurship based on students' responses to Assignment 1 (due today)	
3		Wicked problems and systems thinking	Read Cabrera Quiz 1: Design Thinking and Wicked Problems
		Complete "Draw Toast" activity	
		MODULE 2—INNOVATION	
4		Problem solving and problem finding	Read Michalko—all Read articles: "Sitting is the New Smoking" and "The Best Chair is No Chair" Assignment 2—The Chair Problem
		Problem-solving activity Discussion of "the chair problem"	
5		Lateral Thinking	Assignment 3: Easy Company Tea—a Rube Goldberg Puzzle
		Discuss student results on "the chair problem" Share Assignment 3, Parts 1 and 2; complete Part 3 in class. Assignment 2 due	
6		Critical thinking and computational thinking	Assignment 4: Strategies for Ideation Quiz 2: Strategies for Ideation

FIGURE 5.2 Design Thinking for Entrepreneurs—Schedule Excerpt

YOUR TURN: WRITING YOUR ASSESSMENTS, REVISITED

Before we move on to developing individual lessons, this might be a good opportunity for you to write the assessments you've scheduled. Remember: Everything that happens in your classroom should lead directly to student learning, and all learning should be measured. It is your responsibility to ensure that your assessments fairly and accurately reflect your students' accomplishments in your course. This necessarily varies between disciplines, topics, focus areas, and even individual instructor's preferences. Furthermore, it's best to use a variety of assessment mechanisms rather than relying on two high-stakes tests administered as midterm and final exams.

You should also develop detailed student resources with specific instructions and expectations for all projects, papers, presentations, or other product-based assignments and assessments. These resources should be attached to your course syllabus so that students can prepare to meet these expectations from the very first day of the course, including any rubrics or checklists you plan to employ when evaluating their work, clearly indicating all criteria that could result in penalties to a student's grade and linked to the course objectives and program expectations.

Creating a large number of related documents can complicate the task of course planning. I've discovered that it helps to create a course map that lists everything needed for each week of the course, with columns for Readings, Assignments, Assessments, Student Resources, and Instructor Resources. I keep this document open on my computer as I'm planning, listing each item in the correct column by week. Of course, not every assignment needs a separate document for instructions, nor does every assignment necessitate creating a student resource such as a note page or instructor resource such as a grading rubric. I've found, though, that these documents tend to pile up and become disorganized as I'm planning, especially if I start rearranging the course content as I go. By keeping track of them on something like a spread sheet, I can be more productive. It's also a great tool while teaching the course because it provides both you and your students with a quick reference guide for where to find the materials or information planned for each week.

Creating a well-planned course seldom progresses sequentially. We begin with our outcomes and objectives, and then we envision the assessments we'll use, but once we go deeper into the actual planning and developing of readings, assignments, and resources, we engage in a process of iteration, revision, research, and creativity that moves between and among these steps in order to arrive at the final design of the course.

For instance, I determined that students' first assignment in Design Thinking for Entrepreneurs would be to read an article I'd found on the *Forbes* website called "30 Under 30"—the magazine's yearly list of notable young entrepreneurs. Then I set up an assignment grid for the syllabus titled "Written Directions for

Assignments" dividing it into three columns: when the task would be assigned, when it would be due, and a short set of bullet-point instructions, entering this assignment as the first item in the grid, along with a hyperlink to the article, as shown in Figure 5.3.

Because this first assignment is relatively simple, I decided that I didn't need to provide a template or a separate set of written instructions that students could download from the course web page.

Later in the planning process, I wanted students to complete a short reflective summary of the strategies for innovation we'd been studying. I find it's easier to grade students' work if their papers are substantially the same, so I created a very simple template for them to use for that assignment. I also created a quiz covering the content of that module and an answer key for the quiz. Week 6 of the course also marks the beginning of the course project. Figure 5.4 is an excerpt from the course map, showing each of the items for the week. (Note: the "Readings" cell is blank because I didn't assign any new readings for this week. Students had quite enough to do without reading added on to their workload.)

Students have access to the Project Documents folder from the first day of the course, but we explain the relevant documents during our discussion section in Week 6. The project has been thoroughly resourced in an attempt to eliminate as much confusion and ambiguity as possible and to maximize students' successful completion of this task. Therefore, the Project Documents folder contains (1) a blank business canvas document; (2) detailed written instructions; (3) a grading rubric for the project; (4) a form that students will complete when they submit their project, summarizing their work; (5) instructions for creating and uploading the required video documenting their work on the project over the duration of the course.

Assigned	Due	Description
Week 2 Class 1	Week 2 Class 2	**Assignment 1: 30 Under 30** • Read "30 Under 30: Social Entrepreneurs, 2017" www.forbes.com/30-under-30-2017/social- entrepreneurs/#4a368d385752 • Choose one of these social entrepreneurs: what was most remarkable about this person? • Write a short (150–200 word) statement. • Be prepared to discuss this person in the Discussion Group this week. Submit written response to instructor at the end of Week 2, Class 2

FIGURE 5.3 Design Thinking for Entrepreneurs—Week 2 Syllabus Excerpt

Wk #	Readings	Assignments Due and/or Project Task to be Completed	Assessments (in Assessments folder)	Student Resources (in Student Resources folder) A = Assignment ** = must complete using document provided SR = Student Resource	Instructor Resources (Instructor Resource folder also includes copy of all items in Student Resources and Assessments folder, including answer keys)
6		A4: Strategies for Ideation ** Form project groups	Quiz 2: Strategies for Ideation	• A4: Strategies for Ideation** • SR6-Critical Thinking • SR7-Computational Thinking • Project Documents Folder	• Week 6 Lecture • Week 6 Lesson Plan • Quiz 2: Strategies for Ideation

FIGURE 5.4 Design Thinking for Entrepreneurs—Course Map Excerpt

LESSON PLANNING

Instructional planning begins with the broadest strokes, working backwards to the finest details. Once you've determined what your students must learn during the course you're planning and how you will measure their acquisition of this knowledge and skill, we turn our attention to what we, as teachers, will do during each class period. This, too, begins with planning.

Mentioning the phrase *lesson plans* conjures up the notion of K–12, something faculty tend to meet with indifference or even disdain. Nevertheless, skillful instructors in higher education can benefit from planning their teaching activities beyond the general weekly level, determining the specific activities that will occur in each class period.

While I'm planning each week of a course, I create the PowerPoints for my lectures. These don't provide a fully formatted script for what I'll say in the classroom, but they give me a conceptual framework that allows me to make sure that my instruction aligns with the assignments I've planned. It also reminds me of resources I might want to create for students, and it helps to ensure that students will have been exposed to all of the relevant course content prior to administration of the planned assessments.

As I mentioned previously, Design Thinking for Entrepreneurs is held twice a week, with the first class period devoted to lecture and the second to discussion and active learning. My lecture PowerPoint sets out the main ideas I want to highlight, drawing from or building upon the assigned readings or prior assignments. I don't create a PowerPoint for the discussion sessions, but I do write an outline for myself that includes questions I plan to ask and basic directions for any student activities.

Crafting a lesson requires thoughtful preparation resulting from working knowledge of good teaching. It's likely you've already addressed these key considerations while you completed the overall design of your course, but they apply equally to the plan for an individual class period as they do to the map of the entire progression of study. In all you do as a teacher, keep the following points in mind:

A. *Rationale and Objective*: *What's the point* of the planned instruction? In other words, *why* is it important, *how* will you convey these ideas to your students, and *what* do you expect your students to know and be able to do after they've received this instruction?

B. *Instructional Context*: Where does the planned instruction fit into the *overall design* of the course?

C. *Learner Support*: What common student *misconceptions or errors* can you anticipate?

D. *Enrichment*: How might you *extend* student learning or *challenge* your higher-achieving students?

E. *Assessment*: How will you know if your students have *learned* what you intended to teach them during the class period?

Instructional Components

Good instruction usually includes five components: (1) the lesson objective; (2) a "hook" that grabs the students' attention; (3) teaching, including both lecture and active student participation; (4) checking for understanding; and (5) independent practice.

(1) **Objective**: Just like the course as a whole, each lesson has a unique objective. In other words, we need to ask ourselves *what's the point* of what we're teaching? What should students know and be able to do by the end of *this class period*, not just by the end of the course or program of study?

Even if it's strictly for your own reference, it's helpful to create an outline of the major points you want to address during each class period. You might decide to provide these outlines to your students, freeing them to participate actively rather than focusing their attention on taking notes. This also serves to keep the day's instruction on track. Instructors who use presentation software such as PowerPoint, Keynote, Prezi (and so on) can create a note-taking copy for students or they might post an electronic copy of the lecture to the course website. That way, students who are absent can make up for the missed lecture, or students can review it to remember key concepts prior to an exam.

The day's objective can be stated on the outline or course notes for the individual lesson, and it should also clearly relate to the outcomes and objectives of the course, as stated on the syllabus. Remember: *every* lesson and *every* assignment and *every* assessment should clearly and specifically relate to the outcomes and objectives of the course, and these should all be evident on the course syllabus.

The lesson outline should include key vocabulary terms and definitions appropriate to the day's discussion. It's easy to lose sight of the fact that it took us years to acquire the level of knowledge we now possess because the language of our disciplines has become second nature to us. I've spoken to many faculty members who hold high expectations that their students use correct disciplinary terminology from the first day of class. This is logical in an upper-division course. However, the instructors of introductory courses, even those designed for majors, must deliberately teach the language of the discipline in order for students to be successful in the course.

(2) **Hook:** An excellent lesson should begin with a "hook" that captures the students' attention. If you view any TED Talks on YouTube, the most effective and engaging speakers use this technique. The hook should only take the first 5 minutes of class and can include (among other things):
   — Alarming statistics
   — An interesting fact (related trivia)
   — A story or anecdote
   — Personal experience
   — Literature
   — Exaggeration
   — An image, artwork, a map, or other visual element
   — Audio recording/media clip
   — A graphic organizer (Venn diagram, concept web)
   — Questions
   — An example
   — An artifact
   — A riddle, joke, or funny anecdote

Note: Distributing copies of the lesson outline does *not* count as a hook, nor does saying, "Okay, Class, today we're going to talk about _____." That said, if

103

you're continuing the discussion from a previous lesson, you can just remind students of where you left off and then proceed. *But,* if you're presenting something new, a hook is highly recommended. It establishes the tone of the lesson and puts students in a receptive frame of mind.

(3) **Teaching**: Once you have the class's attention, you can begin your lecture or instruction. Instructional activities can include, but are not limited to, lecture, discussion, demonstration, active student participation, project-based learning, or a combination of these and other approaches. (In-depth discussion of such pedagogical activities will be the subject of Chapter 8.)

(4) **Check for Understanding**: It's not enough to end your daily instruction with, "Any questions?" A student who's confused won't usually speak up, and students might not realize they've failed to grasp the material until the test. One simple method of checking for student understanding is to use an exit slip: a half-sheet or quarter-sheet of paper containing one or two questions that students must answer prior to leaving the classroom. The same purpose could be accomplished by requiring students to post a response to your class web page or to send you a quick email. You don't have to grade these exit slips (although you do have to read them), but they allow you to see what your students know or don't know, guiding your plans for the next lesson. If many students exhibit the same lack of understanding, you can adjust your plans to address the problem during your next class period. This technique is especially valuable in courses where the day's instruction contains pivotal concepts that students must grasp to understand subsequent course content, as frequently occurs in science and mathematics. Any time you intend to hold students accountable for any content, or when that content is foundational to subsequent learning, checking for understanding is definitely a best practice.

(5) **Independent Practice**: This is the purpose of assignments. Make sure that the tasks you ask students to do
   — relate to what you've taught in that class period,
   — touch on one or more of the course objectives, and
   — are within the students' ability to accomplish independently.

Timing

Although you're not required to plan your lessons down to the minute or script your lectures and questions ahead of time, it's good to get a rough idea of how long you intend to spend on each part of your lesson.

- Hook: 5%–10% of class
- Lecture or Demonstration: 25%–50% of class
- Active Student Participation: 25%–50% of class
- Guided Practice: 25%–50% of class
- Wrap-Up/Assignments: 5%–10% of class

Example 1

Given a 90-minute class period, the distribution of time might be scheduled in this way, but many variations exist.

- Hook: 5 minutes
- Lecture/Demo: 45 minutes
- Student Participation: 30 minutes
- Wrap-Up/Assignment: 10 minutes

Without a doubt, it takes some work to develop strong lesson plans for an entire course, but the time you invest is well spent. You'll not only create a working document that you can reuse each time you teach the course in the future, but you'll be engaging in professional practice exceeding the standards of a typical course.

Example 2

Figure 5.5 is a sample lesson plan for a week of Design Thinking for Entrepreneurs. I created a lesson plan template and then used this tool to plan each week's instruction.

Lesson plans such as these don't require the level of detail expected in K–12, where many teachers must script their every question and tie instruction to state-mandated standards. Most fortunately, we in higher education retain our academic freedom in this regard. However, creating lesson plans remains a best practice at every level because it helps us to anticipate the actions we'll take, and subsequently allows us to develop or gather any resources, materials, and equipment we'll need.

Lesson planning requires a substantial investment of time and energy, without a doubt. Once the task is completed, though, the semester is likely to go much more smoothly. You're also moving beyond common practice, taking your teaching to an advanced level, which is definitely an admirable and worthy goal.

If you'd like to learn more about how to achieve excellence in teaching, I recommend George Kuh's *High-Impact Educational Practices: What They Are, Who Has Access to Them and Why They Matter* (2008). The Association of American Colleges and Universities (AACU) offers an excerpt from this pivotal resource, including a chart of these high-impact practices.[3] Kuh echoes many of the ideas we've been discussing, including

LESSON PLAN—WEEK 6

LECTURE	CLASS 1
Week Number/ Topic	6—Critical Thinking and Computational Thinking
Lesson Objective	Students will acquire new strategies for innovation through deeper understanding of critical thinking and computational thinking.
Materials and Equipment	Computer Projector/projection system/microphone PowerPoint presentation Internet connection
Hook	Visual example—is the glass half full? (Slide 2 of ppt)
Instruction	Compare critical thinking and computational thinking Critical thinking as a life skill Steps to critical thinking Define computational thinking Turn and Talk: High school track repair scenario Preview: Quiz 3 due before the Week 7 lecture Assignment 4—Strategies for Innovation due in this week's Discussion class period.
DISCUSSION GROUP	CLASS 2
Materials and Equipment	Print out and make copies of the project requirements and grading rubric. Distribute to students.
Questions for discussion	What might you be interested in working on for your course project? What are the requirements for the course project?
Guided Practice	Review the project requirements with students Emphasize the requirement that groups document their process. This could involve appointing a note-taker, using video, taking still photos, etc. Remind students that they may work alone, but that those choosing this option will be considered a group during discussions and worktimes even though they're pursuing different projects. Allow student time to walk around and talk to each other freely, discussing their preliminary project ideas. By the end of the period, students should have determined their groups and begun to discuss possible project topics. Group members should exchange contact information so that they can confer outside of class.
Independent Practice/ Assignment	Students may conduct some independent, exploratory research in order to decide on their project topic.
Assessment	Quiz 3 should be completed on D2L prior to the Week 7 lecture.

FIGURE 5.5 Design Thinking for Entrepreneurs—Lesson Plans Week 6

- First-year seminars and experiences
- Common intellectual experiences
- Learning communities
- Writing-intensive courses
- Collaborative assignments and projects
- Undergraduate research
- Diversity and global learning
- Service learning and community-based learning
- Internships
- Capstone courses and projects

Several of these topics will be examined at greater depth in subsequent chapters.

SCAFFOLDING INSTRUCTION

Most instructors have encountered situations where we notice that our students display misconceptions or lack basic disciplinary knowledge, hampering their ability to learn what we're trying to teach. For instance, university faculty members frequently mention that their students don't know essential disciplinary vocabulary or complain that students lack basic skills or subject-area knowledge they "ought to know." But how can we hold students accountable to know what they've never been taught? Students attending a live theatrical performance, for example, may lack basic knowledge of polite audience behavior simply because they've never been in this situation before.

Therefore, no matter how obvious or basic they may seem to us, we must systematically and deliberately *teach* these fundamentals regardless of whether we believe that students *should* already possess this foundational knowledge. We also need to deliver direct instruction in necessary skills, providing concrete examples and incorporating opportunities for students to practice these new skills before expecting them to perform at a level of mastery.

This may necessitate building additional lessons into your syllabus beyond the specific content you intend to cover. Such lessons might address

- Essential vocabulary
- Instruction in new or foundational skills
- Overt instruction in appropriate behavior during discussions, presentations, performances, and in laboratory or studio activities

Furthermore, it's usually not enough to simply *tell* students how to do something. We need to provide deliberate, systematic, concrete instruction, building in opportunities for practice, for *everything* we expect students to know or be able to do. This is sometimes called *scaffolding instruction,* which can be understood to occur in three phases.

107

- *Demonstrate*: Direct instruction using models and examples of the skill students must acquire
- *Facilitate*: Guided activity, often in a group setting, involving supported student practice of the skill
- *Evaluate*: Independent practice of the skill, assessed separately from a content-area assignment

Example: Let's say you're teaching an introductory film course in which students will be expected to write a critical analysis of a particular film. You decide to plan a lesson teaching students how to meet this expectation successfully.

- *Demonstrate*: Provide explicit instruction in how to write film criticism by giving students step-by-step directions, sharing examples of professional criticism, and clarifying the specific criteria you'll expect the students to meet.
- *Facilitate*: Divide the class into small groups and give each group a different prompt featuring a film that most students are likely to have seen in the past, such as *Star Wars*, along with the step-by-step directions you demonstrated in the first part of the lesson. Walk around the room, helping groups as they work together to complete the task. At the end of the allotted time, have groups share their critical analyses with the class, while you provide commentary and immediate feedback.
- *Evaluate*: Allow students to choose a film they've seen before and ask them to write their own critical analysis as a homework assignment. This is a formative assignment, so it should have a low-point value and be graded only based on the student's demonstration of skill rather than the broader criteria you'll use in grading more important student work.

A simple way to understand how to scaffold instruction is to think of it as:

Walk through: Walk students through the skill by demonstrating how to do what you expect them to do (demonstrate).

Talk through: Guide students as they practice the skill together under your supervision (facilitate).

Drive through: Independent student practice (evaluate).

Scaffolding is sometimes also shortened to: *I do* (demonstrate); *we do* (facilitate); *you do* (evaluate).

This approach is especially helpful for instructors teaching beginning-level courses or those open to non-majors, providing essential vocabulary, background knowledge, or disciplinary skills through the course's plan of instruction. Admittedly, this seems very basic, and instructors often resent having to spend valuable class time teaching things they think students "should already know." Think, though: How often have you been frustrated at students' apparent lack of crucial knowledge and skills? Didn't you wish someone else had taught them the things they need to know to succeed in your class? Whether or not this *should* have occurred, it clearly did not. That's why it's up to *you* to step in and provide this important learning experience, thereby enhancing your students' chances for success in your classroom and in their subsequent coursework as well.

YOUR TURN: PLANNING YOUR LESSONS

Before completing this chapter, you should verify that you have accomplished the following tasks:

1. Aligning your outcomes, objectives, assessments, and assignments
2. Selecting instructional materials and experiences such as textbooks, supplementary readings, field work, trips, guest lectures, etc.
3. Creating modules organizing your course content, each ending in an appropriate assessment
4. Preliminary planning of individual lessons, including lecture, demonstration, and/or active student participation
5. Completing the assessment mechanisms such as quizzes, exams, projects, presentations, or written assignments that you've planned and creating written student resources such as directions or expectations for each task that your students will be asked to do during the course

The time we invest in planning our instructional activities is never wasted. The more organized we are, the more deliberate and informed our pedagogical choices, then the better prepared we are to meet our students' learning needs and to enhance their opportunities to acquire the skills and knowledge we intend to teach them to meet both our course objectives and our program outcomes.

Remember:

- Planning for effective instruction increases your potential success in meeting your course outcomes and objectives and helps to ensure continuing accreditation and strong instructor evaluations.
- A plan is always a work in progress. Each time you teach the course, you can modify and adapt the plan to reflect your growing expertise as an educator.
- Planning begins with the development of assessments, working backwards to the level of individual lessons. Know where you want your students to go, and then plot the course that will best help them to arrive at your destination.

Identify →	Ideate
Why do we need to create a comprehensive plan for our course instead of allowing it to evolve organically? Since our first priority is to ensure that our students will meet our course objectives and program outcomes, we need to plan and organize our instruction so that all of the content we plan to cover is addressed by the end of the semester and everything we do supports that priority.	How can we possibly plan everything before the course even begins? We need to take a strategic and systematic approach to our teaching, creating a plan of instruction and then digging deeper into each week's planned content to anticipate our students' learning needs, then developing each of the resources we will need in order to support them in achieving our outcomes and objectives.
Iterate ←	Implement
When you teach, keep track of the times when you notice that an additional resource would have helped your students to be more successful, where you need to change the schedule, or noting any other changes you should make prior to teaching the course again.	What resources do we need to develop? Minimally, every assessment needs a rubric (or other grading tool) and a set of explicit written instructions. Each class period should have at least a rough lesson plan outlining what you intend to teach, along with any materials or resources you'll need to do what you've planned.

FIGURE 5.6 Chapter 5 Design Connection

Notes

[1] Thomas, M. (2017). What is the average reading speed and the best rate of reading? *HealthGuidance*. www.healthguidance.org/entry/13263/1/What-Is-the-Average-Reading-Speed-and-the-Best-Rate-of-Reading.html

[2] Interviewees in the Mellon Research Project were not identified by name in compliance with the University of Michigan's Institutional Review Board protocols for the project.

[3] Kuh, G. (2008). *High-impact educational practices: What they are, who has access to them, and why they matter*. AAC&U. Excerpt available at www.aacu.org/leap/hips

Chapter 6

Writing as Instruction and Assessment

CHAPTER SUMMARY

- Professional Communications
- Writing-to-Learn, Writing-to-Communicate
- Proofreading and Providing Feedback on Student Writing
- Best Practice
- Your Turn: Incorporating Writing in Your Assignments and Assessments

---

Writing is as ubiquitous as speaking and listening in higher education. However, its very ubiquity means we cannot address it only as a tool for learning or assessment.

College courses usually include written assignments. Unless you're a faculty member in the Department of English, though, it may sound strange to consider adding specific writing *objectives* to our courses. Why should we consider taking this step? After all, isn't our primary goal to convey disciplinary skills and knowledge, not to teach writing?

The answer to the last question is yes, but we also want to improve students' abilities to engage in theoretical, philosophical, and practical discussions within a specific disciplinary context. Our students should become proficient in the discourse of our fields. They should be able to write and speak coherently about their professional practice, and they should develop their potential to make substantive intellectual contributions to the discipline. Therefore, every course should incorporate meaningful writing assignments that allow students to acquire the skills they need for professional written communication.

This is especially true if you're designing a writing-intensive course, which might include the following characteristics:

1. Writing should be integrated throughout the course, tied to the course's outcomes and objectives.
2. Instructors should provide substantial feedback on students' writing, allowing revision in response to that feedback.
3. Explicit instruction in the modes and expectations for writing within your discipline should be integral to the course.

PROFESSIONAL COMMUNICATIONS

Most institutions in higher education mandate that students complete writing courses as part of their general education requirements, so we generally presume that the instructors of these courses have taught our students how to write. Why, then, do our students fail to write well in our classes?

We can identify a few reasons for this frustrating situation. First of all, students tend to compartmentalize their learning, seeing writing as something occurring in an English class but not necessarily as important in their other courses. This is not entirely incorrect: Many fields do not ask students to write very much. In fact, students might encounter their first substantial writing task, such as a 10- or 20-page research paper, only near the end of their undergraduate experience or perhaps not even until they reach graduate school (depending, of course, on their major).

Next, every discipline has its own expectations for professional-grade written communication. This goes beyond the choice of APA, MLA or Chicago style guides. The vocabulary we use, the way we construct an argument, whether we use or avoid personal pronouns, whether passive language is acceptable or anathema— all these factors and more influence the norms and practices of our written communication. We might identify this as a disciplinary dialect, or as I said in *Surveying the Landscape: Arts Integration in Research Universities* (2015, p. 86), "The norms, methodologies, literatures, and histories of academic disciplines comprise the foundation from which new knowledge arises, giving rise to highly specialized modes of thinking and speaking known as disciplinary vernaculars." Students must assimilate these vernaculars and become proficient in this specialized communication to become disciplinary practitioners. However, this does not necessarily happen automatically.

When we shake our heads in bewilderment at our students' apparent lack of skill as writers, we must recognize that part of their problem arises with us. First, our own sensibilities have become so finely tuned to our own disciplinary vernacular that our students—who do not possess this same level of proficiency— seem to produce poorly written work. Second, we seldom consider that we must actively and deliberately assist our students in developing the fluency we expect, yet students rarely become skillful in these specific disciplinary norms without receiving direct instruction. We must teach them that writing is essential to all professions yet differs quite significantly between them: Part of becoming a philosopher is learning how to *write like* a philosopher, just as much as learning how to be a scholar of Latin requires learning how to read and write in Latin.

An effective strategy for teaching our students disciplinary communication should exhibit five major characteristics that engage both the cognitive and affective domains of understanding (Sejnost and Thiese, 2001):[1]

- Foster critical understanding. Students' development of skill in critical thinking is among the most important learning tasks of their university experience. If the texts we assign them to read, and the writing we ask them to do, merely involve rote assimilation of facts and repetition of those facts in their assignments, then we cannot truly say that they have learned. Rather, they must critically engage with the information we present and apply higher-order thinking to it to demonstrate a more advanced understanding.
- Engage readers and writers in the process of revision. Both reading and writing rely upon revision, as does the design process itself. Few of us fully assimilate a text upon reading it once, and perhaps even fewer of us write a perfect first draft of a paper. Repeated reading of texts and revision of written work allows for deeper learning.
- Provide steps that allow students to thoroughly assess, monitor, and implement their prior knowledge of the topics they're studying. Knowledge is cumulative: The more we know, the more we are then able to learn. Our students know comparatively little about the content of our courses, which (of course) is why they're enrolled—to acquire knowledge they don't already possess. However, because they don't have the same preexisting knowledge as their instructors, they can't efficiently incorporate new learning without building background knowledge or linking to things they already know. Our task is to lead students to recognize when they lack background knowledge and to act upon this insight to seek out the missing information. Indeed, most of us don't know what we don't know—we don't recognize the gaps in our own knowledge unless we build our capacity for introspection and awareness of our own thought processes.
- Encourage students to engage with the topics contained in the course readings and writing assignments by making choices, taking positions, or viewing topics from different perspectives. Student choice is crucial to engagement in the learning process—the more personally invested we are in an academic task, the more likely we are to learn from it. Novelty, such as being asked to consider a topic from multiple perspectives, also increases engagement and therefore enhances student learning.

113

■ Ask students to examine, assess, utilize, and analyze their personal reaction to the topics under study. Students learn best if they can develop the ability to become aware of their own thoughts and reactions to the material under consideration in the course and then to understand and analyze these responses. This self-awareness supports critical thinking, the willingness to engage in repeated revision, and engagement in the learning process. Journals or blogs are an effective tool for fostering this crucial skill, as are classroom discussions that invite students to engage with course content on a personal, affective level.

WRITING-TO-LEARN, WRITING-TO-COMMUNICATE

Within an educational context, writing serves two purposes: instruction and communication, which we can understand as "writing-to-learn" and "writing-to-communicate." In *Teaching Writing Across the Curriculum* (2006, pp. 9–10),[2] Art Young explains the matter like this: writing-to-learn gives students "an opportunity to explain the matter to themselves" whereas writing-to-communicate "challenges the student to explain the matter to others." These two purposes are closely linked, since all of us must understand a topic for ourselves before we can explain it to someone else. Writing-to-learn and writing-to-communicate are neither binary nor dualistic. They merely represent two different and interconnected purposes for writing, both leading to discovery and critical understanding (see Figure 6.1).

	Writing-to-Learn	Writing-to-Communicate
Audience	Self and others with whom the writer is already acquainted	Broad public audience
Characteristic	Creativity, exploration	Analysis, critical thinking
Language	Informal	Formal
Instructor's Role	Facilitator	Representative of professional community
Point of View	Subjective	Objective
Sample Types	Journals, field notes, rough drafts, blogs	Essays, reports, business letters,

FIGURE 6.1 Writing-to-Learn—Writing-to-Communicate

114

Writing-to-Learn

Most students first encounter expectations for college-level writing in their English classes, where their teachers pay close attention to spelling, grammar, punctuation, structure, organization, transitions, and numerous other considerations. However, when students engage in writing-to-learn, these niceties take second place to the process of learning by means of the writing assignment. Only when transitioning from writing-to-learn to writing-to-communicate does it become important to ensure that students' work adheres to the conventions of college-level English and exhibits features common to written communication within a given discipline.

Writing is an excellent tool in assisting students to deepen their learning, because it requires that they understand a topic well enough to put it into written language. The physical and mental act of writing enhances retention of knowledge, even when the written product isn't a professional-quality text. I'm reminded of the countless hours I spent taking notes as an undergraduate student. At times, I'd wonder why I bothered to take those notes, since usually I remembered the material from class fairly well without looking back at what I'd written. Then one day, I accidentally left my notebook in my car, so I just sat and listened to the instructor's lecture. I found I didn't remember it half as well as I usually did, which convinced me of the power that note-taking had on my memory. I also relied on note-taking as a learning tool in the aesthetic philosophy courses required in my doctoral program. The articles I was required to read for these classes were extremely difficult to comprehend. By taking each article one paragraph at a time, then pausing to write a sentence summarizing the paragraph I'd just read, I was better able to understand the material. Further, I ended up with a fairly good summary of each article that proved useful not only in preparing for exams, but in my later scholarly writing. I often recommend this technique to students who struggle with their college-level reading assignments.

Instructors must determine how they will incorporate writing into their courses, as is the case with all course-planning activities. Writing-to-learn can serve as a formative assessment, including rough drafts that later receive a final, summative evaluation. Here are two suggestions for beginning to incorporate writing-to-learn activities in your teaching:

- *Reading Journal*: Require students to keep a journal of their readings throughout the course, assessing it periodically.
  - You don't need to read every word of the journal, nor should you mark student's errors in spelling or language mechanics.
  - To lessen your grading burden, you could ask students to flag a given number of entries they'd like you to read closely, and provide feedback on the content of just those selections.

115

- You only need to spot-check the rest of the journal to make sure students have met expectations for the number and type of entries.
- *Summary and Response*: Ask students to write a short summary and reflection at the end of a given lesson, especially one that presented important content.
  - Option 1: The instructor could collect and read these summaries herself.
  - Option 2: Students could exchange these summaries and provide written commentary about one another's work with the intention of helping their peers to reach an understanding of the essential concepts presented in class.
    - Students could then photocopy their notes, returning the original to their peer during the next class period and giving the photocopy to the instructor.
    - The instructor should read these copies but need not comment on them individually. Rather, she could provide a "collective response" to the whole class, addressing common misconceptions or needed clarifications regarding course content.

Young (2006) provides many suggestions to help instructors across all disciplines incorporate writing-to-learn into the courses they teach. The academic institution for which you work is likely to have a number of other resources available in its Center for Teaching and Learning or similar entity.

Even fields not typically seen as writing intensive can and should require students to write as a regular part of their educational experience. The list below provides suggestions for writing in disciplines that seldom assign writing. These suggestions should certainly not be considered an exhaustive catalog, but rather to serve as a place to begin thinking about the types of writing tasks students could perform.

1. Project Statement
2. Analysis of a professional work (i.e., scholarly article, professional lecture, performance)
3. Critical review of a project, product, or performance
4. Biographical profile of an influential individual in the academic discipline of the course
5. Research into the history, theory, or criticism of the discipline
6. Narrative heuristic writing: self-narrative of one's own disciplinary practice

Variations on these same assignments could be utilized in many disciplines, tailored to the specific context. Business students could critique a business plan.

Engineering students could write analyses of mechanical systems. Health care students could write a review of a hospital. Students in virtually any discipline could write a biographical profile of a notable contributor to the field, reflecting on how he or she has made a difference in the world. The possibilities are limited only by the instructor's ability to envision how best to incorporate writing into students' educational experience. Furthermore, many of the suggestions above ask students to go beyond simple reporting, tapping into the upper levels of Bloom's Taxonomy by asking students to analyze and evaluate the topic at hand. This, too, is demonstrative of high-quality teaching and learning.

Writing in Online Courses

Writing becomes even more important in an online course, because nearly all communication between students, or between a student and the instructor, occurs in written form. Most online instructors establish expectations for these interactions: prohibiting "text speak," asking students to proofread their posts for obvious spelling or grammatical errors before hitting "submit," and so on. They also clarify expectations for what constitutes an adequate peer response, banning empty phrases such as "I like your work" or "good job," and insisting on substantive and thoughtful replies. Few instructors, though, treat a discussion post as a writing assignment per se, focusing on the content of the response rather than its language mechanics unless the latter are so problematic that the reader cannot understand what the writer is attempting to say. We'll discuss writing in online courses further in Chapter 7.

Writing-to-Communicate

Writing-to-communicate takes a somewhat different approach than writing-to-learn or the kinds of writing common to online learning, seeking to foster students' mastery of disciplinary knowledge and its applications, leading toward the goal of becoming an effective practitioner.

To paraphrase Young (2006), this does not mean that a professor of philosophy must suddenly become an English teacher. Rather, professors of philosophy should teach philosophy, including its particular ways of communicating knowledge and means of utilizing written language in the teaching and learning *of* philosophy. The same, of course, is true of any academic discipline.

All such assignments should support student learning, expanding and refining their mastery of disciplinary knowledge with an emphasis on communicating with an external audience. This remains closely linked to writing-to-learn, since the writer must first go through the process of drafting—explaining the matter to herself—before being able to create a final draft capable of explaining the matter to others.

Our students will achieve greater success if we provide explicit, direct instruction in how to conduct this type of professional communication. We cannot expect them to transfer their learning from freshman English composition to a setting they may perceive as completely alien to their prior writing experiences. Instead, "the teaching of writing happens—or should—within a deep field of practice, theory, and research," according to Doug Hesse (2017), president of the National Council of Teachers of English.

Your syllabus can be the first step in this journey, providing concrete expectations for formatting, a hyperlink to the preferred style guide used in your discipline, and detailed instructions for all summative writing assignments.

Not all writing within every discipline could possibly be addressed within a book such as this. Writing a script for a play differs wildly from constructing a philosophical argument, just as writing an analysis of a software application bears little resemblance to writing a historical account of events that occurred in ancient Greece. The point is that you—as a skilled and knowledgeable disciplinary practitioner—must apply your expertise to the task of building your students' communication abilities in the ways that matter within the field you have made your life's work.

Regular exposure to professional-caliber written communications in your discipline facilitates increased proficiency in writing as students develop a familiarity with the writing style and conventions typically used in your discipline. Each discipline has a particular dialect, or disciplinary vernacular, and the more exposure students receive, the more they develop an "ear" for the cadence and conventions of your field, including its jargon and idiosyncrasies. Reading professional journal articles, for example, also helps your students to become acquainted with typical publication outlets in your field, which is especially beneficial to graduate students, or to undergraduates who aspire to graduate school.

Here are a few suggestions for incorporating professional writing into your classroom:

- Begin the class period with an interesting excerpt from an "article of the week," possibly offering extra credit for students who read the article in its entirety and write a short response paper.
- Post links to articles or websites containing topics of current interest in your field to the course web page, or send students a weekly email with these links.
- Use professional articles as part of your course's required readings. Remember to change the assignments each time you teach the course so that the material doesn't become outdated or stale.
- Require students to cite at least one peer-reviewed journal article whenever writing a research paper. This actually serves two purposes: Beginning researchers don't know how to find appropriate sources so this

points them in the right directions, and it acquaints them with professional-level writing in your discipline.

■ Hold a "current events" class period in which students must find a professional journal article that interests them and bring it to class to share with their peers.

Reading and writing are undeniably linked. When we provide models of good writing for our students to read, they will become better writers themselves because they will come to know what "sounds right" in this very specific genre of written communication.

PROOFREADING AND PROVIDING FEEDBACK ON STUDENT WRITING

Writing is always a creative process, even when it yields an informational text. Therefore, the most important instruction occurs through the same type of interaction common to other creative settings: one-on-one critique. Instructors provide essential feedback either through written commentary on a marked copy of the student's paper, or in an individual tutorial situation. This is not to say that you must evaluate your students' every word for every assignment. Sometimes, though, students should receive the benefit of your expertise through personal evaluation of their formative drafts so that they can revise and improve their work prior to submitting a summative assignment, much the same as students in the arts receive regular instructor critique of their artistic products or performances.

When we read students' formative drafts, we're usually either proofreading or editing, which are two distinctly different activities. When proofreading, we look for *errors*, particularly in spelling, grammar, punctuation, capitalization, and other mechanical aspects of writing. Editing, on the other hand, looks at the *content, message, or meaning* of the document, considering things like structural elements, organization of ideas, transitions, and whether the writer's ideas are clear to the reader. Initial feedback tends to focus on proofreading, while critique of subsequent drafts centers on editing.

Proofreading can be tedious, without a doubt. The following section outlines some strategies instructors might employ to manage this task.

1. Paper and Electronic Options
   a. If you ask students to submit a *paper copy* of their first draft, you can mark this using a highlighter, simply indicating the errors you found. *Do NOT fix the errors! That's the student's job.* You can verbally discuss these errors in person or annotate the margins where you feel comments are warranted.

    b. If you choose to proofread electronically, highlight the errors using the tools in Word. *Again, don't fix the errors, just mark them for the student.* Insert comments using the Review Toolbar.

2. Staying on Task

    a. It's very easy to fall into skimming the student's work rather than reading every word carefully (especially if you're bored), causing you to miss important errors.

    b. If you're working from a paper copy of the student's paper, mask the paper below the line you're reading by using a blank sheet of paper or manila folder. It will help you to focus on the line you're reading.

    c. If reading the student's paper on a computer, enlarge the text so that one line of text fills the screen from side to side, but shrink the window top to bottom so that only a limited portion of the screen is visible below each line. You should be able to see three or four whole lines of text, but not be able to glance too far ahead.

3. One-on-One Tutorials

    a. You do not have to meet with students individually to discuss *every* writing assignment, but you should schedule one-on-one appointments with students to discuss the most important writing assignment in your course, providing direct, personal critique of their work.

    b. Proofread the student's draft *before* this critique, which frees you to use the meeting to discuss the problems you marked previously and to talk about your proposed changes.

4. Additional Help

    a. Offer extra credit for students who visit your institution's Writing Center prior to submitting their drafts and/or final papers.

    b. The more help students get from the Writing Center, the less onerous your task in evaluating their writing will be.

Peer Editing

Frequent opportunities for feedback and revision are important, but not all of this has to come from the instructor. Peer editing is a good option for assignments you can't proofread yourself. It gives students the opportunity for revision, but spares you from reading their papers twice. Papers less than 5 pages long can usually be critiqued in class. Papers longer than 5 pages require more class time than you're probably willing to devote to this activity, so students will need to do this on their own time.

Option 1: Small-Group Critique

    a. Assign students in groups of three. Each student should have two different colored pens. (Say, red and blue.)

    b. Take a few moments to instruct students in the process of peer editing: Look for and mark errors; make note of areas that need more explanation; be sure to comment if something is particularly good; check that sources are appropriate, etc.

       i. Trade papers. Read and mark the papers using the red pen.

       ii. Pass papers to the second reader. Read and mark the second paper using the blue pen.

       iii. Return the papers to the author. Take a few moments to read through the marked copies.

    c. Allow time for discussion.

    d. The whole activity should take approximately 30 minutes or less, depending on the length of the papers.

Option 2: Whole Group-Critique (for papers of 2 pages or less)

    a. Project the paper on the screen while the student author reads it aloud.

    b. Provide a few minutes for peers to comment. Allow the student to annotate the projected paper as comments are made.

    c. Group critique of writing will usually occupy the entire class period. If this is a large class, break up into groups of five to 10 students. Move between the groups to keep discussions on track.

Option 3: Peer editing can also occur outside of class. Groups of three students schedule their own time to meet, or they can trade their papers via email. However, some time in class will still have to be allotted to instruct students in this process. When peer editing occurs outside of your classroom, you'll need to hold the students accountable for completing this task since you won't see them at work. For example, you could ask to see the marked drafts at the next class period. You don't have to evaluate the students' editing work, only record their completion of the task.

Option 4: Students can work with the Writing Center, providing proof of this interaction.

Option 5: Students can find their own proofreading and editing partner, providing evidence of this interaction. (This is the last choice option due to potential unreliability of the selected editor.)

As another strategy for teaching students to recognize good writing characteristic of your discipline, you can provide examples of both good and bad writing throughout your course. This could be a brief 5-minute opening exercise for a given class period, or it could occupy an hour or more. The length of time you devote to these discussions is up to your professional discretion as an educator.

1. Begin the class period with a short (one-paragraph) sample, discussing why it's good or bad writing in your field.

2. Cull and anonymize examples from students' papers, (preferably not from the same section of your course—try not to embarrass anyone) and use these to begin a conversation about the strengths or weaknesses of those examples.

3. Teach your expectations *explicitly*. Never presume that students already know what you want them to do, nor that they possess the background knowledge you think they should have acquired prior to entering your classroom.

    a. If you require students to use disciplinary vocabulary, provide them with a glossary of terms you expect them to know. Quiz them on these terms. Use them in your lectures. Award bonus points for using them in written work.

    b. At the time a writing project is assigned, provide a rubric, checklist, or other grading schema. Take a few moments to review expectations with students when you explain the project itself. If possible, provide good and bad examples of student work to illustrate what you want them to do. They need to know what success looks like and sounds like before they can produce similarly successful documents. It's helpful to approach this as though your students only know as much as you've taught them yourself—don't presume they already possess any level of familiarity with your expectations unless you've made these explicit.

    c. Teach students about the types of research sources appropriate to your discipline. Ensure students know which sources are unacceptable and why. As a few general examples:

        i. Never cite Wikipedia or other wiki pages, but use them as a starting point for initial investigations, mining the bibliographies of specific articles to find the original sources for the information contained in the article.

        ii. URL's ending in. org,. edu, and. gov tend to be more reliable than those ending with. com.

        iii. Blogs and self-published materials should be cited only in moderation as they generally reflect opinion rather than fact.

        iv. The bulk of evidence in a paper should be provided through professional journals, published books, or discipline-specific authoritative sources (provide examples specific to your discipline).

4. Teach students about the style guide you expect them to use (MLA, APA, Chicago, etc.). Provide resources for quick reference to common tasks (e.g., correct header and page numbers; how to cite various sources.) Provide examples of correctly formatted papers for student reference. The more resources you offer, the greater the chances that they'll produce the kind of document you expect.

5. Evaluate student work promptly. You should proofread and return assignments for revision within 48 hours, if possible. Virtually nobody likes grading student writing, but procrastination leads nowhere.

6. Remember: The more pages you assign students to write, the more pages you must read and grade. Keep assignments reasonable and manageable for both your students and yourself.

7. Provide students with a writing guide to help direct their work, tailoring it to the needs of your class and in alignment with your particular assignments.

Example

In Design Thinking for Entrepreneurs, the majority of the students' grade is based on their design of a business model addressing a "wicked" social problem. However, there are also several written assignments that serve to reinforce student learning through the weekly lectures and readings. This course is not centered in a particular discipline, so its purpose is not to prepare students for professional practice in an academic field. However, employers across virtually all career fields seek candidates who demonstrate proficiency in written communication, which is why incorporating written assignments into the course is simply a best practice. I also wanted to extend my students' learning beyond several of the course lectures and to foster their abilities for introspection and reflection on their learning, which you'll see is the main emphasis of several of these assignments. Figure 6.2 is an excerpt from the course syllabus. (Assignments that did not require a written response have been deleted for the sake of brevity.)

You'll see that I provided students with templates to help them complete Assignments 4 and 7. They're not hard to create, and they help to keep students' work organized, making the task of grading much easier. The list above provides only a sketch of what will be required in each assignment. The template for Assignment 7 is presented in Figure 6.3.

Because students in this course will download the form from the class website and type directly into it, their information remains organized more clearly than if I'd simply written a paragraph containing the directions. In the absence of a structure such as this, students each tend to put their own interpretation on assignments, meaning that the instructor has to sift through their submissions to confirm whether they've met the given criteria. It only takes about 10 minutes to create a template like this, and it allows me determine at a glance whether or not they've included each of the assignment's components, making the task of grading much less onerous than if I left students to their own devices when organizing their papers.

Assigned	Due	Description
Week 2 Class 1	Week 2 Class 2	**Assignment 1: 30 Under 30** • Read "30 under 30 2016" www. forbes.com/30-under-30-2016/social-entrepreneurs/#1433d8427600 • Choose one of these social entrepreneurs: What was most remarkable about this person? • Write a short (150–200 word) statement. • Be prepared to discuss this person in the Discussion Group this week. Submit to instructor.
Week 6 Class 1	Week 6 Class 2	**Assignment 4: Strategies for Ideation-Reflection** • Following the lecture, write a short reflection about the strategies for innovation that we've discussed thus far in the course. (Use the template in the Student Resources folder). • Submit at beginning of Class 2.
Week 8 Class 1	Week 9 Class 2	**Assignment 5: Business Canvas Reflection** • Reflect on the Business Model Canvas process you're working on with your group. (200-word statement) • What is exciting and going well? • What is difficult/confusing/not going well?
Week 10 Class 1	Week 11 Class 1	**Assignment 6: Project Management** Read the two articles about Millennium Park after Week 10 Class 1, but before the Week 10 Class 2. Answer the following questions after the Class 2 discussion. • What criteria should be used to determine whether Chicago's Millennium Park project was successful? (e.g., on time/on budget, or other metrics?) • List three ways that design is essential to Millennium Park. • (bonus) If you've visited Millennium Park in person, please describe your impressions.
Week 13 Class 1	Week 14 Class 2	**Assignment 7 Leadership** Find, watch, summarize, and evaluate at least two TED Talks about leadership using the template provided in the Student Resources folder.

FIGURE 6.2 Design Thinking for Entrepreneurs—Writing Assignments

ASSIGNMENT 7: LEADERSHIP
Directions
Find, watch, summarize, and evaluate at least two TED Talks about leadership (200 words).
BE SURE TO CHANGE THE FILE NAME TO INCLUDE YOUR LAST NAME WHEN SAVING THIS DOCUMENT.

URL (copy/paste)	
Title of TED Talk (by) speaker's name	
Summary (explain the main idea of the talk)	
Evaluation (explain what you thought about this talk and what you learned that was valuable)	
URL (copy/paste)	
Title of TED Talk (by) speaker's name	
Summary (explain the main idea of the talk)	
Evaluation (explain what you thought about this talk and what you learned that was valuable)	

Submission Instructions
- Save this document *as lastname_firstinitial_A7.doc* (or docx).
- Upload to the Assignment 7 area on D2L.

FIGURE 6.3 Design Thinking for Entrepreneurs—Instructions for Assignment 7

Since I want to eliminate common causes of ambiguity or misunderstanding, I provide brief instructions for all assignments in the syllabus, and I post extended instructions to the course website, all of which are available from the first day of class. Of course, during my lecture about leadership in Week 13 Class 1 (when I introduce the assignment), I could simply say, "By the end of next week I want you to find, watch, summarize and evaluate two TED talks about leadership on YouTube. Make sure you include the URL for the talks you watch." This method yields much poorer results than taking a more organized and proactive approach; however, and the marked inconsistency of students' responses makes the task of grading their work unnecessarily difficult. Time spent creating and uploading the template is far outweighed by the benefits it provides to me as the instructor.

Research Papers

Students in Design Thinking for Entrepreneurs don't write research papers because it is a project-based course, but I do assign research papers in other courses I teach. Experience has taught me that even graduate students approach this task less consistently or reliably than I'd originally presumed they would. If I want my students to produce a product that meets my grading criteria, therefore, I need to provide clear and comprehensible instruction in why they need to meet the requirements, how to do so, and what I expect.

For example, I taught an online senior seminar course titled Professionalism and Project Management in which students wrote a research paper formatted according to the guidelines for submission to a specific peer-reviewed journal. Despite the fact that students in this course are seniors, few had any previous experience with research writing. To address this deficit, I built three lectures about the paper into the course. The first contextualized the research paper requirement, reviewing the importance of professional publication and introducing students to research techniques. The second lecture focused on finding appropriate research sources. These two lectures occurred within the first 2 weeks of the course, followed by a short quiz on research methodologies to hold students accountable for the lecture content. Students then had 3 weeks to search for appropriate sources and complete an annotated bibliography of their findings. The third lecture, delivered just after midterm, presented a detailed overview and explanation of correct formatting, for which I provided resources and explanations. All of this material was available to students in a Writing Guide posted to the course website from the first day of class. I also incorporated check-in points throughout the semester, each included in the paper's final grade. The annotated bibliography was due during Week 5, an outline for the paper during Week 9, and students conducted a peer review of one another's first drafts in Week 12, giving them time to revise and improve their work prior to the final paper's submission in Week 14 of the semester. Each of those check-in points had a set of written instructions and was explained in the course lectures. I also offered bonus points to students who provide proof that they'd worked with the university's Writing Center

Students who paid attention to the lectures, followed the guidelines and instructions provided, and met those check-in points produced much better research papers than those who did not. Colleagues expressed surprise that I went to such great lengths to scaffold this assignment for my students, but they also complain about the quality of their own students' written work, while mine ended up achieving better results. It seems self-evident to me that we must directly and deliberately teach students about our expectations, providing them with instruction that enables them to achieve success on whatever tasks we assign. After all, we cannot live in the world we think ought to exist—we work to create that world for ourselves. Undoubtedly, my students *ought* to know how to write a research paper by the time they're seniors in college, but they don't. It's up to me to teach them *how* to do this if it's *what* I expect them to do.

BEST PRACTICE

Doug Hesse, in "We Know What Works in Teaching Composition" (*Chronicle of Higher Education*, January 3, 2017),[3] offers the following advice about what writing "looks like in the best writing courses, informed by decades of research":

- Students have ample opportunities to write. Professors expect them to write frequently and extensively, and we demand and reward serious effort.
- Professors carefully sequence writing tasks. The idea is progressively to expand on students' existing abilities and experiences.
- Professors coach the process. We offer strategies and advice, encouragement and critique, formative and summative assessments.
- Courses provide instruction and practice on all aspects of writing. Attend to the form and conventions of specific genres? Yes. Talk about creativity, invention (how to generate ideas), grammar, and style? Certainly, but also discuss things like logic and accuracy in writing, and how to fit a piece to various audience needs and expectations.
- Courses use readings not only as context and source materials (which is vital in the academic and civic spheres), but also as models—and not only static models of form, but also as maps to be decoded as to how their writers might have proceeded, why, and to what effect.
- Professors teach key concepts about writing to help students consolidate and transfer skills from one writing occasion to the next. But we recognize that declarative knowledge is made significant only through practice and performance (see Bullet No. 1).
- Student writing and student writers are the course's focus. Everything else serves those ends.

Professor Hesse was speaking of courses in which the primary purpose is to teach writing, but many of his suggestions echo those included in this chapter. Writing need not be our sole instructional focus to lead our students toward proficiency in the written disciplinary vernaculars of our academic fields, whether we just want them to generally become good writers or to be capable of producing scholarly

127

articles for peer-reviewed publications. We do, however, need to be systematic and deliberate in our teaching of writing, and to accept our responsibility in this area rather than merely complaining to our colleagues that, "These students just don't know how to write."

YOUR TURN: INCORPORATING WRITING IN YOUR ASSIGNMENTS AND ASSESSMENTS

Now that you've considered the importance of writing in your classroom, take another look at the plans you've developed for your course.

- Are there any areas where you could add lessons that include writing activities?
- Can you identify any written assignments where you could schedule opportunities for individual feedback prior to students' submission of the final paper or project?
- Have you included direct instruction in the norms of written communication in your particular discipline, including key terminology, vocabulary, preferred style guides, and resource materials?
- Have you built in opportunities for students to read and analyze professional writing in your discipline?
- Could you develop your writing assignments more fully, providing resources, templates, outlines, or other scaffolding that will allow students to meet your expectations successfully?

If you cannot answer these questions in the affirmative, consider revising your course plans to include writing as learning and as assessment. Not only is this a best practice in instruction, but it will prepare your students to be proficient and professional communicators in your discipline.

As one last word of advice, I'd like to share this final quote from Ed Young (2006):

> **Assign only writing that you want to read** . . . . *If you have little interest in reading student writing, chances are that students will have little interest in writing it. Under such conditions, we teachers create a situation in which writers who don't want to write, write for readers who don't want to read, and we do this in the name of improving communication. . . . Rather, writing across the curriculum suggests that we begin by creating assignments in a classroom environment where students and teachers are eager to read one another's work.*
>
> (p. 32; emphasis added)

Identify ⟶	Ideate
Why should I include writing among my course objectives if I'm not teaching a writing course? Every discipline contains specific expectations for written communication and the ability to write well is among the hallmarks of an educated person. By teaching writing in the context of our disciplines, we better prepare our students for professional practice.	How can I fit writing into my course if it's already planned out? Writing doesn't need to dominate your course, but you can minimally add some instruction about appropriate writing in your discipline to one or more of your lectures, you can provide your students with resources that will assist them in creating written work that meets disciplinary norms, and you can include assignments that require students to write according to these norms to support their acquisition of this important skill.
Iterate ⟵	Implement
When you teach your course, try to watch for points where you could insert further writing-related instruction or assignments. The more deliberation we apply to this important task, the greater our chances of producing students who can write competently in their professional lives.	What should I add to my course? Look over your plans and find points where you could build in the following three things: (1) a lecture where you could add an example of good writing in your discipline; (2) an assignment that could include a written component; (3) a way to approach that assignment that allows for instructor feedback and revision to produce a piece of professional-quality writing suitable to your disciplinary norms and expectations.

FIGURE 6.4 Chapter 6 Design Connection

Remember:

- All disciplines have particular norms and expectations for written communication (disciplinary vernaculars). In our courses, we need to teach these to our students so that they can think, write, and speak in a professional manner.
- Writing can be formative (writing-to-learn), summative (writing-to-communicate), or both, depending on your instructional choices.
- Writing should enhance the students' learning experience and enrich your teaching.

Notes

[1] Sejnost, R., and Thiese, S. (2001). *Reading and Writing Across the Content Areas*. Arlington Heights, IL: SkyLight Professional Development.

[2] Young, A. (2006). *Teaching Writing Across the Curriculum*, 4th ed. Upper Saddle River, NJ: Prentice Hall Resources for Writing.

[3] Hesse, D. (January 3, 2017). We know what works in teaching composition. *Chronicle of Higher Education*. www.chronicle.com/article/We-Know-What-Works-in-Teaching/238792

Chapter 7

Incorporating Engaged Learning

CHAPTER SUMMARY

- Collaborative Learning
- Getting Started: Level 1
- Groups: Level 2
- Problem-Based or Project-Based Learning: Level 3
- Example
- Other Active Learning Strategies
- Your Turn: Incorporating Collaborative Learning in Your Classroom

---

The phrase "engaged learning" broadly indicates any situation in which students actively participate in their own acquisition of knowledge or skill. Collaborative learning methods such as problem-based or project-based learning can be identified as engaged learning, among other pedagogical practices such as increasing the frequency of instructor feedback, incorporating writing across the curriculum, and establishing learning communities. Therefore, engaged learning is not specifically linked to any single instructional approach but refers to

- active learning (engagement in the learning process),
- experiential learning (engagement with the object of study),
- multi/interdisciplinary learning (engagement with multiple disciplinary contexts), and
- service learning (engagement with social or civic contexts).[1]

Phrases such as *student engagement* or *engaged learning* appear frequently in mission statements, departmental goals, programmatic outcomes, or strategic plans. Collaboration, interdisciplinarity, service learning, or community engagement also occupy prominent positions in these documents. This isn't necessarily as daunting as it may seem: Sometimes a single activity can satisfy two or more of these purposes or meet multiple expectations. However, we must first consider this: Why should we depart from our relatively comfortable, familiar habits to build these activities into the plans we're making for our courses? Why is lecturing for 90 minutes twice a week no longer sufficient when it has been the norm and expectation for quite literally more than 1,000 years?

The short answer is that our two primary means of communicating necessary course content to our students—listening and reading—require students to be passive recipients of transmitted information, as though we could externally fill our students' heads with all the knowledge we decide they need. These practices lie at the root of an instructionalist educational philosophy, or instructor-centered pedagogies. As we saw in Chapter 2, however, other educational theories and our own personal experience contradict instructionalism. We know that our students learn best when they're actively engaged in the learning process, as we saw in our exploration of the theories of Malcolm Knowles (andragogy), John Dewey (education as experience), and many others. Most of us know, too, that we ourselves learn best by doing, not be listening or reading.

A study conducted by the University of Missouri found that participants initially heard, understood, and retained 50% of what was said in a 10-minute oral presentation, but 48 hours later, participants remembered only half of that original knowledge, or one-fourth of what had been said. Nevertheless, we continue to expect students to acquire 85% of their knowledge by listening to lectures.[2] Engaged learning strategies counteract the discrepancy between our knowledge of best educational practices and traditional approaches to pedagogy.

Think of it this way: If you needed heart valve replacement surgery, would you want the surgeon to have sat in hundreds of hours of lectures and read dozens of textbooks about surgery, or would you want someone who had performed the procedure successfully hundreds of times? You might argue that surgeons have likely done both—learning in the classroom as well as learning experientially, and you'd be right. The point is that abstract theory alone is insufficient preparation; direct experience must also be part of the equation.

COLLABORATIVE LEARNING

The 21st century workplace is increasingly collaborative, as businesses move away from individual cubicles to open, flexible workspaces in which employees solve problems in teams rather than in isolation. This trend is fueled by technological developments enabling employees in diverse locations to work together in real time, or through the use of internal corporate tools such as a social intranet, discussion forums, company wikis, or cloud-based document creation, not to mention instant messaging and other digital communications tools. Tech giants such as Google lead the way in this endeavor, but it's actually nothing new: More than a century ago, Henry Ford worked with a development team of Clarence Avery, Peter Martin, and Charles Sorenson in inventing the assembly line.[3] Many innovations that seem to have been the work of a lone genius were actually group efforts. Thomas Edison, for instance, built a team of dozens of inventors in his Menlo Park lab, allowing him to work on numerous innovations simultaneously. Indeed, some historians have said Edison's greatest invention was not the light bulb, the phonograph, or motion pictures, but the research and development laboratory.[4]

Just as teaming in the workplace allows companies to achieve superior results, collaboration among students has a positive impact on learning. Students who work in teams develop better oral communication, self-management, and leadership skills. Team-based or cooperative learning increases the quality of student–faculty interactions, bolsters students' self-confidence, and allows them to gain a greater understanding of peers from diverse backgrounds or perspectives.[5] Collaborative learning methods are "based on the assumption that learning is an active, integrated, and constructive process influenced by social and contextual factors"[6]—an idea supported by research such as a 2015 study at the University of Haifa revealing that emotions occurring during social behavior directly influence the brain's processes of learning and memory.[7]

Incorporating collaborative activity into the classroom is not a tremendously difficult change to make in our pedagogical practice, but it does require some background knowledge and prior planning in order for these learning experiences to work well for students. It's important to understand that there is no one-size-fits-all method of introducing collaboration in the classroom. Countless approaches exist, and none is superior to the others.

Collaborative learning can occur within a lecture-based instructional approach, it can complement lecture, or it can serve as the primary pedagogical method for a course. We might understand this as varying levels of collaboration. A brief description follows, with practical suggestions for implementation later in this chapter.

Level 1: Short-Term Partnerships or Groupings

Using this approach, an instructor builds brief student interactions into a given class period, which may last for just a few minutes or up to one or two entire class periods. Short-term group activities tend not to be graded or to comprise only a small percentage of the student's grade. Examples include turn and talk, Think-Pair-Share or Write-Pair-Share, Jigsaw, and case studies.

Level 2: Discussion Groups/Study Groups

Students meet on a regular basis to discuss course content, complete assignments together, or prepare for exams. Study groups sometimes complete their work outside of scheduled class periods, apart from direct instructor supervision. Discussion groups more typically meet during regular class times, often with the instructor or a graduate assistant. The purpose of these groups is to support learning presented during lectures or through students' assigned readings, allowing students to more deeply assimilate the course content through small-group interaction.

Level 3: Problem-Based and Project-Based Learning

As these names suggest, student groups are presented with a problem to solve or project to complete. This differs from the Level 1 and Level 2 configurations listed above in several important aspects, which we'll examine in the pages that follow. Perhaps most importantly, Level 1 and Level 2 collaborative learning strategies can easily exist within a traditional lecture-based course structure, but Level 3 strategies generally represent a more student-centered or learning-centered educational philosophy that does not rely on lecture as the primary method of instructional delivery.

GETTING STARTED: LEVEL 1

The key to success in collaborative learning is prior preparation. For those educators who seldom step away from the lectern (so to speak) these small steps may be a good way to begin to incorporate collaboration into the classroom.

- Turn and Talk
  - Plan 1 or 2 questions or discussion prompts for each of your lectures, coinciding with points where you most want students to internalize the content or make a connection to the ideas you present.
  - For example, let's say you were delivering a lecture about the importance of leadership in your specific discipline. You could say to the students, "Turn and talk to someone near you about a leader who has had a positive impact on your experience in [this discipline]. What was the most important lesson you learned from this person?"
  - Allow students 4 or 5 minutes to discuss, and then bring their attention back to your lecture. (Using a bell or similar auditory cue

133

is a good way to signal that it's time for students to end their conversations and return their attention to you. Some instructors project the image of a digital timer on the presentation screen, if using these technologies.)

- Think-Pair-Share
  - This strategy also works well with a primarily lecture-based format. After you introduce concepts that require students to analyze or evaluate ideas, pause and ask students to think for a moment about this idea and write down their reactions. Wait for 1 or 2 minutes to allow them sufficient time to think about the questions you've asked.
  - Then instruct students to share their ideas with someone sitting nearby. Pause for 1 or 2 minutes again.
  - Now direct student pairs to join another partner pair, making a group of four, who share their ideas. Pause for about 5 minutes to allow this conversation to take place.
  - Ask the groups to appoint a spokesperson to share the result of this discussion with the entire class. If you're teaching a very large group, you'll only be able to have a handful of student groups share their responses, but this still serves to enhance all students' learning.
  - Although Think-Pair-Share is more time consuming than the Turn and Talk strategy, it encourages deeper interactions among students and helps them to better connect with the course content through their exchange of ideas.
- Jigsaw / Case Study
  - Divide the class into groups.
  - Assign each group a portion of the content you want the entire class to learn, such as a chapter from a course textbook, one of a series of related journal articles, or one of a set of similar case studies.
  - Allow sufficient time for the group to work together to learn their assigned content and create a way to present it to the whole class. Depending on the amount of material they must read and discuss, and the length of the presentation you want them to create, this may require anywhere from 30 minutes to more than one class period.
  - Once the student groups have prepared their presentations, allow sufficient class time for the presentations to occur.
  - You might consider asking each group to write a quiz question or two about their presentation, submitting these directly to you. You can aggregate these questions and administer the quiz during the class period following the presentations. Providing for this measure of accountability helps the audience members to focus on their peers' presentations.

GROUPS: LEVEL 2

Student study groups are nothing new, nor is it atypical to incorporate discussion groups into the structure of a course, especially one with challenging academic content. As instructors, though, we can facilitate these groups' success by providing a framework for their activities.

- Study Groups
  The purpose of a study group is to reinforce students' learning of material presented in lectures and assigned readings. They might share notes from lectures, discuss concepts in the readings, or work collaboratively on their assignments.
  - Study groups generally meet outside of regularly scheduled class periods and do not typically receive direct support from the instructor, nor do students usually receive a grade for their participation in a study group. Presumably, students are motivated to engage in these groups in the hopes that it will enhance their learning and therefore help them achieve a higher grade for the course overall.
  - Consider assigning students to these groups based on their relative levels of ability or achievement in the course so that each contains a balance between high-achievers, average students, and those who will probably require additional help.
  - Provide an outline or study guide containing specific questions for discussion, lists of available resources, and specific instruction as to which chapters or sections of course texts are the most important.
  - I utilized the study group strategy in an aesthetic philosophy course I designed. Assigned readings in this course were notoriously difficult for students to comprehend, and the study group format provided a structure for students to read and discuss as they went through each assigned reading together, generating a set of shared notes and using their conversations as a tool to facilitate better comprehension. Each discussion group had an appointed leader who made a brief report after the group's meetings, allowing me to remain informed of their progress even though they met outside of the regular class periods.
- Discussion Groups
  This approach to student collaboration provides opportunities to interact with course content in a smaller setting than a lecture hall. Students can share their ideas more freely, ask questions, and receive help from their peers.
  - Discussion groups are more structured than study groups, often meeting during regularly scheduled class time with support from the instructor or a graduate teaching assistant who can facilitate discussions and other learning activities.

135

- For example, a typical course meeting twice per week might devote the first class period of the week to lecture and the second to discussion groups and active learning such as role-playing, case studies, or game scenarios that are not possible in a lecture hall.[8]
- Students generally receive a grade for their participation in a discussion group, especially those that occur within the class period.

PROBLEM-BASED OR PROJECT-BASED LEARNING: LEVEL 3

This approach significantly minimizes the role of lecture in student learning, with the activities of student groups occupying the majority of the course's clock hours. Some characteristics of this type of instructional strategy include the following.

- The instructor's primary role is that of facilitator. Direct, whole-group instruction may continue to be part of such courses, but it usually takes a backseat to students' independent investigations.
- Problems or projects tend to be assigned before instruction, which reverses the typical approach of giving students a problem to solve only after we've taught them how to do it. Instead, students must take the initiative to seek out the knowledge they need to address the problem they've been given rather than passively waiting for the instructor to tell them what they're supposed to know.
- Problems or projects vary in length or importance, lasting anywhere from a single class period to multiple weeks or even an entire semester.
- Problems or projects include genuine connections to the world outside of the classroom. They often require students to interact with community members, industry partners, or various other individuals or groups external to the university.
- Problems are not tightly structured. The most effective problems
  - Require students to seek out more information than they possess at the start of the project
  - Hold the potential for multiple paths to a solution or multiple solutions
  - Change as students gather new information
  - Prohibit one simple or correct answer
  - Spark students' interest and cause students to ask questions
  - Are open-ended and complex enough to demand collaboration and higher-order thinking skills
  - Maintain authentic connections to one or more disciplines or areas of professional practice

- Students should receive grades for their work, but methods of assessment vary: In some cases, the group receives a shared grade, sometimes students receive an individual grade, and sometimes the instructor uses a combination of both approaches. Group critique of projects, self-assessment, and traditional quizzes and exams can also factor into students' grades, depending on the course content and instructor's preferences.
- Emphasis tends to be on students' *depth* of knowledge rather than the breadth of material to be covered.
- In my experience, problem-based or project-based learning works best in classrooms with fewer than 50 students. Larger enrollments are more difficult to manage in terms of physical space and the fact that the instructor's attention could not be divided equitably among so many students. Use of graduate assistants can help with this, but the issue of space would still need to be addressed if the course is scheduled to meet in a large lecture hall rather than a classroom where the furniture can be moved to accommodate student groups.

Forming Teams

There are several methods of forming groups or teams. Team size can vary depending on instructor preference, but between 3 and 6 students per group is generally effective. Groups larger than six have trouble reaching consensus and individual students can be more easily pushed aside or left out unless they are fairly assertive.

- The easiest method of dividing a class into teams is to allow students to choose their own teammates. However, this doesn't always yield the best results because students will nearly always decide to work with their friends or people with whom they have something in common. It also inevitably ends up that a few students are left out and the instructor will have to assist them in joining a group, which can be awkward.
- You can also choose to sort students into teams according to their aptitude or ability. For example, you can use data gathered through a pre-course survey to sort students by their self-identified familiarity with the course subject, ensuring that each group has at least one member who is a strong student, at least one who is likely to need some additional help, and at least two others who provide necessary balance. The same task could be achieved by ranking students based on their performance on a quiz or exam that you've administered early in the course.
- Students generally consider random assignments to groups as "fair" and these often result in a better mix of students on each team than allowing

students to choose their own teams. Suggestions for random grouping include:

- — Arbitrary alphabetical assignments: The first four students on your class list are Team 1, the next four are Team 2, etc.
- — Mixed majors: In a class open to students from different colleges or schools, form teams in which each student is from a different academic field. This encourages students to interact with people they normally wouldn't associate with, and the groups' discussions might be richer due to these individuals' divergent perspectives.
- — Random sort: As students enter the classroom, hand each person a playing card from a standard deck. Instruct students to find the other students in the room who are holding the same numbered card as they are. (You'll have to make sure your deck of cards has the same number of cards as you have students and that you have complete groups of four of each card.) The same task can be achieved by passing out pieces of colored paper or candy and then instructing students to find all of the other people who are holding an orange card or a blue Jolly Rancher. Again, some preparation is necessary to ensure that you have the correct number of items to distribute.

Team Management

Beginning: Once you've divided the class into teams, the projects can begin. Investing some time in establishing a good foundation is important because it can help teams function cohesively.

- ■ Students need some time to get to know one another the first time they work in their project groups. This could involve icebreaker activities or just simple introductions.
- ■ If the team will be working together for an extended period of time, encourage them to establish team norms or ground rules (e.g., We agree not to interrupt one another during discussions; we will arrive for our group prepared to work, etc.). Students may wish to draw up a team contract that outlines these rules specifically, signed by each group member.
- ■ Students should determine their own group norms. You can suggest that students create a division of labor, assigning roles such as coordinator, timekeeper, note-taker, materials manager, etc. Roles could rotate periodically or remain the same for the duration of the project. However, students should retain ownership of their group's operation unless instructor intervention is warranted should the group become dysfunctional.

- Introduce the task, providing enough information to get students started, but not so much that they can do the task without conducting any background investigations.
- Provide students with a detailed set of expectations *at the onset of the project*, including a timeline for completion and any interim assessments or benchmarks. A calendar with check-in points or due dates is helpful.
- Make sure students understand how their work will be graded: What criteria will you look for? How is individual participation weighted against group results? Determining the answer to crucial questions such as these prior to assigning the project, and communicating these expectations to students up front reduces the likelihood of conflict at the end of the semester.

Middle: While the task is underway, the instructor's role becomes decreasingly visible. The goal is for teams to function independently, while you provide support but not direct instruction.

- Check in with groups frequently.
  - Move between groups throughout the class period.
  - Avoid telling students what to do—suggest, recommend, or guide them to additional resources, but make every effort not to subvert their discovery process. Intervene only when absolutely necessary. *Note: This is difficult to accomplish!* We tend to want to step in and "fix things" when we see something wrong, or to just hand students the right answer to their questions. Optimal learning, though, requires students to discover answers on their own, so even if you literally have to walk around the room with your hands in your pockets, don't step in unless asked to do so, and then only provide nondirective advice and support.
  - Try to answer students' questions with another question. For instance, if a group asks, "What should we do next?" respond, "What do *you* think the next step should be?" or, "What strategies have you already tried?"
- Keep anecdotal records of your observations as students are working, especially if you've tied student participation to their course grades. The level of detail you choose to employ in this task depends on your personal preference. You could simply make notes, or you could use a point sheet, awarding either groups or individual students a daily or weekly score for participation.
- Remind students of project benchmarks frequently, so they aren't taken unawares by approaching deadlines.

139

- Incorporate peer and self-assessment at several milestones throughout the project. This allows you to recognize emerging problems and gives you the opportunity to intervene if necessary. For example, it's a good idea to hold an interim critique about halfway through the project's timeline in which each group shares its progress and receives feedback from you and their peers. It's also advisable to provide a means of confidential communication so students can report problems in the group's interpersonal dynamics. No individual should dominate the group, nor should nonparticipation by any group member be acceptable.

End: Collaborative learning generally concludes in a presentation of the group's work.

- Presentations can take several forms:
  - Website or wiki
  - Video, posted to YouTube or saved to a flash drive and handed to the instructor
  - Written report
  - Visual display or tangible artifact accompanied by verbal description or explanation
  - In-class presentation or performance, sometimes using multimedia
  - Pecha Kucha[9]
- Provide students with confidential opportunities to evaluate one another's contributions to the group. These can inform your grading process, but should not factor too heavily into an individual student's final grade.
- Evaluation should include both a collective grade on the group project and a separate grade for students' individual contributions or participation, based on your own observations and confidential peer input. This helps to prevent a high-achieving student from being disproportionately penalized for the work of a low-performing group and also mitigates a low-performing student's impact on an otherwise high-functioning group.
- Communicate your grading schema clearly (e.g., 75% of the grade will be based on the group project and 25% on the student's individual participation or contribution.)

EXAMPLE

Design Thinking for Entrepreneurs employs several of these collaborative learning strategies. Most lectures include at least one turn-and-talk question, and the second class period each week is primarily geared toward discussion and active learning. Students complete hands-on, engaged learning activities featuring design thinking, lateral thinking, problem solving, and peer critique, among others.

Students also engage in a long-term collaborative project in which they create a business model canvas using design thinking and other ideation strategies to envision a business or nonprofit organization that addresses a complex social problem. The schedule of instruction front-loads ideation strategies, so the project begins in Week 6 and concludes Week 15 with formal presentations. Student groups must meet various check-in points along the way.

- Week 6: Form student project groups.
- Week 7: Project brainstorming and background research
- Week 8: Complete business canvas.
- Week 9: In-progress critique
- Week 11: Produce a business document.
- Week 12: Develop marketing/branding strategy using social media.
- Week 13: Present to a small section of the class, receiving initial feedback.
- Week 14: Post required video documentary of the project to the class YouTube channel.
- Week 15: Formal presentation of projects to whole class; peer critique; self-assessment

The project is evaluated at each point listed above. This is also built into the course structure. For example, Assignment 8 asks students to evaluate their group using the form presented in Figure 7.1.

The group will also receive a collective grade on the project as a whole using the rubric presented in Figure 7.2.

Finally, Assignment 9 presented in Figure 7.3 requires students to view and critique other groups' videos, posted to the class YouTube channel.

Requiring students to critique and evaluate their peers' work does more than provide important feedback. It also holds them accountable for paying attention to other groups. Furthermore, these three approaches to evaluation combine to form a more complete picture of the projects' success, making assessment somewhat less subjective by supplementing the instructor's observations and yielding information about the group's dynamics when the instructor wasn't watching. A beautiful presentation could be the work of only one student on a team, but that student would likely complete the peer evaluation of her project group differently than those who sat passively by and allowed her to do all of the work. Likewise, group critique gives the instructor a mechanism to gauge audience response to the presentations. The instructor may have thought a given presentation was merely average, but it might really resonate with the audience. Upon reading those critiques, the instructor's opinion may change. Similarly, the instructor may think a given presentation was excellent, but it could receive a lukewarm reception from the audience. When a

ASSIGNMENT 8: PEER EVALUATION OF PROJECT GROUP

Please complete this form in class. Hand it directly to the instructor prior to leaving the classroom today. Your responses will remain confidential and will not affect your course grade.

Statements Choose a response in the column at right to indicate your level of agreement with the statements below.	Rating Scale (Circle one). 1 = strongly disagree 2 = disagree 3 = neither agree nor disagree 4 = agree 5 = strongly agree
1. My group functioned well as a team.	1 2 3 4 5
2. Every member of my group contributed equally to the group's success.	1 2 3 4 5
3. I gave my best effort to this project.	1 2 3 4 5
4. I feel that our project could be successful if we actually had the opportunity to implement it.	1 2 3 4 5
5. The members of my group shared leadership of the project.	1 2 3 4 5
6. We did not experience any significant problems in our team dynamics.	1 2 3 4 5
7. We were able to meet the due date without trouble.	1 2 3 4 5
8. We addressed all of the project requirements.	1 2 3 4 5
9. We actively utilized design thinking.	1 2 3 4 5
10. We actively utilized entrepreneurial processes.	1 2 3 4 5

FIGURE 7.1 Peer Evaluation of Project Group

discrepancy exists in perceptions, it's wise to reconsider our initial opinions prior to assigning an important grade.

OTHER ACTIVE LEARNING STRATEGIES

Civic Engagement/Service Learning

Both civic engagement and service learning connect the student with the community in some capacity. Although they are not necessarily collaborative or

PROJECT EVALUATION RUBRIC

		Possible	Score
INNOVATON STRATEGIES Score 0 = not present 1 = minimal 2 = present	Critical thinking	2	
	Computational thinking	2	
	Design thinking	2	
	Lateral thinking	2	
	Problem finding/problem solving	2	
	Systems thinking	2	
ENTREPRENEURIAL PROCESS Score 0 = not present 1 = minimal 2 = adequate 3 = outstanding	Recognize opportunity	3	
	Determine how to capitalize on this opportunity	3	
	Identify needed resources	3	
	Develop branding and marketing strategies	3	
	Discuss future implementation strategy	3	
	Predict the outcome of the project	3	
VIDEO PRESENTATION Score 0 = not present to 10 = outstanding	Length: Video is long enough to communicate needed information but does not exceed time limit.	10	
	A/V quality: The audio and visual presentation conveys the intended message without significant errors.	10	
	Focus: The purpose of the project is clear.	10	
	Message: The presentation delivers an interesting and engaging message.	10	
	Each group member's contribution to the project is evident.	10	
MATERIALS PACKAGE Score 0 = not present 1 = minimal 2 = needs improvement 3 = good 4 = outstanding	Project Summary document	4	
	Business Model Canvas document	4	
	Screenshot of website's home page	4	
	Screenshot of social media marketing or branding strategy	4	
	Business letter, grant inquiry or application, or other business document	4	
TOTAL		100	

Instructor Comments:

FIGURE 7.2 Project Evaluation Rubric

ASSIGNMENT 9: PEER CRITIQUE OF VIDEO PROJECT PRESENTATIONS

Directions:

- Complete this form for three groups' video presentations.[1]
- Type your answers into the cells below.
- Submit this form to your instructor prior to the final exam.
- Please limit your comments to 100 words in each cell of the chart, below.

Project name	
Demonstration of strategies for innovation	
Demonstration of entrepreneurial process	
Video quality	
Feedback on the best aspect of the project—and why you felt this was successful.	
Feedback on an aspect of the project that could be improved—and how you think this should have been changed.	

[1] Note: To avoid repetition, only one grid is show here, but the form that students access through the course web page has sections for all three presentations.

FIGURE 7.3 Peer Critique Form

team-based pedagogical strategies, tasks assigned to students in problem-based or project-based learning frequently involve engagement in the community- or service-oriented learning opportunities. We cannot count civic engagement or service learning as collaborative learning per se, but these approaches can coexist or overlap with collaborative pedagogies.

Higher educational institutions frequently establish programs, centers, offices, or other official structures that provide students with options for civic engagement, service learning, or other pathways to interaction with groups or individuals outside of the institution. The College of William and Mary's Office of Community Engagement, the University of Notre Dame's Center for Social Concerns, Vanderbilt University's Office of Active Citizenship, and George Washington University's Center for Civic Engagement and Public Service serve as but a few examples of these organizations.[10]

We don't need an institutional structure to employ this learning strategy in our classrooms, though. You have many options for incorporating service learning or community engagement into your course.[11]

- *One-time group service projects* involve all students and the instructor working collaboratively with a community group or organization to achieve a mutually beneficial outcome.
  - Example: Students in an architecture course design a community recreation center in collaboration with a team of individuals who will be the users of the facility
- *Optional course components* can take the place of a more traditional research paper or group project through which students participate in a community-based project, documented through an experiential research paper or personal journal. This could be accomplished through existing co-curricular community service groups.
  - Example: Students in an education course volunteer to tutor elementary school children who live in a disadvantaged neighborhood, writing about their experience in lieu of a formal research paper about an educational theory
- *Required course components* are built into the framework of the course, mandating that all members of the class engage in a service experience that supports the course's outcomes and objectives. In most cases, these are prearranged by the instructor through partnerships with external groups or organizations.
  - Example: Students in a marketing and promotions coursework with a nonprofit community youth orchestra to create and implement a fundraising campaign using social media
- *Action research projects* engage students within the community through research in address of identified needs. This option not only involves students in research, but can support ongoing faculty research as well.
  - Example: a professor of biology works with the county forest preserve district to identify and eradicate invasive species of plants. Students research and implement various approaches to controlling the plants' growth, trying different methods until they find an effective strategy. The students' investigations support the professor's ongoing research into this topic, eventually leading to a paper for a peer-reviewed journal.
- *Capstone projects* promote students' authentic engagement in a professional context suitable to their major field of study as they explore the intersection of disciplinary expertise and community needs. These generally occur in students' senior year of undergraduate study and may embody the entire purpose of a course.
  - Example: Students nearing completion of a major in community health work with a local social service organization on a campaign to raise awareness about a health issue pertinent to that organization's target population

- *Multiple-course projects* are the most ambitious of these strategies, with projects spanning either sequential semesters of the same course or occurring across a group of simultaneous courses in which students and faculty collaborate on the same community-based project.
  - Examples: The action research project involving the professor of biology could exemplify this strategy if the research spans multiple semesters. A transdisciplinary project in which students create a theatrical performance designed to teach high school students about a concept in physics could involve the coordinated efforts of students and faculty across several courses including physics, playwriting, acting, costume design, education, music composition, and graphic design, all working in concert to create this educational experience.

Implementing community-engaged learning will require a larger investment of advance planning than you may be used to. The following is a partial list of actions that instructors considering taking this step should think through prior to deciding to embark upon this best practice in teaching.[12]

1. Identify and establish a relationship with a community partner, determining through open discussion how your students can best meet one or more of their needs or serve their target population meaningfully.
2. Write outcomes and objectives for your course that students will achieve through their involvement in the planned learning experience.
3. Address any ethical issues that may pertain to your project, ensuring the just and benevolent treatment of all persons involved. You may need to work with your institution's Institutional Review Board to be certain that requirements have been satisfied.
4. Determine how you will handle any logistical issues such as
   a. Transportation of students or project materials to and from the work site
   b. Liability concerns, including drivers' licenses or insurance for those providing transportation
   c. Media coverage, either by informing the local media of the project, creating posts to social media, or publicizing the project through campus communication channels
   d. Clarifying the roles of all participants and providing for student supervision and oversight
   e. Scheduling the project, creating a master calendar and agendas for each meeting, maximizing participants' time while at the job site
   f. Training or orientation that might be required by the partner organization before students can engage in the project
   g. Establishing contingency plans for when things don't go as expected, and also ensuring that proper procedures for handling emergencies are in place

5. Express any expectations and assumptions so that students, community partners, and the instructor all understand what each party hopes to gain from the project. Participants should also verbalize any concerns so that these can be addressed before they become problematic.

6. Include all necessary information, documentation, and written materials in the course's design, incorporating them into your syllabus, and providing these to all participants. This may encompass the following:

   a. Information about required training, the work to be performed, what will occur after the completion of the project

   b. Broad issues related to the project such as the demographics and histories of the target population, including contextualization such as discussions of power and inequality

   c. All planned activities related to the project, calendars, schedules, and logistical information

   d. Incorporate instruction in problem solving, critical thinking, analysis, application, theorization, and reflection

   e. Plan for how you will assess student learning and how you will assign grades for students' involvement in the project

7. Communicate regularly with the partnering organization, visiting the project site, monitoring progress, and ensuring that students are functioning appropriately within the project setting.

8. Incorporate separate opportunities for debriefing and reflection for students and for participants in the partnering organization, allowing each person to think critically about their experience, relate it to larger social contexts and issues, recognize their involvement in the project's challenges and successes, and prepare for future engagement if possible.

This approach to instruction is undoubtedly labor intensive. It is also among the most interesting, most rewarding, and most beneficial actions you can take as an instructor. A well-planned and successfully executed service-learning or community-engaged project can become a transformative experience for your students as they see the theory of the classroom made tangible through their work with the partner organization. Despite the greater investment of your thought and energy in bringing this to life, it is well worth the effort.

Practical Experience

Numerous degree programs incorporate practical experience as a standard part of student learning. Education majors complete student teaching, nursing students are required to complete clinical hours, and business students complete internships in corporate settings, as just a few examples. Even though this book is more directed toward individual instructors' course planning rather than program-level decisions, our courses can nevertheless incorporate practical experiences for our students.

In "Connecting the Dots," a paper I wrote for the Conference on the Liberal Arts (Jackson State University, 2016), I argued that schools of business have practiced this strategy for decades, sometimes resulting in extraordinarily high job placement rates. For instance, 99% of the of the graduates of Babson College, a small business school in Massachusetts, acquire full-time jobs within 6 months of commencement, as do 98.6% of graduates of the University of Pennsylvania's Wharton School of Business, and 98% of graduates of Emory University's Goizueta Business School.[13] If these results merely indicated that there are more jobs available in the business sector, we could expect to see similarly stellar job placement rates at all schools of business, but this is not the case. Students who major in business management experience an unemployment rate of 4.8% overall, just 1% lower than the 5.8% rate for liberal arts majors.[14] Rather, these institutions achieve outstanding results for their graduates by maintaining a laser focus on preparing students for the workplace through industry partnerships and by incorporating career training into their curriculum.

Many universities offer excellent career services centers, but when students receive direct classroom instruction in the professional expectations of their disciplines, including topics such as navigating the present job market, creating resumes, and practicing interviewing techniques, it dramatically increases the likelihood that they will secure good jobs after graduation. This instruction can be incorporated into any course. It doesn't have to occupy the majority of your time, but by making deliberate connections between the content of your course and the workplace your students will encounter after graduation, you maximize their potential for success.

As we've seen in other areas of engaged learning, practical student experiences can exist in many different configurations. The following terms are sometimes used synonymously, but differences between them do exist in practice. Understanding this terminology can help us to set a direction for our course preparation when considering adding practical experience requirements.

- *Internships* involve a short-term, usually part-time, position with a company or organization related to a student's field of study. These can last from 2 or 3 months to an entire semester or even a full academic year. Interns usually function as employees of the organization, with designated duties and some level of responsibility. Interns may receive pay or a stipend, which varies depending on many factors. It is not unusual for an internship to lead to permanent employment, since employers are able to witness the student's work ethic and job-related skills.
- *Externships* also involve a student in a practical work experience but are shorter in duration, lasting anywhere from a day to a week, or occurring

over the summer or spring break. Externships are typically unpaid and often consist of workplace observations or job shadowing. Therefore, an internship provides a more authentic work experience for students than an externship, but externships can still help students begin building a network of professional relationships. They may also lead to later internships with the same organization. Because of their limited nature, externships are perhaps the best option for instructors who aspire to incorporate practical work experience into their students' course of study. For example, you might choose to require students to shadow a disciplinary professional for a day when they're home over Spring Break, or you could organize similar 1-day opportunities with a partner organization near campus, rotating students throughout the semester.

- *Cooperative education* (co-op) is a specialized type of internship that provides career training, sometimes with pay, as students work with professionals in their major field of study. Depending on the field, a co-op placement may necessitate that the student take a semester or more away from their studies, especially if it is a full-time paid position. Co-op students have more opportunity to become an integral part of an organization, to work on important projects, and to receive an authentic work experience. Co-op is most common in technology and engineering, but it also exists in other fields such as business and the liberal arts.[15]

- *Volunteer work* related to a student's field of study can also expose students to practical experience in your discipline. Co-curricular or community-based organizations abound, and most are eager for volunteers. There are also plentiful volunteer opportunities on most campuses. A student majoring in marketing could help design the advertising campaign for an upcoming production put on by the Theater Department, or a chemistry major could volunteer to tutor high school chemistry students. You might consider requiring students to engage in a volunteer experience as part of your course content, holding them accountable through the writing of a reflective report at the end of the semester.

Preparing to include practical experience requirements in your course is somewhat simpler than establishing a service-learning or community-engaged learning option because these occur outside of the confines of your classroom.

- Option 1: Identify and build a relationship with community partners willing to host externship students for 1-day job shadowing. You can simply provide students with a list of these organizations and information for a contact person with whom the student must schedule their experience, or you could work with the partner organization(s) to create a schedule and assign students to particular days.

■ Option 2: Create a list of possible volunteer options related to the purposes of your course. Inform students of the requirement that they select and work with one of these organizations during the semester and create a means by which the student will report on this experience. The syllabus should clearly state each detail of this requirement and how it will be assessed.

■ Option 3: Require students to identify and conduct their own job shadowing or volunteer experience while on an extended break from school (generally over Thanksgiving or Spring Break). Students must make these contacts on their own, undertake the experience, and then create documentation to show that they have met this requirement. Again, the syllabus should clearly state each detail of this requirement and how it will be assessed.

What follows is a sample report, and a student reflective report form appears in Figures 7.4 and 7.5.

Job Shadow Reflective Report

Student Name: _____

Name of Organization: _____

Name and Position of Employee Shadowed: _____

Date of Observation: _____

Please describe your experience, focusing on the following questions. Your response should be between 200 and 300 words in length.

■ What is the primary business or purpose of the organization?
■ Who did you shadow and what is this person's role within the company?
■ What did you observe?
■ What did you do in addition to your observations?

Please reflect on this experience, focusing on the following questions. Your response should be between 200 and 300 words in length.

■ What was the most important lesson you learned during this experience?
■ Did this experience change your opinion or perception of working in [name of discipline]?
■ How do you think that this experience will help to prepare you for professional engagement in [name of discipline]?

FIGURE 7.4 Job Shadow Experience Reflective Report

Volunteer Experience Reflective Report

Student Name: _____

Name of Organization: _____

Name of Administrator: _____

Phone Number: _____

Email Address: _____

Dates and Hours Worked: _____

Please describe your experience, focusing on the following questions. Your response should be between 200 and 300 words in length.

- What is the primary purpose of the organization?
- With whom did you work?
- What did you do?

Please reflect on this experience, focusing on the following questions. Your response should be between 200 and 300 words in length.

- Why did you select this organization?
- What was the most important lesson you learned during this experience?
- How do you think that this experience will help to prepare you for professional engagement in [name of discipline]?

Student Signature: _____

Administrator Signature _____

FIGURE 7.5 Volunteer Experience Reflective Report

Syllabus Text: Instructor-Arranged Externship

- In this course we will explore professional practice in [name of discipline] by working with [name of organization]. Each student will have the opportunity to spend a day job shadowing an employee to gain firsthand workplace experience that will deepen and broaden your studies.
- A schedule has been posted on our course website [insert URL]. Before the end of Week 1 of our course, please enter your name in one of the available spots. Students who have not done so by the due date will be assigned to the first available spot thereafter.

151

- Within 48 hours of your job shadow experience, you must complete and post the Job Shadow Reflective Report form, available on our course website. (Figure 7.4 is a sample form for this purpose.)

Syllabus Text: Volunteer Experience

- In this course we will explore professional practice in [name of discipline] by volunteering with a campus-based or community organization.
- A list of possible volunteer opportunities is available on our course website [insert URL] including links to each organization.
- You must complete and document at least 10 hours of volunteer experience with the organization you select.
  - Week 8 (midterm): You will verbally report on your choice of organization in class, describing your activities to date.
  - Week 13: Volunteer hours must be completed.
  - Week 15: You must complete and submit the Volunteer Reflective Report form, located on our course website. (A sample of this form is shown in Figure 7.5) Please note that this form must be printed out and physically signed and dated by a person of authority in the organization with which you choose to volunteer. This hard copy must be handed to the instructor no later than the last regularly scheduled class period of the course.

YOUR TURN: INCORPORATING COLLABORATIVE LEARNING IN YOUR CLASSROOM

Now that you've been introduced to the benefits of collaborative and engaged learning, how might you adapt these strategies to the course you're planning?

- Are there any lectures that might benefit from the addition of Turn and Talk or Think-Pair-Share?
- Can you identify any lessons that might fit well with Jigsaw activities?
- Could you establish study groups or discussion groups to better facilitate student learning?
- Have you considered using problem-based or project-based learning for at least a portion of the course content?
- How might you incorporate service-learning or community-based learning into your course?
- Would adding a requirement for practical experience such as volunteering or externships add depth to your students learning in this course?

If you can answer any of these questions positively, it's time to adjust the plans you're making to include engaged learning opportunities for your students. Not only is this

Identify	➜	Ideate
Why is it important to incorporate engaged learning into the course you're planning? Lecture remains the primary instructional method in higher education, yet it has proven to be among the least effective pedagogical practices. By engaging your students through multiple instructional activities, you can provide them with a better learning experience.		How can I utilize engaged learning in my classroom? This chapter has set forth a broad menu of options for instructors who want to enhance their lectures or move beyond the lectern to involve their students in active, hands-on, and practical learning experiences.
Iterate	⬅ Implement	
When you teach your course, keep track of points where you might be able to change a lecture into a more active learning experience the next time you teach. Before the next semester begins, revise your course plan to include those activities.	What should I do to get started? If you're not yet comfortable with engaged learning, start small. Work a few Think-Pair-Share questions into your lectures. Choose several professional journal articles, distribute them to small groups, and ask students to present the content of the articles to their classmates. Observe a colleague who regularly incorporates engaged learning in his or her classroom. The more you give this a try, the more confidence you'll gain and the better your teaching will become.	

FIGURE 7.6 Chapter 7 Design Connection

a best practice in instruction, it will better prepare your students for their eventual roles in the workplace as well as enhancing their learning in your course.

Remember:

- Collaborative learning and other engaged learning strategies help prepare students for the increasingly team-based workplace they will face after graduation.
- It has demonstrably positive impact on students' acquisition of knowledge and skill.
- Engaged learning activities can be short term or long term. They can enhance or support lecture, or they can provide a student-centered or leaning-centered alternative to traditional instructor-centered pedagogical practices.
- Preparation is crucial to the success of collaborative learning: planning questions; gathering materials; and creating resource lists, schedules, grading rubrics, study guides, and calendars of project benchmarks require an outlay of the instructor's time and effort when first implementing these strategies. However, the results are well worth the investment.

Notes

[1] Bowen, S. (2005). Engaged learning: Are we all on the same page? *Peer Review: Association of American Colleges and Universities*, 7(2). www.aacu.org/publications-research/periodicals/engaged-learning-are-we-all-same-page

[2] Lee, D. (1993). *Listening: Our most used communication skill*. University of Missouri Extension. https://mospace.umsystem.edu/xmlui/handle/10355/50293

[3] Motavalli, J. (February 16, 2016). 5 Inspiring companies that rely on teamwork to be successful. *Success.com*. www.success.com/article/5-inspiring-companies-that-rely-on-teamwork-to-be-successful

[4] Bellis, M. (August 16, 2016). Thomas Edison's 'Muckers'. *ThoughtCo*. http://inventors.about.com/library/inventors/bledisonmuckers.htm and Padgett, K. (n.d.). *Thomas Edison's Research Laboratory*. http://agilewriter.com/Biography/EdisonLab.htm

[5] Cornell University Center for Teaching Excellence. (2017). *Collaborative learning: Group work*. www.cte.cornell.edu/teaching-ideas/engaging-students/collaborative-learning.html

[6] Stanford University "Speaking of Teaching" Winter 2001 Center for Teaching and Learning. PDF.

[7] *Science Daily*. (August 6, 2015). How emotions influence learning and memory processes in the brain. www.sciencedaily.com/releases/2015/08/150806091434.htm

[8] For more information on gamifying your classroom, see www.scoop.it/t/games-gaming-and-gamification-in-higher-education.

[9] Pecha Kucha generally takes the form of a PowerPoint or similar slide-based presentation of 20 slides shown on screen for 20 seconds each accompanied by verbal narration.

[10] Top 25 universities for nonprofit and community service ranked by return. (2017). *Best Value Schools*. www.bestvalueschools.com/non-profit-and-community-service-ranked-by-return/

[11] Enos, S., & Troppe, M. (1996). Service-learning in the curriculum. In B. Jacoby (ed.), (1996). *Service-Learning in Higher Education: Concepts and Practices*. Jossey-Bass: San Francisco, CA, 156–181.

[12] Band, J. (2017). *Community engaged teaching step by step*. Vanderbilt University Center for Teaching. https://cft.vanderbilt.edu/guides-sub-pages/community-engaged-teaching-step-by-step/

[13] Jones, R. (2017). 30 colleges with the most impressive job placement rates and career services. *Online School Center*. www.onlineschoolcenter.com/30-colleges-impressive-job-placement-rates-career-services/

[14] Federal Reserve Bank of New York. (January 11, 2017). *The labor market for recent college graduates*. www.newyorkfed.org/research/college-labor-market/college-labor-market_compare-majors.html

[15] Boyington, B. (March 21, 2015). Understand the differences between a co-op, internship. *U.S. News: Higher Education*. www.usnews.com/education/best-colleges/articles/2015/03/31/understand-the-differences-between-a-co-op-internship

Chapter 8

Teaching Effectively

CHAPTER SUMMARY

- Pedagogical Tasks: Lecture, Discussion, Student Participation, and Demonstration
- Online Pedagogies
- Interaction and Communication
- Providing Feedback for Formative Assessment
- Informal Feedback and Interactions With Students
- Establishing Classroom Policies
- The Teachable Moment
- Improvisation and Serendipity
- Teaching for Diversity, Equity, and Inclusion
- One Last Thought

Many faculty members approach pedagogical tasks intuitively, with varying degrees of pedagogical accomplishment. However, we've probably all had the misfortune of sitting in a classroom where the professor stood at the lectern, never looked up from his notes, and droned on for 90 minutes twice a week for the whole semester. There's so much more to being an excellent teacher than earning a terminal degree. Skilled instructors must also know essential teaching practices such as classroom management techniques, effective methods of instructional delivery, and how to provide valuable feedback on students' work.

Nearly every faculty member was first a student. At minimum, we've probably spent 4 years as undergraduates and 2 or 3 years in graduate school to earn a masters' degree, with some of us investing even more time to earn doctoral degrees. This means that most of us have rich stories to tell about both the excellent educators in whose classrooms we were privileged to sit, and memorably bad instructors who serve as the embodiment of our own cautionary tales—individuals whom we hope never to emulate.

Some people are born teachers. They possess an innate skill in holding an audience's attention, they know how to form high-quality professional relationships with peers and students, their courses receive consistently excellent student evaluations, and there's always a wait list for their courses at the start of each semester. Despite the seeming ease with which those educators approach their work, every faculty member can acquire similar skills and knowledge. Moreover, no one is such an expert that he or she cannot improve his or her pedagogical practice to at least some degree.

PEDAGOGICAL TASKS: LECTURE, DISCUSSION, STUDENT PARTICIPATION, AND DEMONSTRATION

Curriculum planning takes place outside of the classroom, usually well before the first day of class. Pedagogical practice, on the other hand, occurs whenever you and your students interact with one another. During scheduled class times, instructors tend to engage in one of four primary approaches to instructional delivery: lecture, discussion, student participation, and demonstration. The sections that follow contain advice gleaned from thousands of hours of formal observation and personal experience.

Lecture

Lecture is the most ubiquitous of pedagogical practices, to the point that it's become cliché in higher education. Nevertheless, we instructors possess information that our students need to know, and lecturing is among the most direct ways of conveying this knowledge.

As you lecture, you should be aware of the following considerations.

- Remember that you're the center of attention.
  - *Your own enthusiasm for your topic and passion for your discipline are the most powerful pedagogical tools you possess.* When you demonstrate this passion, it's contagious—it's what draws students into the lecture and keeps them engaged in the course as a whole.
  - The dark side of this attention is that students see and remember every little thing that you do, even if you have a habit of absent-mindedly scratching your nose. Your appearance and unconscious physical and verbal mannerisms can significantly distract from your ability to be an

effective lecturer. Regardless of whether you're teaching a small group of students or standing before a packed lecture hall, you always need to be mindful of how you look and sound to your audience.

- To improve my own skills as a public speaker and lecturer, I've devoted a significant number of hours reviewing videos of effective speakers, studying their verbal cadence, posture, facial expressions, and so on. Just speaking personally, I want to be remembered for the infectious passion and inspiration I communicated about my discipline, not because I habitually did something odd during my lectures or had trouble communicating the point of my presentation to my audience.

■ Don't read your notes or your PowerPoint slides verbatim. Look up frequently and make eye contact with students. Nothing is as boring as a teacher who merely reads aloud and never looks up or speaks extemporaneously.

■ Don't talk too fast or too slow; don't shout or whisper—maintain a conversational, friendly tone of voice and a volume at which everyone in the room can hear you clearly. Use a microphone if necessary.

■ Use stories, anecdotes, examples, and other conversational devices to hold students' interest and make your points relevant.

- The human brain needs to connect new learning to prior knowledge. By deliberately helping students to make these connections with frequent examples, analogies, and stories, you're far more likely to increase your students' opportunities for success.

- Here, TED Talks can serve as some of our best models. Akash Karia[1] studied more than 200 of these presentations and discovered that the most successful speakers used storytelling to capture and maintain audience interest. They began their talk by jumping immediately into a personal narrative that related directly to the subject of their presentation and used this story as a touchpoint that shaped the presentation's structure from the first sentence to the last.

■ Don't just sit at a desk or stand behind the lectern for the entire class period. Move around the classroom sometimes.

■ Stay on point. You have a limited number of minutes to present the material you intend to teach that day. Going off on a lengthy tangent about a favorite activity, last night's sporting event, or the latest campus gossip might make for an entertaining conversation, but it won't accomplish your instructional goals.

■ Use multimedia, visual aids, audio clips, or other means of adding interesting content to your lecture.

- Students cannot sit and listen to you for an hour or more with nothing but the sound of your voice to occupy their attention. They grew up in

a fast-paced multimedia environment where their attention is frag-
mented every moment they're outside of your classroom.
  - Using multimedia requires advance preparation along with projection
    systems, audio equipment, etc.
  - Don't use a new technology for the first time when students are in the
    room—set it up in advance and test it to make sure it works.
- PowerPoint and other presentation software (Keynote, Prezi, and so on)
  are great tools for lecturers and presenters. However, we need to use
  technologies judiciously.
  - When you're presenting in person, your slides should not contain
    a script that you read verbatim. They serve to convey only the most
    important points you want to communicate to the audience, or to
    give the audience a visual image that supports what you're saying. Your
    spoken words should be the main focus, not the text on the slides.
  - Use a clean, simple design template that won't distract the audience
    or overpower your message.
  - Ensure that all text is legible for all viewers, even those at the back of
    the lecture hall.
    • Dark text on a light background is easier to read than light text on
      a dark background.
    • Use a plain, standard font.
  - Avoid visual clutter, sound effects, or flashy transitions between slides.
    The goal is to maintain visual interest, while avoiding distraction.
  - Animations can help you control the flow of your message by bringing
    content onto or off the screen one point at a time or to emphasize
    different aspects of the presentation. Be careful, though: It's easy to
    overdo this.
  - Select images thoughtfully and be sure to create a citation or a credits
    page if you use photographs, artworks, or other visuals that were not
    expressly your own creations. We should model the kind of ethical
    scholarship we want our students to emulate, even if we only want to
    begin our presentation with a funny meme.

Discussion

Discussion is among the most crucial of classroom activities, where the flow of
ideas can enrich the learning experience for both the students and the instructor.
However, it's very easy for a discussion to be derailed by student behaviors. The
following suggestions can help to deepen your discussions, keep the conversation
on track, and avoid having one or two students monopolize your attention, while
others sit passively.

■ Ask students to justify or clarify their contributions to the discussion or critique their peers' answers, re-state what a peer has just said, or provide a rationale as to why they agree or disagree with a peer.

■ Be sure to call on different students each time—don't limit your interaction to the few who raise their hands.

■ Keep all discussions or activities on point.

■ As often as possible, respond to students' questions with a question rather than an answer or a statement. This technique is as old as Socrates himself, but it's just as effective now as it was in ancient Greece. Answering a question with a question causes students to think more deeply about the subject at hand and extends their learning beyond their initial query. If you reflexively provide a simple answer, the conversation stops. If you respond with a counter-question, you put the responsibility for learning back on the student and invite greater engagement in the topic at hand.

■ Don't let one or two students monopolize the conversation. It's okay to interrupt someone who's rambling on for too long, politely saying, "Excuse me, that's a very interesting topic and I'd be happy to continue that discussion after class, but for now we need to move on to ____."

■ Likewise, if just one or two students are struggling to grasp a new concept, make arrangements to work with them outside of class and proceed with your planned instruction.
  – You don't need to force the whole class to review something that only a couple of students have failed to grasp.
  – If the entire class, however, doesn't understand, you may need to adjust your lesson plans to include additional instruction for everyone.
  – This is where we see the power of utilizing formative assessment throughout your course. When you determine which students have acquired the necessary skills and knowledge to move forward and which have not, you can tailor your instruction to best meet all students' needs.

Active Student Participation

As we saw in our discussion of engaged learning in Chapter 7, you should plan to incorporate active learning strategies during your lesson even if most of your teaching involves lecture. These can include:

■ Small-group discussions/break-out sessions
■ Turn and Talk
■ Hands-on activities
■ Collaborative projects

- Cooperative problem solving
- Role playing
- Case studies or jigsaw presentations
- Project-based/problem-based learning

Whenever students are working independently or in small groups during the class period, you should move around the classroom and facilitate their discussions or activities, keeping them on task, answering questions, or giving feedback. Don't just sit at a desk.

Demonstration

Of course, not every lesson requires a demonstration component, but they're very common in lab-based or studio-based courses. Keep in mind that modeling a new process or procedure, showing the correct use of equipment and materials, or engaging in other similar tasks requires that students have a clear line of sight to what you're doing. Use a projection system or other technology if necessary to ensure that everyone can see what you're doing and how you're doing it.

If a lesson requires demonstration, you must also provide students with opportunities to practice these new skills in class while you're there to guide and re-demonstrate one-on-one or work with a small group of those who need a bit more help. Depending on the lesson, guided practice may use as much as half of the class period or more. Remember the strategy of "I do, we do, you do."

ONLINE PEDAGOGIES

Teaching an online class demands a different set of skills than teaching on campus. We have to do even more advance planning and preparation for an online course than for an on-campus course, since everything needs to be available to students the first time they log into the virtual classroom. Talking and listening—the bedrock of face-to-face learning—are notably absent online, forcing us to approach instruction differently than we're used to. Online learning also differs from the traditional face-to-face environment in several important aspects.

- *Time*: Nearly all online interaction between the students and instructor occurs in writing, and this is subject to time delays between someone's original post and someone else's reply.
- *Authorship*: The content of an online course is often built-in and predetermined by the course developer rather than the instructor.
  a. You may be allowed to modify it or to adjust it to your preferences as the instructor, but you're generally following someone else's script.

b. If you're instructing a course you did not design yourself, you'll need to invest some time in reading all of the materials embedded in the course so that you're familiar with what students have been taught and what they've been told to do.

■ *Information Delivery*: online lectures tend to be presented as PowerPoints or similar slide-based formats, with or without embedded verbal narration, but they may also be presented as videos. If you're the course developer, you'll need to create these resources prior to the course launch. If you're teaching a course that was developed by someone else, you should read or watch all of the lectures so that you know what the students have learned through these resources.

■ *Written Instructions*: everything you want your students to do, from discussion posts to important assignments must include step-by-step, explicit instructions. All expectations must anticipate potential misunderstanding, be explained clearly, and be easily accessible within the online classroom.

In the beginning of this book we took a brief look at the Quality Matters standards for higher education:

1. Course Overview and Introduction
2. Learning Objectives
3. Assessment and Measurement
4. Instructional Materials
5. Course Activities and Learner Interaction
6. Course Technology
7. Learner Support
8. Accessibility and Usability

We've conducted an in-depth examination of Learning Objectives in Chapter 3. Now we'll turn our attention to the other standards and consider how they relate to instruction in an online context.

1. Course Overview and Introduction

The first thing your online students should encounter upon entering your classroom is a statement summarizing the course so that they have a clear idea of what they'll learn and how they'll learn it. The simplest option is to post a written statement, but many instructors also provide a short introductory video or other verbal and visual presentation.

Your students also want to know who you are and what you're like as an instructor. When we teach in a traditional bricks and mortar classroom, this is obvious in the first 2 minutes of the class, but online, we have to make more of an effort to introduce ourselves. Creating a video in which you make the same introductory remarks to your online students as you'd deliver in a regular class is a good idea. Students like to see your face and hear the sound of your voice. It makes you seem more approachable and human than just being the disembodied person behind the words they read in your announcements, emails, and discussion posts.

Students also need to learn about one another. That's why the first assignment in many online courses asks students to introduce themselves. To generate greater engagement than the standard "name, hometown, major, and reason you're taking this class" criteria, you might ask a more probing question that requires a narrative response. Asking students to "tell about a time when you felt a strong sense of academic accomplishment," or "describe an experience you've had during your studies that was personally transformative" can lead to more fruitful discussions and also help to build a sense of community. Our stories are what make us human, and sharing them is what begins to establish peer-to-peer rapport. Be sure to post your own response to the question to lead off the discussion thread. I always share my story about returning to full-time study in higher education when I was 40 years old, undergoing a complete career change and completing my bachelor's degree, while simultaneously running my own business full time, commuting 80 miles per day, round trip, to attend classes. Students often comment that this story encouraged them to pursue their own goals—if I can do it, they say, then they can, too. It lets them see more of who I am as a human being, instead of thinking I'm just a judgmental, faceless critic who grades their work.

Along with the self-introduction, it's helpful for students to post a photo of themselves, and the instructor should also follow suit. Some Learning Management System (LMS) providers include an option for each user to personalize their own avatar or profile image, a feature that allows the instructor to see the face of each student alongside every one of their posts or replies rather than just their name. I've found this to be quite helpful as an instructor, and students have commented that they liked seeing my face alongside my comments as well.

3. Assessment and Measurement

Beyond the ideas covered in Chapter 3, online learning environments might require you to adapt your preferred assessment methods, especially if you rely heavily on exams to determine your students' grades. Cheating is unfortunately a significant problem in online exams. True, you can require that students take exams in a proctored setting, or you can specify that they use a lock-down browser option if they're taking an exam unsupervised, but neither of these options is foolproof. It's best, therefore, to diversify your assessment mechanisms so that you form a more accurate picture of student learning than you can determine with two high-stakes tests.

Students can't easily cheat on their discussion board posts, so these might be more likely to reflect their genuine learning, even though it's a qualitative assessment rather than something that's easily quantifiable like a multiple-choice exam. Assessments that require original thought, creativity, or synthesis of information also make it more difficult for students to cheat, since they can't share answers or easily find a correct response on Google. Furthermore, nearly all objective exams measure students' acquisition of facts rather than their ability to apply those facts to a problem or situation. We want our students to be able to mobilize the knowledge they've gained under our instruction and put it to use outside of our classrooms, so a simple measurement of factual recall should not be the only way you measure their learning. I could memorize Planck's Constant, for instance, and be able to choose it among a group of similar-looking mathematical expressions on a multiple-choice exam, but this does not mean that I actually understand what it means or how to apply it to a problem in quantum mechanics. My physics instructor would need to find additional means for me to demonstrate my knowledge of this crucial concept for me to prove that I had truly learned it.

4. Instructional Materials

Students need to have all of the resources necessary for them to be successful in the course and for these to be easily accessible within the online classroom. Online instruction is generally organized both by modules and by weeks within the module, although other terminology can be used for these divisions as well. For example, I taught in an online program that organized the course content into "milestones" instead of weeks and named students' work as "tasks" rather than assignments. The point is that you need an organizational structure of some kind, which is sometimes dictated by the LMS, that your institution has chosen such as Blackboard, Canvas, D2L, Brightspace, e-College, and so on, or by your department or institution itself.

In my own planning for online instruction, I organize everything by week, and then I group those weeks into modules, posting a folder for each one. Then I make a subfolder for each week that contains everything that each student will need to complete the given tasks successfully. For example, the Week 10 folder for the online version of Design Thinking for Entrepreneurs contains the Week 10 PowerPoint lecture, two PDF articles that students are required to read, written instructions for Assignment 5, Student Resource 10, and a link to the grading rubric found in the Assessment folder.

I also post a "resources" folder that contains a copy of all of the materials in the weekly folders plus additional items such as a student writing guide, the course syllabus, copies of any PDF articles students might be asked to read during the course, grading rubrics, assignment instructions, and so on, each organized into subfolders by type (assignments, assessments, supplementary reading, and so on).

This seems redundant, but it's intentionally so. For example, I'll post a given rubric in the Assessment area, in the weekly folder in which the assignment to be assessed is assigned and the weekly folder in which the assignment is due, as well as in the Resources folder. This way, students always have the needed item easily accessible no matter where they decide to look for it. I don't want to send my students on a scavenger hunt every time they need to refer to something, so I anticipate where they'll logically look for things and provide them with those resources in those locations.

Online lectures should contain more text than PowerPoints you'd create for live presentation unless you provide a voice-over narration of your lecture just as you'd deliver it in a regular classroom. It's very important to think through what you want students to know and ensure that all of those ideas are presented on your slides. If you're using verbal narration, make sure it's clearly audible. If the sound quality is at all fuzzy or distorted, you might want to provide captioning or a written transcript of the sound track. The same formatting rules apply to all presentations and written materials: They should be clean, simple, legible, and clear. Be sure to proofread your text carefully and make sure any animations or sound files work appropriately. Students might not notice your mistakes when they're listening to your lecture in person, but when they can view your lecture over and over again, those errors really stand out.

When I design a course, I post the directions for each assignment in at least three places. First, I explain the assignment in the lecture for the week when it's first introduced, including a summary of benchmarks, deliverables, or deadlines as appropriate. Next, I post detailed written instructions in the Assignments area of the course where students will submit their work *and* in the weekly folder for the week the assignment is introduced. It's also a good idea to post the instruction document in the folder for the week in which the assignment is due, especially if students will have more than two weeks to complete their work. Last, I'll email a copy of the instructions as an attachment to my weekly communication with students. Taking the time to build in this redundancy can save aggravation down the road, preventing you from having to reply to repetitive student questions about where they can find the instructions, when the assignment is due, or what is expected. If you don't want to re-post the same document in multiple areas, you should at least provide a hyperlink to each document or a reminder of where the document is located so that students can access it with minimal difficulty.

Beyond instructions, it's helpful to provide students with examples of what you expect in each assignment, showing them what high-quality work should look like. For instance, some students inevitably exhibit difficulty in formatting citations correctly in their research papers. I proactively provide an excerpt from an annotated sample paper so that students can see exactly how to create a correct citation. Similarly, a course I formerly taught asked students to write a paper formatted to an exact set of requirements that they routinely misinterpreted.

I couldn't change the assignment itself because I was not the course developer, so instead I created a supplementary handout with a more thorough explanation of the instructions, and I also provided a sample of a paper that had been done correctly so that students had a reference to guide their work. Taking this step dramatically improved the quality of subsequent students' work.

Communicating due dates for online instruction can be a bit more complex than in a face-to-face course. Everything is available to students all at once in an online classroom, whereas we tend to distribute actual materials from week to week when we're teaching on campus, which allows us greater flexibility. Subsequent sessions of online courses are generally copied over from one semester to another, but if you've included due dates or deadlines on your actual course materials, they'll no longer be accurate when you teach the course again. It's tedious to manually revise every item to reflect the new dates, so I recommend referring to due dates in your instructional materials by weeks and days instead of by date, then creating an updated course calendar for each time you teach the same course. (Many online instructional systems offer this as a built-in tool.) Students can refer to the calendar for specific due dates rather than expecting to see these on the materials you created.

5. Course Activities and Learner Interaction

Instructional materials are closely tied to course activities, and online activities will be supported by some form of written explanation or documentation since we're not physically present to deliver this information to students in real time. These are very similar to the activities found on campus but still contain important differences.

Activities

- *Discussion boards:* students must reply to a question posed by the instructor and comment on a set number of their classmates' replies.
    a. Discussion frequently follows assigned readings, enhancing student engagement with the ideas and information they've read.
    b. It holds them accountable for completing the assigned readings, especially if the discussion response requires citation of evidence from the text.
    c. Students are used to treating online communication very casually. If you hold a higher standard, you'll have to teach your expectations, such as prohibiting "text speak" or insisting on the use of proper English in discussion posts.
    d. Make your expectations for students' participation in discussion very clear. For example, you might want students to respond to two of

their peers in every online discussion and require that those responses be at least 100 words long to receive full credit.

e. You might require students to include a reference to the week's readings or provide support for their statements by citing external sources.

- *Written assignments*: Students can generally post their written work to the online classroom in one of two ways: (1) for the instructor alone to see, or (2) posted to a shared forum such as a discussion board where class-mates can see one another's work and comment upon it.

- *Individual projects*: As with written assignments, these can be posted in an assignments area that only the instructor will see, or posted in a public forum where students can view and comment upon one another's work.

- *Non-graded activities*: Students interact with course content to reinforce or extend their learning, such as practice quizzes over assigned readings that serve to prepare students for important exams.

- *Live discussions or presentations*, carried out through tools embedded in the course or via external services or applications such as Skype or GoToMeeting.

a. Live discussions can help students to feel more connected to one another and can encourage peer-to-peer interaction as well as making the course seem less impersonal. They are an extremely important tool in building rapport between the students and instructor, and in facilitating peer-to-peer interactions. The earlier in the course the first live discussion can be held, the better the results will be. Ideally, the course will contain several of these sessions, which can be either formal or informal.

b. However, they can be difficult to schedule for maximum participation.

    i. Many students choose online learning over attending courses on campus because they have challenging schedules and commit-ments, which can be ideal for working adults, parents of young children, or students who just prefer to work at odd hours.

    ii. This flexibility, though, means that it's unlikely that all of your students will be able to attend a live session when scheduled.

    iii. It's important to provide students with an alternative learning experience if they can't be present in real time, or to record the session so that they can view it at a later time and still earn credit for their participation.

      • I don't believe that any online student should be expected to call in sick to work or miss out on a family commitment (their child's parent–teacher conference, for example) to participate in an online class session unless there is an exceptionally com-pelling reason for them to do so.

- It's much better to exercise compassion and to allow some flexibility in how they can best meet your expectations when these conflict with students' prior obligations, rather than imposing an arbitrary penalty for "missing class" that day.

■ *Group projects*: There are many benefits to collaborative learning, as we've discussed in other chapters.

   a. However, online group work is prone to particular complications. A few students usually fail to uphold their responsibilities to their assigned groups, making the learning experience difficult or unproductive for their teammates.

   b. For example, I assigned students to groups of three to conduct a peer review of one another's research papers prior to the final due date. They were to exchange email addresses, send each other their drafts, create an annotated copy of the papers using the review tools in Microsoft Word, and then return the edited papers to their original authors. Several of the students contacted me repeatedly, reporting that one or more of the members of the group was not responding to their email, had failed to edit their papers, or was causing problems in some other way. I took steps to intervene on their behalf, also attempting to contact the silent students, but to no avail. Of course, the students who had abstained from participation received a zero for the assignment, but it was clearly not fair to penalize the students who had been ignored by their peers. I asked these students to take screenshots of the messages they'd sent and gave them credit for the activity even though they had neither been able to edit their peer's paper nor to have their paper edited in return.

   c. This type of problem crops up often enough that I try to provide alternatives to group work for those who find it frustrating. For example, in the on-campus version of Design Thinking for Entrepreneurs, students work in groups to complete the course project, but they have the option of working alone if they so choose. In the online version of the course, however, the opposite is true. Students complete the project individually; working in groups is a voluntary option. If students choose to work together, they must sign a participation contract that outlines the expectations clearly.

■ *Other Considerations*:

   a. Certain activities that work well in an actual classroom don't easily translate to online learning. Role playing, Turn and Talk, or Think-Pair-Share activities that enliven lectures delivered in in a classroom don't work in an asynchronous online environment.

   b. If your course includes instruction in processes or skills, it's a good idea to create video content demonstrating what you want students

167

to learn or how you want them to do it. You might consider enlisting additional help in filming yourself doing these things, or you can find videos of these processes online, sharing the clip with your students. Some institutions also partner with a tutorial provider such as Lynda.com to offer students supplementary instructional content on demand.

INTERACTION AND COMMUNICATION

Our interactions online are obviously different than when we meet with our students face to face. We have to think carefully about the words we type and to consider how the student will interpret what we're saying. This is especially true because students can't hear the tone of your voice or see your face. If I'm discussing a student's project in my actual classroom, I might offer the same criticism that I'd offer online, but in person the student could hear that my tone and expression were kind and respectful, which softens the impact of the words. Typed into an online forum, though, those exact words could come across as much more negative or harsh than I'd intended them to be.

Some online instructors find that using emoticons helps to soften a critical message or to give posts a friendlier tone, but this should not be overdone. Our communications with students should always be appropriately professional. In fact, we should insist upon this in all communications within the online classroom, holding ourselves and our students to the standards expected of business-like, adult written communication. This means that expressions like "LOL" or "OMG" are unacceptable, as is not capitalizing the word "I", using "u" instead of "you" and not writing in correct college-level written English. It also includes proofreading our own comments before clicking "post" or "submit." Accuracy is important. We always notice our student's errors, but they notice *our* mistakes even more acutely. Adhering to these expectations helps to ensure that our messages are clear, but perhaps even more importantly it sets the standard for proficient communication that students will be expected to meet once they begin working in the professional sector.

Online learning environments typically require the instructor to post comments in discussions and on assignments. These can be written, but you can also use tools such as Jing or features built into the LMS that let you post a short audio or video clip. (We'll explore the idea of feedback in greater depth later in this chapter.) Your comments are a powerful tool for enhancing your students' learning. Indeed, this is where you do most of your real teaching online, through the information and guidance you offer beyond the built-in components of lecture and assignments. It is also a key point of contact for strengthening your rapport with your students.

Online, we lack the physical presence and visual cues that we take for granted in a face-to-face setting, so we have to compensate for this by being much more deliberate in our interactions with students. Successful strategies[2] include

- Providing frequent and immediate feedback
- Sharing personal information; being open and approachable
- Engaging in non-course-related off-task chat
- Demonstrating friendliness in communication (e.g., beginning an email with, "Good morning, Students! I hope that all of you had an enjoyable weekend. Our first task this week is . . ."
- Getting to know students' socially or through their social media (with permission)
- Ensuring that communication is comfortable
- Making personal contact; reaching out by phone to students who are struggling or who have "disappeared" from the classroom
- Offering to help students improve poor work they submitted and to resubmit for a better grade
- Providing sincere positive reinforcement, encouragement, or praise
- Ensuring that students know how to contact you and that they feel comfortable doing so
- Answering all student communications promptly
- Using humor whenever possible
- Admitting your mistakes and offering an apology
- Showing care and concern, especially if students report personal problems that have prevented them from turning in their work on time or participating according to expectations
- Using technologies with which students are familiar such as instant messaging or text messaging

I've also found that addressing the student by name in each discussion response is a good tool for establishing and maintaining relationships. It's the written equivalent of making eye contact while you're speaking to someone. As much as possible, I'll use the student's preferred name or nickname, too, if they've shared that with me, and I ask them to sign their posts with that name if it's different than the one that the LMS automatically tags their posts. If Elizabeth Jones shares in her introductory post that she prefers to be called E. J., then my comments to her will be something like this: "You're right, E. J.—one of the most important aspects of leadership is taking on the role of active listening. When do you think that a person in a position of authority could best demonstrate this trait?"

If a student asks a question in a bricks-and-mortar classroom, the instructor can respond immediately. When a student asks a question in an online discussion forum or via email, they must wait for the instructor to notice the question and to compose an adequate reply. This is why it's essential to check your online classroom and your linked email frequently and to respond to queries promptly. You should post comments on student work within 48 hours of the due date, and should grade their work within 48 hours of the end of the module, as well. Even more importantly, you should wait no longer than 24 hours to respond to an email or to a post in your course's "problems and solutions" or "questions for the professor" area. This is especially true if the student is asking you for information about how to complete an assignment, since a delay in your response means that they cannot post their work on time or correctly.

Email to students is also essential, as are course announcements. I typically send my online students an email just before the beginning of each week with reminders of due dates, helpful information about upcoming assignments, and additional resources such as links to websites or document attachments like study guides or templates for assignments. I might also address common problems or misconceptions that I've noticed cropping up in their work. I also send a quick email to students after I've posted their grades for each assignment so that they can let me know if there are any problems. To simplify the task of weekly communication, I keep a file of the main text of these regular email messages and announcements. Then I only need to copy and paste into the course announcement page and into a group email, making any modifications necessary before sending or posting. This considerably streamlines the process.

If your course includes a discussion board component, students genuinely appreciate their instructor's engaged participation in these discussions. Discussions are a valuable opportunity to provide individualized instruction and to share your own experience and disciplinary expertise with the group. Instructors with 20 or fewer students in the course should try to post a comment or reply to each of student in every required discussion. This is going above and beyond expectations, I know, but students notice the instructor's extra effort. However, if your course has more than 20 students, it might not be possible. In that case, your goal should be to respond to at least 20 students in the discussion overall, commenting on the posts where you notice a particularly good point being made, where you find you should address a misconception, or to recognize students who have received no peer comments on their posts.

Online students are unfortunately prone to disappearing. Some just forget they registered for the class altogether, others become overwhelmed by the work involved, and a few lose track of the course in the day-to-day demands of their busy lives. When I notice that students have not been participating in the discussions, have missing assignments, or have not logged into the class in an unusually long time, I send them a friendly email reminder, and if that goes unanswered I also contact their academic advisor. Some universities have an Academic Warning system for such occasions that automatically emails the student and his or her advisor.

When grading students' work online, communication is also essential. Provide an explanation of any points that have been deducted. Using rubrics or checklists can simplify this task, as we discussed in Chapter 4. If students have met the assignment's expectations, it's still good to post positive comments acknowledging their good work or thanking them for their effort.

6. Course Technology

In all likelihood, the technologies involved in your course will be determined by the LMS your institution has chosen to utilize. We've probably all experienced the frustration of learning to use a new computer operating system, or having a software upgrade disrupt our usage of a program we've come to use nearly intuitively. At first, it's awkward and takes a great deal of thought and exploration before we find our comfort level again. You'll find the same is true in online teaching. You won't know where to find things, how to post them, or how to navigate the course until you've used it for a while. Your students will also experience the same frustration. Be patient with yourself and with your students. Make sure you have the email address and phone number for tech support handy, and provide these to your students as well, along with tutorials of how to use the system and a map of where to find the information they're looking for. When students email me with questions about where to find things, I'll take a screenshot of the item open on my computer, annotating the path of how to arrive at the specific location and email this along with a detailed response to the question.

7. Learner Support

Your online classroom should include a section directing students to whatever resources are available within your program, such as the Writing Center, Disabilities Services, and so on, just as you would provide in your syllabus. You should also make sure that students can access tutorials on how to use the LMS and navigate the online classroom.

You should create a post containing your contact information, the best hours to reach you, and your photo. This might also include links to your website, your institutional email address, and your phone number, including instructions on your preferred communication methods. Letting students know when they can generally find you online, when you'll comment on their work, and when you'll post their grades is helpful, too.

Supporting students goes beyond directing them to the appropriate resource. As instructors, we should be dedicated to our students' success, and this sometimes means that we need to modify assignments, extend due dates and deadlines, or even excuse students from some of the course's expectations. For example, a student in an online course I taught a few years ago had fallen very far behind.

He really didn't have a good excuse for this, but he was very contrite and made a herculean effort to get his missing work done before the deadline. Despite his best efforts, though, he was going to fall short and earn a failing grade, and since it was the last semester of his senior year this would prevent him from graduating on time. I decided to exempt him from the discussion posts he was still missing, especially because his classmates would never have seen his late comments, anyway. This allowed him to earn a C− in the course and graduate as scheduled. Of course, I'd have been within my rights to fail him, but what purpose would this have served? Demonstrating compassion and understanding made a much more positive and lasting impression on this young man than a hardline approach ever would.

Flexibility and respect for our students also means being aware of their identity preferences. For instance, some individuals choose to employ plural pronouns even when referring to a singular subject because the plural version is gender-neutral whereas the singular is gender-specific. Strict grammarians may determine this usage to be incorrect, yet it has become increasingly common in our culture, and it is a matter of tremendous importance to these students. Rather than deducting points from a student's work for incorrect pronoun usage, we should mobilize our understanding of their identities to respect their grammatical preferences.

8. Accessibility and Usability

In any course we teach, it's important to meet the documented needs of our students with disabilities such as those who require accommodations for extra time on tests and assignments. Online courses, however, pose particular challenges for students who have difficulties hearing, seeing, or typing. If you have a student who is hearing impaired, but your lectures are primarily delivered through audio narration of bare-bones PowerPoints, you'll need to create a transcript of the lecture and make this available to the student. The concept of Universal Design[3] takes this a step further, based on the principle that an accommodation that's good for one person may be beneficial to all. Posting a transcript of your lecture isn't just good for the hearing-impaired student—all students could benefit from having access to this important information, freeing them from taking notes, while they watch and listen to your lectures. It's a win-win for everyone. Similarly, a visually impaired student might need verbal narration of visual content, but since we know that the human brain learns best when information is presented in more than one receptive modality, everyone could benefit from both seeing and hearing the content of your lessons. A student who cannot type might need to submit comments to discussions as an audio file attachment rather than text entry. If all students were allowed this response method, it might stimulate better discussion posts, since it's generally easier to talk than to type.

As you plan your course, consider how you could incorporate the elements of Universal Design into your lectures, activities, and discussions. The time spent in preparing these additional resources may help all students to be more successful, not only those with a disability.

PROVIDING FEEDBACK FOR FORMATIVE ASSESSMENT

Instructors in many disciplines regularly provide feedback to students by means of informal meetings with individual students or more formalized group critique sessions. This process can also apply to student writing or class presentations in any discipline, whether on campus, online, or in hybrid classes.

Educators hold a variety of views regarding this pedagogical task. Some instructors become notorious for being impossible to please, a reputation they cultivate deliberately because they believe it motivates students to work harder and achieve more. Other instructors maintain a belief that only blunt appraisal of a student's work will help him or her to grow, so if the work is not up to expected standards, they say so, sometimes quite harshly.

The primary goal of any assessment should be an honest appraisal of a student's learning relative to a given academic task. As we discussed previously, evaluation is crucial in every academic area, including substantive diagnosis of the strengths and weaknesses of the student's work. However, this should occur without resorting to destructive or disheartening negativity. This is not to say that assessment should be sugar-coated, but neither should it be an exercise in oppositional contrarianism.

Providing Feedback

Feedback should take place throughout many courses, especially with regard to formative tasks. When we begin with a positive comment, it sets a constructive tone for the rest of our remarks and allows the student to accept our evaluative statements without immediately becoming defensive or demoralized. Admittedly, this seems contrary to many instructors' natural inclinations: Our trained eyes first spot all of the student's errors, and it's very tempting to begin our comments by addressing those deficits.

The problem with this approach is that students naturally focus on the first thing you say. When this is negative, they can easily become discouraged. This is certainly not to suggest that instructors should give every student a metaphorical pat on the head and an insincere, "Good job!" Feedback *should* be fair and honest, and if the work needs improvement, you should say so. However, very few student works are so terrible that *no* redeeming feature or successful attribute is identifiable.

High-quality feedback should include three components: recognize success, suggest improvement, and make a personal connection.

- *Recognize Success:* Whether or not a student's work was successful overall, your comments should begin with a statement recognizing *something* that was good in comparison to the entire project.
  - In other words, what is the best thing you notice about the student's work?
  - If you genuinely cannot identify anything the student did well, it's still possible to recognize the student's effort or the fact that they met a given criterion for the assignment, even if their execution of this requirement was merely adequate.
- *Suggest Improvement:* Realistically, most student work will demonstrate several areas in need of improvement. The way you address this in your comments can allow students to receive your criticism with open minds and to implement your feedback to make their work better.
  - Phrasing your recognition of the flaws in their work as suggestions for improvement rather than highlighting their failures makes a significant difference in the way students will perceive your comments or act upon your recommendations.
  - It's also important not to overwhelm students with negativity. Even if you can identify dozens of flaws, try to limit your suggestions to five, at most.
  - This might require a second meeting with the student to re-evaluate the work after he or she implements the recommended changes, making further suggestions for improvement at that point.
  - Furthermore, if the students' work is noticeably deficient in some area, provide guided instruction in the particular skill or concept with which they're struggling.
- *Personal Connection:* Just as the beginning of your feedback sets the tone for what follows, the way you choose to end your comments affects how the student perceives this interaction as well. Some suggestions:
  - Ask the student a question about their experience in completing the project.
  - Share an anecdote or make a personal connection related to the work.
  - Provide some advice about how the student could implement your suggestions, such as directing the student toward some helpful resources or offering to work with the student one-on-one in order to rectify the problem.

Students should leave each encounter with a sense that you believe in their ability to succeed, you respect them as individuals even if their work was not entirely successful, and you will support their efforts toward becoming better at what you are trying to teach them.

Example

The following is a student's response to an assignment in which they were asked to find a grant for which they might apply. Students were instructed to conduct research into the selected granting organization, and to write a 3-page letter of inquiry for this grant utilizing a planning template provided by the instructor. The paper was to be formatted according to specific requirements for a business letter, which were provided in a printed handout. When explaining the project, the instructor emphasized that attention to detail was crucial, as was creating a concise, convincing, and professional product following the granting organization's specifications, including submission by the stated due date. The student who submitted the following letter clearly failed to meet most of these expectations.

To Whom It May Concern,

I am writing to inquire about whether your organization would be willing to provide a lot of money to turn a vacant lot near a downtown elementary school into a playground because all the school has is pavement all around it and nothing for kids to play on. The land belongs to the city and is available for us to do this project, if we can get funding and enough volunteers to make it happen. This project will bring community members, university students, and the members of the school's staff and parents together to build the playground. We are an all-volunteer group and we really need the money in order to buy the materials and rent the heavy equipment that will be necessary to get the job done.

I know that I'm submitting this after the due date for this grant, but I really hope that you will be able to give us these funds anyway. We're a small group of all volunteers and none of us know much about how this process works. We also don't know yet how much money we'll need. We'll be able to figure this out after we get started, but we thought that maybe we could build our budget around the amount you might be willing to give us?

Thanks so much for thinking about our request. We really need this money if our project is going to succeed. I hope that we'll hear from you soon.

Sincerely,
[student name]

Obviously, this student's work has quite a few problems. The letter is far too short, too vague, and too casual, among many other flaws. In fact, the instructor's justifiable first reaction might be to fail the student outright, since this paper did not come close to meeting the assignment requirements.

A better approach would treat this assignment as a first draft and provide concrete feedback giving the student explicit instruction into how to improve the letter to meet the assignment requirements successfully the second time around.

Here's a sample of how the instructor might go about that task by way of written commentary on the student's paper, remembering to (1) begin with a positive comment, (2) suggest improvement, and (3) make a personal connection.

> *(1) Thank you for submitting your grant inquiry letter. I think that the collaboration between your organization, university students, and the elementary school is a very promising idea. (2) However, your letter needs more detail to both meet the assignment requirements and to develop its potential to convince the granting organization that this is a meritorious proposal. (3) First, I'd like you to consult the writing guide I provided for this assignment and to compare those instructions to the document you submitted. Then I'd like to schedule a meeting with you where we can go over the criteria for the proposal and we can address the other areas of your letter that need revision. I'm happy to help you revise your letter, but as it stands I'm unable to give you a passing score if you choose not to make these changes. I would be available to meet with you during my office hours after class on Thursday.*

This approach validates the student's initial efforts and basic idea but leaves no doubt that the assignment is presently unacceptable. It also includes an offer of support so that the student can become more successful in the task upon revision.

LBNT

Besides learning how to receive instructor feedback with an open mind and employ it constructively, students should become adept in assessing their own work. We can teach this through a simple mnemonic device: LBNT.

> LB stands for "Like Best": What does the student like best about his or her work?
>
> NT stands for "Next Time": What would the student do differently the next time?

Again, we're focusing on the positive and on identifying actionable steps for improvement, rather than making a list of flaws. Students often know the shortcomings of their work quite well and tend to perseverate on their mistakes, so learning how to begin with a statement about what they like best—what's the most successful aspect of the work—sets a constructive tone for the conversation. Similarly, couching discussion of errors in terms of what the student would choose to do differently the next time turns the conversation into a learning experience rather than a fault-finding exercise.

This is a useful strategy in other instructional contexts, too. Following a group presentation, you can guide the class's discussion by asking the group members, "What do you like best about your project?" and "What would you do differently the next time?" You can similarly ask the audience members to critique the presentation using a peer evaluation form structured around these key questions.

INFORMAL FEEDBACK AND INTERACTIONS WITH STUDENTS

Educators provide feedback to our students all of the time, even when we're just answering a question. The way we respond to our students has a tremendous impact on their learning experience. Let's look at this through several scenarios, considering two ways the instructor could react that either shuts down learning or fosters it.

Scenarios

Scenario 1: Student A sends the instructor an email asking for clarification about how to format a research paper. The instructor is somewhat annoyed with the student's question, since it clearly indicates that the student could not have read the instructions that were provided weeks earlier.

Poor Response: The instructor sends a curt reply: "Full instructions for this assignment were provided in the course syllabus."

Better Response: The instructor replies to the student's email, saying, "The answer to your question can be found in our course syllabus, where complete directions for the paper are provided on page 15. In answer to your question, though, the paper should conform to MLA guidelines, including a heading, works cited page, and footer with your full name and page numbers. If you need help with MLA formatting, you might want to check in with the campus writing center, or you can try the OWL at Purdue at https://owl.english.purdue.edu/owl/resource/747/01/

Why this is better: This response reminds the student of the original expectation but also addresses his concern directly and provides additional information that might help the student to be successful.

Scenario 2: Student B fails to turn in an assignment in an online class.

Poor Response: The instructor marks the assignment as a zero.

Better Response: The instructor sends Student B an email, saying, "Dear B, I see that you did not submit the assignment that was due on Monday. If you have questions about this assignment or if there's any information I can provide that might help you to complete it, please let me know."

Why this is better: The instructor would certainly be within her rights to simply mark the missed assignment as a zero, but reaching out to the

177

student and offering to help is a more empathetic choice and more likely to result in the student doing the work. If this email went unanswered by the student, the instructor should also take the next step of informing the student's academic advisor of the problem.

Scenario 3: Student C constantly interrupts class to ask questions or provide very opinionated remarks about the course content.

Poor Response: The instructor begins to ignore Student C in class, refraining from calling on him when he raises his hand and changing the subject without responding to his comments.

Better Response: The instructor asks Student C to stay after class, inviting him to sit down and discuss his classroom behavior. This could include an approach something like this, "I'm really glad to see that you're so engaged in our class, C. But it seems to me that your contributions are edging other students out of the conversation. I'm happy to continue our class discussions with you after class, but I'd like for you to try to tone down your rhetoric a bit when other students are present so that they still feel like there's room for their own questions or comments. I'd like to make a private agreement with you that I'll call on you no more than three times during the class period. Does this seem reasonable to you?"

Why this is better: Ignoring the problem student will not cause his behavior to change. He may be unaware that he is a disruptive influence in the classroom, so bringing the problem to his attention is a good first step. Further, having this discussion privately rather than calling the student out for the bad behavior in front of the other students is more respectful and therefore more likely to meet with the desired result.

Scenario 4: Student D is frequently late for class, remains silent during discussions, and has difficulty staying awake during lectures.

Poor Response: The instructor penalizes Student D's class participation grade but says nothing to the student, choosing to address the behavior indirectly through the poor grade.

Better Response: The instructor meets with Student D during her office hours, explaining that her behavior has a negative impact on the other students, reminding her that this could affect her grade, and asking for her explanation about why this has been happening. When Student D replies that she has been very tired because of working the late shift in the computer lab, the instructor offers to help her strategize ways to maximize her schedule given the conflicting demands of expectations of her work and her classes.

Why this is better: Although it's easy assign a low grade for these behaviors, attempting to find the cause of the problem is more likely to solve the problem. If the conversation does not resolve the problem, it might be wise to seek the input of the student's academic advisor, who could move the student to a different section of the course that meets at a more advantageous time of day for the student, or who could advocate for a change in the student's work schedule so that she's not so exhausted in class.

ESTABLISHING CLASSROOM POLICIES

Most educators establish a set of policies applicable to their classrooms. Carefully thinking through this set of student expectations is good professional practice: Students should know exactly how you expect them to behave in your classroom and what the consequences for running afoul of those expectations will be.

We commonly tell students that they should power off their electronics, for example, and require them to use polite, respectful communication with their peers. We may limit their freedom to eat and drink in our classrooms, or we may impose penalties for excessive tardiness or for skipping class. When these expectations are set forth in writing, posted clearly on your syllabus, you mitigate distractions and establish a classroom climate that's conducive to learning.

Establishing a policy for late work can help motivate students to complete their assignments on time. A common practice is to inform students that they might incur a penalty of up to 10% of the assignment's total value for each day the work is late. In theory, this could result in the student's reaching a state of failure in a mere 5 days. Most instructors also include a set of caveats, listing exceptions to this rule if the student provides documentation of serious illness, a death in the family, or military deployment, for example.

We know that students will sometimes try to take advantage of these policies and their exceptions. In 1990, biology professor Mike Adams penned a tongue-in-cheek research report stating that students' grandmothers were 10 times more likely to die before midterm exams and 19 times more likely to die before finals.[4] Nevertheless, students really do sometimes have to deal with a death in the family, they face countless personal hardships, or they encounter circumstances beyond their control that make it difficult or impossible to meet your expectations.

When such things happen, we're within our rights to assess penalties for their late work. But we should also ask ourselves if this is actually a best practice in education. Remembering that this book is written from a learning-centered standpoint, what approach toward students' late work will result in the greatest possibility for the student's learning?

Let's consider some typical justifications for penalizing late work:

- Students must learn to be responsible.
- Meeting deadlines is part of adult life, so we prepare students for the real world by holding them accountable for our classroom deadlines.
- Making exceptions is not fair to the other students who worked hard to turn in their work on time.

When we hold onto rigid late work policies because we believe that we should help our students build character or acquire life skills, we should also remember that our job is to teach students the *specific disciplinary content* of our courses, not to be their parent. It's true that adults encounter penalties for lateness in our everyday lives, such as incurring a fee if we pay our credit card bill beyond the stated due date, or facing disciplinary action from a supervisor if we're habitually late to work. These penalties motivate us to pay our bills on time and to arrive at our workplace promptly. In the same way, our policies about late work motivate students to submit their assignments on time, which ensures that we can evaluate their work in a timely manner and with a higher degree of consistency.

However, teaching character or life skills are not truly within our sphere of influence as university educators unless these behaviors are (1) directly related to our course content, (2) clearly listed among our outcomes and objectives, or (3) tied to expected professional conduct within the discipline. For example, I recently read a syllabus for a graduate course in Business Administration where students were required to dress in business attire for every class period. Expectations were clearly laid out in the syllabus, such as the requirement that male students must wear a pressed shirt with a tie, the shirt must be tucked into dress pants worn with a belt, and the student must wear dress shoes with dark socks. Because this course was specifically about professionalism in the workplace, the requirement for professional dress was overtly tied to the course objectives and part of the instructor's teaching on the first day of class. Your policies should be similarly made clear to your students and overtly taught by linking them to the professional standards and expectations of your discipline.

The idea that fairness involves treating all students the exactly same is difficult to support, since the words *fair* and *equal* have been proven repeatedly to be very different ideas.[5] However, treating students experiencing the same *situation* in the same way makes sense, such as allowing an exception to your late work policy for one student who suffered a devastating computer malfunction and then extending the same grace to another student with a similar problem. Consistency is also an important standard, but this should be applied by responding to similar circumstances in comparable ways rather than making a habit of enforcing the letter of the law every time without exception, or conversely approaching every situation differently.

Therefore, when a student explains that she could not turn in her assignment that day because _____ (fill in any reason), your decision of whether or not to accept the work late and/or whether or not to assess a late penalty should take several factors into account beyond reflexive imposition of the stated penalty:

- How crucial is the due date within the overall schedule of the course? If it's the last week of the class and you're under pressure to grade the paper and post final grades, you won't have as much flexibility as would be possible earlier in the course.

- Is this the first time the student has asked for an extension, or is this a habitual problem? If the student repeatedly submits work late, additional steps to find the root of the problem might be more appropriate than either leniency or assessing a late penalty.
- Is the student's reason legitimate? A litmus test for legitimacy is this: Would you personally find it difficult to meet an external deadline if you were faced with the same situation that the student is experiencing?
- Would accepting the student's work late violate any disciplinary or professional standards overtly tied to the assignment? In our example regarding instructor feedback on a student's grant letter, meeting a specified deadline was among the criteria necessary for success on the assignment, so lateness was legitimately penalized. After all, a granting organization would be highly unlikely to take the sender's reason for a late submission into account.
- Have you made exceptions for other students experiencing similar difficulties in the past?

Best practice with regard to classroom policies, especially late penalties, involves a return to one of the most important considerations when planning instruction: We need to ask ourselves, "*What's the point?*"

- We create assignments because we want our students to learn disciplinary content by means of the planned experience.
- We assess their work to evaluate their learning of this disciplinary content.
- Whether or not the work is late, students who actually complete the work successfully should receive appropriate assessment.
- Unless the performance of this task by a firm due date explicitly ties to a disciplinary standard, programmatic outcome, or course objective, the student's demonstration of learning through the assignment should still be paramount. If the student successfully completed the assignment, even if it was late, the grade should reflect their learning, not be entirely overridden by late penalties.
- This is not to say that late penalties cannot apply. But if we keep the point of the assignment in mind, we should weight our acknowledgement of the student's learning over punitive measures for lateness, even when a published policy states that such consequences will be imposed.
- We are just as much within our rights as educators to respond with compassion, empathy, and wisdom as we are to enforce rigid policies for their own sake.

181

That said, loss of points to a student's grade may be unavoidable unless the instructor is willing to make accommodations for the student. Let's say an instructor is teaching an online class that includes extensive online discussions. The student is hospitalized for 2 weeks, missing a group discussion. In this class, the discussion board automatically closes at a fixed date, prohibiting late responses. This student, therefore, cannot earn points for the discussion even though he had a legitimate excuse. It would therefore be up to the instructor to take one of several actions.

- Depending on the online classroom's technological structure, she may be able to exempt the student from the assignment altogether.
- She may offer the student an alternative assignment or extra credit to make up the missed points.
- Or she could choose to do nothing, resulting in a lost learning opportunity for the student and a substantial blow to his grade.

Asking, "What's the point?" leads us to the second choice—offering an alternative assignment or extra credit. In this way the student still engages in a learning activity but does not suffer a penalty for something that was unavoidable. If our goal as instructors is for our students *to learn*, then our policies and our response to violations of these policies should all be informed by this overarching value.

I believe that we should hold empathy and compassion for our students among our highest values. Not only is this an important part of the design process, but it's also simply among the values we should exemplify as human beings.

Our level of engagement with others who are experiencing a hardship can be represented as a continuum ranging from pity through sympathy, empathy, and compassion. Pity offers the least, most abstracted state of mind, and compassion the most active and direct involvement Figure 8.1 offers additional clarification.[6]

Let's consider how this continuum would apply to a situation in which a student has not turned in several assignments and is now in danger of failing the class. She explains that she has been consumed with anxiety about revealing her identity as a lesbian to her deeply religious family. Figure 8.2 explains possible instructor responses.

It is possible to err too far on the side of compassion if we lose sight of our professional boundaries or make choices that undermine our students' learning, no matter how well-intentioned we might be. If the instructor in the present scenario simply forgave the student's missing work, the student would not learn the course content, which deprives her of the skills and knowledge the course was supposed to provide. If the instructor not only made the appointment with Student Services but accompanied the student to the appointment and then invited her home for dinner, it would transgress reasonable professionalism. Being compassionate shouldn't mean that we're pushovers for every tale of woe that our students try to use as justification for poor performance. We must use

Category	Description	Explanation
Pity	To acknowledge the suffering of others; to feel abstract discomfort at the distress of others. Pity is sometimes condescending or paternalistic; it presumes that the object does not deserve its plight and is unable to prevent, reverse, or overturn it.	We feel pity when we see news reports about or portrayals of persons who are the victims of a disaster or who are experiencing hardship.
Sympathy	To experience personal feelings of care or concern for the suffering of others.	Sympathy can exist apart from empathy. For instance, we can sympathize with the plight of polar bears affected by the melting of the polar ice cap but cannot empathize with them because we cannot know how the polar bears feel.
Empathy	To imagine one's self as experiencing the same situation as someone else based on firsthand knowledge of who the person is and what she is experiencing; to make a personal connection.	We feel empathy when we have had a similar experience ourselves or have a personal relationship with the person in distress. It is possible to experience empathy intellectually, but not emotionally—to empathize, but not sympathize, or to understand how someone feels, but not share actively in their emotions.
Compassion	To be moved by the suffering of others and actively seek to relieve their distress, elevating them to a universal or transcendent experience. Compassion is the primary motivator of altruism.	We feel compassion when we share fully in others' experiences and are motivated to take action to mitigate their suffering.

FIGURE 8.1 *Pity, Sympathy, Empathy,* and *Compassion* Definitions

our professional judgment to discern legitimate hardship from flimsy excuses and to determine the course of action that would best serve our students' social, emotional, and learning needs. Some cases might demand that we hold a firm line on course expectations, whereas others might necessitate that we make radical adjustments to our curriculum. One size does not fit all.

183

Category	Instructor Statement	Explanation
Pity	"I'm sorry you feel so anxious. But rules are rules and you need to turn in the work, subject to late penalties."	This approach recognizes the student's distress but does not take any action to help the student.
Sympathy	"I know how anxiety can be debilitating. My daughter has an anxiety disorder, so I understand something of what you're going through. Now let's make a plan for how you can get this work made up so that you don't fail the course, since I'm sure that's only adding to your struggles right now."	This approach validates the student's feelings through a personal connection and offers limited help in overcoming the problem of the missing work.
Empathy	"I'm so sorry that you're having such a hard time right now. I'd like to help you make a plan to make up the missing work, but first I think we should contact Student Services and make you an appointment with a counselor. When depression or anxiety makes it impossible for us to live our lives, it's time to seek some help. Would you like me to make that call with you now?"	Here the instructor demonstrates greater understanding of the student's problem and offers help on two levels—addressing the emotional distress by offering to assist the student in seeking help and making a plan to make up the missing work.
Compassion	"It's so hard to have to try to hide who you are, especially when you fear that your own family might reject you. I'm glad you want to try and make up the missing work, but I think that first we need to connect you with Student Services, since this has caused such turmoil in your life right now. I'd also like to see how we can streamline your missing work or if there might be an alternative assignment you could do that would let you learn the content you've missed in the short time we have left in the semester. I'm sure you don't need a failing grade on top of what you're already going through. Let's call to make you that appointment with Student Services, and then we'll look at what you're missing and decide on the best way for you to reach the end of the course successfully."	A truly compassionate response demonstrates full understanding and acknowledgement of the student's situation, taking action to mitigate the underlying problem (seeking help for the student's anxiety) and alleviate its effects by making changes to the course's expectations that both facilitates the student's learning and avoids a failing grade.

FIGURE 8.2 Instructor Demonstration of *Pity, Sympathy, Empathy,* and *Compassion*

A real-life counter example played out in the classroom of an instructor who had stated on her syllabus that students' work must be submitted at the beginning of class. A student in this class—a mother who worked full time in addition to enrolling in a full course load—knew that she would be late to class due to a parent–teacher conference for one of her children. She proactively emailed her work to the instructor several hours ahead of the class period. The instructor marked the assignment as late, deducting a substantial number of points, and she also penalized the student for arriving late to class.

When the student spoke to the instructor about the penalties that had been imposed, the instructor was outraged that the student would question her judgment. Naturally, the student protested to me as the program's administrator. I requested a meeting with the instructor, who remained adamant that the penalty she had imposed should stand, even when I pointed out that the student's work had, in fact, been submitted early. She replied that her policy was that all students must turn in their work *only* at the beginning of the class period—not any earlier or later. She also insisted that the student should have scheduled the parent–teacher conference at a time that would not have conflicted with her class and maintained that both point deductions were consistent with her policies as stated on the syllabus. I pointed out that the language on the syllabus was ambiguous and that the student was not free to choose the time of the conference, as it had been prearranged by her child's school. The instructor missed an important opportunity to demonstrate empathy and compassion, compounded by losing her temper when the student raised a legitimate question about the penalty the instructor had imposed. The instructor refused to change the penalty, which she was within her rights to do. However, the entire situation could have been avoided if she had only been willing to approach the student's actions with empathy instead of legalism.

This brings us back to the all-important question: What's the point? If our classroom policies relate to an important professional standard, then penalizing students who fail to meet them is appropriate. However, imagine yourself in the place of the student in the previous scenario. Who among us has not had to make difficult choices between our job and our families? Isn't it better if the person who has authority over us exercises leniency and allows us to come in late to work, leave early, or make up the time we must miss to meet our family obligations? Can we not also extend this same generosity to our students? I believe we can, and we should.

Sometimes, though, holding the student accountable to your standards can be the best lesson you could teach. One of my students skipped an important session of my class because, as he said, "I was tired and decided to take a nap." He had no particular reason for this decision when I asked, saying he "just didn't feel like coming to class." I then enforced the full value of the attendance policy as stated in my syllabus, and during a subsequent meeting with him, I calculated the actual dollar value of his nap, based on the cost of tuition. I asked the student how his parents would feel if they knew that their son had decided to spend $300 to take a nap, which startled him. Enforcing the penalty and holding a further discussion with the student allowed me to seize an opportunity to extend his learning into taking responsibility for his actions.

THE TEACHABLE MOMENT

Teaching occurs every time we interact with our students, not just when we're standing behind the lectern.

- When you ignore students, you teach them that you don't care whether they succeed or fail. This is also true of being inactive in your online courses.
- When you overlook problem behaviors in the classroom, you teach students that you have no control over what's happening or that you're ineffective.
- When you respond brusquely to inquiries, you teach students that you think poorly of them or that you can't be bothered to help them.
- When you treat students with respect, you teach them that they are worthy of respect.
- When you encourage your students, you teach them that they possess the capacity to be successful.

Most students will be more receptive to learning if they believe that their instructor cares about them and trust that they will be treated fairly. This belief is essential to establishing rapport, both in face-to-face or online learning environments. Positive rapport increases student enjoyment of the course, improves attendance and attention, promotes additional enrollment in subsequent courses, affects the broader classroom climate, and reduces classroom conflicts.[7] Online forums such as RateMyProfessors. com reveal the role that rapport, or the lack thereof, can have on students.[8]

> This is by far the worst professor in the entire history of [X] professors. She is un-helpful, un-clear, and extremely odious. She does not like her students at all and had no business in a teaching capacity.
>
> If given the option of having Prof. [X] for this class or Satan, I would definitely choose Satan. Satan probably has more of an interest in seeing you succeed in [this class] than [X] does. He most likely has a better personality as well.
>
> Awesome teacher! She was very helpful, good at explaining things in class, and enjoyed her job to the max. I loved this class. She made [X] even more interesting than I thought it was. She was also willing to help you get better on your papers. Definitely would recommend her.
>
> Wow, just wow! Most flexible professor alive who wants you to succeed and learn and do well. His feedback is actually kind and respectful and not condescending like

every other professor I've ever had ever. [X] should teach other professors how to teach and communicate with students. He's a real human being. And he's there for you, too.[9]

I've never had a professor communicate more. Very clear. Gives you chances to make up work. Explains things good. Nice and friendly, not fake. Treats you with respect.

Our demonstration of caring for our students is reflected in a concept known as *immediacy*, or the overt forms of communication that help to establish the instructor–student relationship. Many of these behaviors mirror the hallmarks of good teaching that we discussed earlier in this chapter.

Physical Immediacy[10]

- Gesture while talking to the class
- Look at the class while talking
- Smile at the whole class while talking
- Move around the room while teaching
- Maintain a relaxed posture or body position while talking to the class
- Smile at individual students while talking to the class
- Use a variety of vocal expressions while talking to the class

These behaviors might seem like they should be self-evident, but they affect the way your students perceive you, enhancing the sense that you're approachable and aware of them personally.

Verbal Immediacy[11]

- Use personal examples or talk about experiences outside of class
- Ask questions or encourage students to talk
- Engage in discussions based on something a student brings up even when this isn't part of the planned lecture
- Use humor when appropriate
- Address students by name
- Engage in conversations with individual students before or after class
- Use phrases like "our" class or what "we" are doing
- Provide feedback on students' individual work through comments on assignments
- Ask students how they feel about an assignment
- Invite students to meet outside of class if they have questions or want to discuss something
- Praise students' work, actions, or comments
- Discuss topics unrelated to class with individual students or with the class as a whole.

These actions show students that you're a genuine human being, relating to them at a more personal level. Witt, Wheeless, and Allen (2004) conducted a meta-analysis of 81 studies involving nearly 25,000 students, which revealed a high degree of association between immediacy and students' positive attitudes toward their instructor and the course, and also positively increased students' perception of their own learning. Instructor immediacy also increased retention of course material.[12]

Here's an example of immediacy from an email exchange I had with a student in one of my online courses. (My replies are italicized.)

Hi Professor,

I didn't turn in my assignment last night, and was hoping I could still do so today. I had everything done early, because we had plans with family, but ended up sick and in bed. It just slipped my mind to put the finishing touches on my paper and submit it last night.

Please let me know if it is ok to submit this evening.

Thank you for your consideration

Yes, of course you may still submit your paper, [student name]. I hope you feel better soon. If you need another day or two, that's okay.

I might have to take you up on that, as I'm headed home sick from work now. If I can't get it done tonight, I will tomorrow.

Thank you so much

No worries, [student name]. Drink some Gatorade (my personal cure for feeling sick) and get some sleep. Do the assignment when you're feeling up to it.

Hi there,

Just wanted to let you know I did submit this assignment, and thank you for your consideration.

My entire family ended up with strep throat—but the Gatorade helped!!

Thanks again

I'm so glad you're better and that the Gatorade helped. Really, I swear by that stuff when I'm sick and my adult kids have adopted the practice, too. I'm glad to share our home remedy with you.

This student and I never met face to face, but by sharing the personal detail about my fondness for Gatorade when I'm feeling sick, I helped to humanize the situation. Furthermore, by extending leniency on the due date for the assignment, I was able to ease the student's worries since she clearly already had enough on her plate caring for a family with strep throat. She likely produced a better paper by waiting until she was feeling better than if she'd turned in a lesser product while she was ill just to meet the arbitrary due date.

This is not to say that an instructor should become personally involved with every student. It's important to set boundaries and to maintain professionalism even as we demonstrate our interest in our students' wellbeing. It's equally important to enforce classroom policies equitably even as we remain compassionate, avoiding the perception that we are lax or overly permissive. Caring does not mean the absence of academic rigor, nor does it mean we must become our students' friend outside of the classroom. This is a difficult concept for many instructors to accept, however. For example, Myers reported an exchange on RateMyProfessors.com in which a professor rebutted a student's criticism that he was "a rude, disrespectful, pretentious snob" by posting a video saying, "We're not there to babysit. We're there to train professionals. If you can't take it, you're in the wrong place. You don't deserve to be in university. Grow up."[13] I'm acquainted with numerous instructors who share this very philosophy, and who resist suggestions that they reconsider their cultivated persona of the remote, brusque, and businesslike professor. They believe that exhibiting personal warmth will undermine their students' respect, and they avoid expressions of compassion or empathy as being "too soft" on students, "mollycoddling" them, or being "too warm and fuzzy," among other things. Each of us must find a balance with which we can feel comfortable.

I've found that establishing rigorous classroom expectations, overtly stated on the syllabus and directly taught in class, allows me to be more generous to students individually without undermining myself as an instructor. The late work policy on all of my syllabi states that assignments will be marked down 10% per day the work is late, and that the only acceptable mitigating circumstances are the death of an immediate family member, the student's own military deployment, a medical or mental health emergency serious enough to require the attention of a health care professional, or a major natural disaster. I intentionally do not list any other possible exceptions beyond a statement encouraging students to contact me if they are having difficulties. When students contact me on an individual basis, I can then make exceptions where appropriate, even if the student's reason doesn't match my stated policy, such as having to work overtime in their off-campus employment, a family emergency, or a personal crisis like breaking up with a significant other. The standard remains firm and applicable to all students. Its application, however, remains flexible, contingent upon my personal judgment and empathy.

I believe we should never underestimate the power of the relationships we build with our students. Poet and author Maya Angelou has been widely quoted as saying, "People will forget what you said; people will forget what you did; but they will never forget how you made them feel."[14] As instructors, our relationships with students are temporary and ephemeral: We teach hundreds, even thousands of students over the duration of our careers, with new faces in our classrooms every semester. For our students, though, that relationship becomes a deeply ingrained memory inextricably tied to their experience in our classrooms. I've never forgotten the way my own instructors made me feel, whether they inspired, encouraged, demeaned, or disheartened me. Furthermore, the problems that I'm called upon to mediate between students and instructors are generally more about emotions than whatever initiated the incident.

Your actions exist within concentric circles of influence like ripples in a pond, radiating out to the program, department, college, school, university, community, and discipline (at the very least). Your choices impact students, sometimes profoundly. You might be the influential person who changes the trajectory of their career for the better, or you might be the person who discourages them from pursuing what was an otherwise bright future. What you say to your students *matters*, sometimes in ways you could never anticipate. In a course I took during the first semester of doctoral study, the professor prefaced her opening remarks with, "When you become administrators of your own programs . . ." I was forcibly struck by the power of this statement. She didn't say "*if* you become administrators someday" but "*when* you become administrators." Her belief in us was transformative and has stayed with me ever since. Conversely, a careless and arrogant statement by a graduate teaching assistant under whom I studied as an undergraduate has also stayed with me, provoking anger at the time and motivating me to continue to prove him wrong throughout my career.

IMPROVISATION AND SERENDIPITY

The phrase *the teachable moment* is admittedly somewhat cliché in educational circles, having been in widespread use for over 60 years.[15] Nevertheless, as instructors we're confronted by many such opportunities to offer additional instruction or input that enhance our students' learning. When we provide high-quality feedback on students' work, treat everyone kindly and respectfully, or not only answer a question, but provide additional resources to extend students' learning, we move beyond being merely adequate instructors, but reach toward becoming excellent educators.

Excellence also sometimes means deviating from our plans when opportunities arise. Course planning is important because it provides a framework within which our instruction takes place. Nevertheless, we're not trying to standardize our teaching, but continue to have the creative freedom to make changes along the way, especially when these might benefit our students' learning in unexpected ways. Just like we might leave the highway to visit a historical site despite the added delay to our road trip, we can follow up on an interesting class discussion, make changes to planned assignments, or change the content of our lectures in response to emerging situations or new information.

Before you decide to change your plans, ask yourself this question: Will the change I want to make still support my students in meeting the course's outcomes and objectives? If yes, then we should feel empowered to seize new instructional opportunities. If no, we should seriously consider whether it is worthwhile.

Academic freedom allows us to teach our students as we see fit, but it does not mean that we can use class time for topics or activities that are unrelated to the course's outcomes and objectives. For example, during my PhD studies, I took a required course in research methodologies in which the instructor used our class periods to promote her own socio-political agenda. I politely requested that she explain the connection between the books she was asking us to read and research methodologies. She testily replied, "That's for you to figure out." Her instruction was not only centered on a controversial topic but was deeply offensive to several students in the class, yet she clung to her own interpretation of academic freedom as the rationale for not teaching us the course content and replacing it with something that was personally important to her but irrelevant to the learning her students needed to achieve.

Similarly, one of my sons took a mandatory university English class in which the instructor required all of his students to purchase a handmade wooden flute, explaining that his friend made these instruments and he wanted to help support his business. Students had to learn to play the flute well enough to perform a short song for the class. How is this related to teaching English? Even if that instructor included some kind of course objective about musical performance enhancing students' ability to communicate, it does not excuse the fact that the purpose of the requirement was not to support student learning, but to help a friend make money.

Whatever we do as instructors should always support student learning aligned with our outcomes and objectives and measured by our assessments. Our course plans ensure that we'll be able to meet these goals by the end of our course. Making a schedule change to take advantage of a serendipitous opportunity, to seize a teachable moment, or to reteach a concept that students did not grasp the first time support the necessity of flexibility and improvisation. Pursuing a personal agenda unrelated to your course content is less defensible and not in the true spirit of academic freedom.

191

TEACHING FOR DIVERSITY, EQUITY, AND INCLUSION

The institutions for which we teach often acknowledge diversity, equity, and inclusion as among their core values or strategic goals. I've often heard administrators declaim, "We need to make diversity a matter of institutional habit." It's an admirable sentiment, to be sure, but mere words have no transformative power. We can inscribe them on t-shirts and bumper stickers, or hang banners from all of the campus lampposts, but without accompanying positive action, such slogans are meaningless. The real work of fostering diversity, equity, and inclusion begins with us, through our everyday interactions with students and colleagues, and in the content of our courses.

Radical Goals

Our classrooms are a rich environment in which we can advocate for the values of radical inclusiveness, radical reconciliation, and helping people live their potential. Radical inclusion means to welcome all persons who are interested in becoming a member of a group, but this presents challenges in light of institutional admission standards or reasonable limits to course enrollment. Nevertheless, we can seek out and develop students who have the drive to succeed even if they are not among those who score well on standardized tests or fit the profile of an "average" student. Gaining access to higher education has a profound impact on "populations at hope"—those students whom others would call "at risk"—providing them with means to succeed and to make a difference in the world. The program I directed served students from among these diverse populations at hope. We admitted thoughtfully and actively recruited from among these populations rather than relying upon institutionally established statistical norms. As individual instructors we have little control over the admissions process. We can, however, welcome all students who want to join our classes, even if they don't meet the criteria we usually insist upon. For instance, one of my courses had several prerequisites, but I admitted students who had not undertaken this prior coursework if they were genuinely interested in taking the course.

Radical reconciliation takes radical inclusion a step farther, offering special consideration or support to persons from populations that have experienced extreme discrimination. This idea began as an attempt to address racial discrimination, but it can be extended to the members of many historically disadvantaged or oppressed groups. Radical reconciliation can take the form of financial assistance, individualized programs of study, or by providing additional supports such as adaptive curricular materials, tutoring, or exemptions from standard admissions requirements. Furthermore, radical inclusion and radical reconciliation need not depend on the existence of favorable institutional policies. Individual educators can facilitate opportunities for all students, paying particular attention to those who would not usually be able to achieve academic success within institutional structures that maintain an implicit bias toward students who mirror traditional expectations.

This leads to the final value of helping all students to achieve their potential. Any of the 24 dimensions of identity (as seen in Chapter 2) may place students at a disadvantage, which must be addressed if we want to facilitate their academic success. Universities' student bodies are projected to become increasingly diverse along with the US population as a whole, with the most substantial changes reflected in growing numbers of Hispanic students and students from low-income families.[16] However, traditional admissions criteria implicitly favor students from more affluent socio-economic backgrounds, demonstrated by their consistently higher achievement on measures of academic readiness such as the SAT. According to Zachary Goldfarb of the Washington Post, "SAT scores are highly correlated with income. Students from families earning more than $200,000 per year average a combined score of 1,714, while students from families earning under $20,000 a year average a combined score of 1,326."

Part of this disparity may result from the fact that our students come to higher education from K–12 systems that tend to be skewed toward one demographic or another. High schools do not deliver equal educational experiences, nor do they all prepare students for college equally well. School districts located in low-income inner-city neighborhoods compare unfavorably to those located in affluent suburbs, and these are also quite different from school districts that serve students in rural areas. Access to co-curricular activities, the availability of tutoring or test preparation assistance, organized sports, or strong arts programs affect the quality of students' education, which then influences their readiness for higher education. Communities invest differing levels of capital into their public educational systems, and this is reflected in the quality of education they provide and the subsequent achievement of their graduates.

The changing face of our student body should cause us to question our underlying assumptions of what constitutes a student who is prepared for college success, particularly as they relate to our students' background knowledge or the lack thereof. When our students come to us from other countries, we anticipate that they might lack the cultural knowledge most of our native-born students take for granted, but the same may be equally true of students who come to our predominantly White middle- to upper-class institutions from non-White or low-income backgrounds. Regardless of race or ethnicity, a student who grew up in the inner city of Chicago, for example, likely had a dramatically different upbringing than her classmate who was raised in an affluent North Shore suburb. Although both students might meet the same admissions criteria, are equally intelligent, driven to succeed, and academically talented, the former's life experiences create a gap not experienced by her comparatively wealthy counterpart.

Income inequality has a wide-reaching impact on students from low-income families, who exhibit other, less visible deficits:[17]

- They are likely to have received poorer health care and nutrition throughout childhood, which can lead to cognitive or physical problems in later life.
- They have experienced lower-quality verbal exchanges with adults and have less language development from an early age.
- They may believe that their ability to succeed is predetermined (a "fixed mindset" such as "I'm not good at math") as opposed to believing they have the power to learn, grow, and succeed academically (a "growth mindset").[18]
- They may not have developed the same cognitive skills or been exposed to the same quality of educational experience as their more affluent peers. For example, they may have had fewer opportunities to engage in creative problem solving or to experience the arts.
- They are more likely to have had adverse childhood experiences such as the loss or desertion of a parent, unreliable availability of food, being the victim of a crime, or facing trauma caused by poor housing or homelessness, any of which cause difficulty in assimilating into social groups or forming high-quality personal relationships.
- They have fewer financial and social resources, lacking the ability to pay for project supplies, take field trips, or even to socialize in the same manner as financially stable peers.

Such students, as well as those from other diverse or nontraditional backgrounds can encounter social isolation, lack an established support network, or face a shortage of mentoring opportunities, particularly when few faculty members come from similar demographic groups. Furthermore, many such students are the first generation in their families to enter higher education, so they do not possess prior knowledge of what is socially necessary for success in academic environments.[19]

What We Can Do

Once we become aware of these problems, we are able to take steps to address them. We can advocate for our institutions to foster open, active, and ongoing conversations about diversity, equity, and inclusion. We can recommend that our programs engage in focused marketing and recruitment of students from diverse groups so that their numbers increase, which minimizes social isolation. Most importantly, all of us who work in higher education should demonstrate sensitivity to the experience of marginalized students. We might even initiate changes to the physical spaces on campus such as signage, artworks, or interior design elements to make the environment more welcoming and supportive to students from many backgrounds.

In our classrooms, there is much we can do to support diversity. Creating a safe space for difficult conversations and ensuring that all voices are heard and all perspectives valued each rank high among inclusive practices that allow us to establish a classroom climate that nurtures diversity.

Employing critical theory to our teaching allows us to reflectively examine common disciplinary norms and practices. Ask your students to join you in identifying underlying assumptions, implicit bias, or exclusionary practices in your discipline and discuss these discoveries as they occur throughout your course. Also, consider the history and practices of your discipline: How has it affected civilization? Does it serve to empower or oppress various groups of people? Is it intrinsically inclusive or exclusive? Does it favor one group over another? Asking questions such as these can initiate conversations that shed light on aspects of our fields that we may have long taken for granted.

Building Interpersonal Connections

We can engage with our students on a personal level by using the 24 points of diversity we discussed in Chapter 2. These could become a useful tool to get to know your students and for them to learn more about one another. For example, you could administer a survey (see Figure 8.3) in which you collect these data during your first class period.

A sample lesson plan for a class period based on these dimensions appears in Figure 8.4.

Beyond devoting one class period to discussions about diversity, equity, and inclusion, we can embed these values into our outcomes and objectives. Sample statements that you can copy and adapt to your syllabus appear below.

Outcome: Students in the _____ (name of program) will engage with diversity, equity, and inclusion within the field of _____ (name of discipline) to prepare for careers in an increasingly pluralistic workplace.

Objective: Students will critically analyze and evaluate present levels of diversity, equity, and inclusion in _____ (name of discipline) by examining current professional practices and the work of leading practitioners, demonstrated in a 5-page summary and analysis essay due _____ (insert due date).

Two-Way Teaching

The inclusion of nontraditional students from diverse backgrounds in our classrooms provides us with opportunities to grow and learn alongside our students. When we practice "two-way teaching," we not only expect that students will learn

Internal Dimensions	External Dimensions	Institutional Dimensions
1. Personality	1. Geographic Location	1. Academic Discipline
2. Gender	2. Income/Economic Status	2. Department, Program, College, School, or Unit
3. Sexual Orientation	3. Personal Habits	
4. Age	4. Recreational Habits	3. Functional Level/ Classification
5. Physical Ability	5. Religion	
6. Ethnicity	6. Educational Background	4. Rank or Seniority
7. Race	7. Work Experience	5. Organizational Affiliation(s)
	8. Appearance	
	9. Parental Status	6. Work Location
	10. Marital/Relational Status	7. Leadership Role(s)

FIGURE 8.3 Dimensions of Diversity Table

what we have to teach, but also remain open to the possibility that students may have something of value to teach us in return. This helps to avoid perpetuating a view that our own culture is dominant and others should simply assimilate our values and practices.[20] Speaking from my own experience, discussions occurring in my Leadership course have allowed me to learn a great deal about leadership practices in other cultures through my international students' contributions. I am delighted to find my worldview expanded and to add new perspectives to my field.

The design process requires that we examine our own motivations behind the solutions we develop and consider how we might apply our prior knowledge of various aspects of the human experience to our interactions with individuals from diverse populations, whether they are our students or our colleagues. For example, we must be especially aware of how our students' dimensions of identity are reflected in the assignments and assessments we ask them to complete. Let's say that an international student struggles with verbal fluency during a required presentation in your class. Certainly, we want our students to communicate clearly because this is a professional expectation in most fields. If the student plans to enter professional practice in her home country after graduation, though, her ability to speak in English is important only to her studies here. Awareness of this fact should influence how you grade the presentation, extending greater leniency for the student's command of English than you normally would for a student who plans to pursue a career in the United States. Your goal as the instructor is to observe whether or not the student successfully demonstrated that they have learned in your course, even if the student's use of American Standard English is imperfect. By placing the determination more on whether the student has learned than on their use of perfect English, you are better able to assign an equitable grade. This also demonstrates two of the most important aspects of the design process: empathy and user experience.

SAMPLE LESSON	24 DIMENSIONS OF DIVERSITY
Week Number/Topic	Dimensions of Diversity
Lesson Objective	Students will deepen their understanding of diversity by considering different aspects of their own lives and use this as a springboard for peer interaction and open discussion.
Preparation	Before class, the instructor should complete the Dimensions of Diversity Self-Assessment for himself or herself. Reflect upon experiences you've had with discrimination. Select a personal experience that you could share with the class.
Materials and Equipment	Student handout: Dimensions of Diversity Self-Assessment (may print paper copies or provide electronically)
Hook	Tell your personal story about experiencing discrimination. Be as open and honest as you can. [Note: The best TED talks begin with personal anecdotes—this is an excellent way to engage your audience's attention.]

Instruction	• After you've told your story, distribute the student handout.
	• Explain that we often think of race or other obvious factors, but we can actually identify many layers and aspects to the parts of our identities that make us unique human beings.
	• Allow at least 30 minutes for students to complete the survey in class. Encourage those who finish early to select a personal experience that they remembered, while completing the survey and to write about it until everyone has finished.
	• Once everyone has completed the survey, group students in pairs. They will conduct a short interview of their partner, asking the following questions and taking notes about their partner's response. Allow no more than 10 minutes for the first partner to ask questions, then reverse roles for another 10 minutes.
	  ○ Question 1: As you worked on the survey just now, which of the dimensions of diversity stood out as the most significant to you personally? Why do you think this is so?
	  ○ Question 2: Which of these dimensions triggered a memory or reminded you of a past experience? Please tell me more about this.
	  ○ Question 3: Which of these dimensions is the most important to your personal identity? Which do you seldom (if ever) think about?
	  ○ Question 4: Of the things we've just talked about, what would you like me to share with the class?
	• At the end of the interview process, come back together as a whole group. Each student will share their partner's answer to Question 4 with the entire class.
	• As students share these stories, encourage peer interaction, allowing for discussion when it arises. However, make sure that one person's story does not take so much time that others are not able to have their stories be told. Each should require about 5 minutes, including related discussion. No one should be left out. If this requires an extra class period, it is well worth taking the time to make sure that everyone is heard and included.

FIGURE 8.4 Dimensions of Diversity Lesson Plan

SAMPLE LESSON	24 DIMENSIONS OF DIVERSITY
Guided Practice	Ask students to complete a short personal reflection on the day's activity and discussion. Depending on the format of your class, this could be written by hand and turned in to you at the start of the next class period, sent to you as an email, or posted to a class website. The reflection should be a communication between only the instructor and the student, not posted publicly. In it, the student should thoughtfully address the following questions: 1. What did you learn from this activity? 2. What was the most surprising thing you discovered about yourself? 3. What was the most significant thing you learned about your classmate(s)?
Independent Practice/ Assignment	Your options for independent practice will vary depending on your class. Some examples: • Biographical sketch about a person in your field whose life or work exemplifies one of the dimensions of diversity. • Creative expression of the student's insights gained during the classroom activity (e.g., write a poem, short story, editorial) • Identify and interview a person in your field whose life or work exemplifies one of the dimensions of diversity.

Assessment	Student learning can be assessed based on any or all of the following:
	
	• Completion of the 24 Dimensions of Diversity worksheet
	• Active participation during
	  ○ The interview activity
	  ○ Presentation of partner's findings
	  ○ Class discussion
	• Completion of the reflective summary
	• Completion of the assignment you choose to require (if any)
	
	Sample Grading Checklist:
	  ○ Student's responses demonstrate a genuine attempt to engage with ideas about identity and diversity.
	  ○ Student actively participated in _____ (name of activity).
	  ○ Student maintained a respectful and open-minded attitude during classroom activities and discussions.
	  ○ Student responses to written questions were thoughtful and thorough.
	  ○ Student met all assignment criteria as stated verbally and in writing.

FIGURE 8.4 Continued

Cultural Tropes

As we work toward the change we want to see in the world, we need to recognize that we bring a great deal of invisible baggage to our interactions with others, but it's difficult for us to set this aside because we often fail to recognize it. An interesting strategy for recognizing cultural assumptions is to examine common tropes. In the simplest sense, a trope is an example of figurative language, like the metaphor "Time is money." In a larger sense, a trope is a plot device common to literature, television, or film. (When you have a chance, take a look at the website TV Tropes [http://tvtropes.org/]. It's not only very entertaining, but it can open your eyes to nuances of pop culture that most of us take for granted.)

A particularly pervasive, if not insidious, trope is sometimes called "The White Savior Complex," which involves the perception that we (affluent/educated/ White/Americans) should be the benevolent benefactors of helpless, unfortunate "others." This is a common literary/media trope as well as a means of alienating the people we're trying to help. Presuming that our own culture and way of life is superior to others is paternalistic, disrespectful, demeaning, condescending, and even imperialistic. It betrays an exaggerated perception of our own superiority or importance, and it undermines the self-reliance and autonomy of others.[21]

Typical media examples of the White Savior Complex trope involve a displaced White European, usually of noble descent, who ends up living with native tribes-people and not only learns their ways, but also becomes their greatest warrior/ leader/representative. Films such as *The Last Samurai* or *Dances With Wolves* exemplify this trope. There's a grain of truth here: Those who had access to nutrition, education, technology, and general skills and experience demonstrated qualities that a native who never traveled further than the neighboring village didn't possess. Such people presumed that they were better because of their culture, beliefs, or genetic stock, rather than their access to tools and benefits derived from hundreds of years of accumulated advantages. We can also define this trope as a "modern" character achieving mastery over "ancient" or "backward" characters, not necessarily with respect to race. A variation on this theme involves a person from a non-White background who is assimilated into a more affluent cultural group and achieves success (as in the film *The Blind Side*, for example).

We're so used to these tropes that it's hard to even be aware of them. When we try to change the world, we generally do so with the purest of intentions. But when we take on the role of the kind, caring benefactor raising the quality of life for someone less fortunate, we risk failing to recognize the repercussions of our assumptions. This is a problem with very deep roots and shifting implications. Therefore, we must first recognize our own biases, presumptions, and the impact of culture in our own lives so that we can genuinely, respectfully, humbly do the most good for the people whose lives we hope to improve. Furthermore, we must remain constantly aware that our way of thinking, cooking, dressing, playing, loving, believing (*anything*-ing) is not superior to anyone else's. Even when we have the most compassionate of intentions, our efforts are meaningless if those whom we seek to help don't want the solution we propose, can't use it, or disagree that what *we* see is a problem is *really* a problem at all.

Relationships Build Bridges

All of our interactions with persons different from ourselves present opportunities to grow in our knowledge of other cultures, backgrounds, personal histories, lifestyles, beliefs, and other factors that cause each of us to be the uniquely valuable individuals we are. Each of the strategies we've discussed thus far will help you to work toward this goal. However, the most direct, most effective means of increasing diversity in our classrooms and working toward social justice happens the most simply—by building personal relationships that transcend the differences that appear to divide us. As we said earlier in this book, humans are exceptionally good at making instantaneous judgments about one another, by which we classify others by the relative threat we perceive (see Figure 8.5).

The more we perceive someone as an enemy, the more likely we are to dehumanize them in order to justify war, murder, or other atrocities.[22] However, when we develop personal relationships with people who are not like ourselves, we grow to care about them, to respect them, reducing our previous fears and insecurities. We begin to experience pity, sympathy, empathy, and even compassion.

For example, the personal struggles of a student in the program I formerly administered inspired empathy in many of her fellow students and instructors, motivating us to engage in political activism on campus, participating in a rally against a federal immigration ban that included this student's home country. The student and her husband (also enrolled in the graduate school) were suddenly prohibited from leaving the country even for a short visit home. Our proximity to this student's hardship made this situation very real to all of us, since it was happening to someone we cared about and wanted to support.

- ■ **No threat:** A person who is a member of my own group
- ■ **Low threat:** A person who is not a member of my own group but is a close neighbor or associate
- ■ **Moderate threat:** A person who is unknown to me but is similar enough that we can communicate with one another despite our perceptible differences
- ■ **High threat:** A person who is unknown to me and with whom I cannot communicate
- ■ **Highest threat:** An enemy whom I must either attack or from whom I must be prepared to defend myself

FIGURE 8.5 Levels of Threat

John Steinbeck wrote, "It means very little to know that a million Chinese are starving unless you know one Chinese who is starving."[23] When we build relationships with individuals from groups different from our own, they cease to be abstract and "other" and become our friends, our coworkers, or our neighbors. I can speak only for myself in this, but I know that my life has been immensely enriched by the relationships I've built and friendships I've made with people from Palestine, Iraq, Iran, Pakistan, India, the Bahamas, and China (among others), as well as friends who are female, Black, Hispanic, LGBTQQIP2SAA, and many combinations of these identities. Their personal histories could not be more different from my own, yet we are friends nonetheless. I am certainly no more immune to implicit bias than anyone else, and I fully acknowledge that denying that one is prejudiced because "some of my best friends are [Black, gay, Jewish, or any other designation]" does not withstand scrutiny. Nevertheless, the more each of us builds relationships that transcend social boundaries, the more we open our hearts and minds to the simple truth that we are all one race—the human race—despite how cliché it admittedly sounds.

The Way Forward

We individual educators are unlikely to change our universities' admissions policies, and few of us have the power to eradicate bias or discrimination from our academic disciplines. We can, however, wield considerable positive influence on our students. If we actively lead our students in questioning their own assumptions and discovering hidden bias in our disciplines, if we remain open to new ideas, and most of all if we diligently work toward establishing our classrooms as places in which diversity, equity, and inclusion thrive, our actions can have far-reaching consequences. Our pedagogical practice and curriculum delivery can reach beyond mere transmission of disciplinary content: lecture by lecture, discussion by discussion, we progress toward a more just society.

Near the end of the Cold War, Sting released the song "Russians" (1985) containing the lyric, "We share the same biology, regardless of ideology/believe me when I say to you/ I hope the Russians love their children too." That thought has stayed with me over the years, not just related to the fears of nuclear war that were so pervasive during my childhood and young adulthood, but whenever the people of the world have been in conflict. People on each side of every human conflict love their families. Each of us wants a life of peace and security. Just so, the concluding words of Abraham Lincoln's second inaugural address issue a universal call to action that we can apply to our goal of achieving diversity, equity, and inclusion in our classrooms and institutions: "With malice toward none, with charity for all . . . let us strive on to finish the work we are in . . . to do all which may achieve and cherish a just and lasting peace among ourselves and with all nations."

201

Taking Lincoln's words a step farther, Franklin D. Roosevelt delivered a speech in 1941 during which he proposed that all people throughout the world should share in "Four Freedoms"—the freedom of expression, freedom to worship as they choose, freedom from want, and freedom from fear. These ideas were later incorporated into the United Nations' Universal Declaration of Human Rights, partially due to the tireless work of former First Lady Eleanor Roosevelt.

Politicians and poets alike have upheld the ideal that all members of the human race should share equally in these freedoms, from Martin Luther King's famous "I Have a Dream" speech in 1963 to Garth Brooks' 1992 anthem of acceptance and inclusiveness, "We Shall Be Free," (re-released as an updated music video in March 2017). Yes, we have made significant progress as a society over the past 100+ years, from the establishment of the 19th Amendment to the US Constitution finally granting women the right to vote (1919), to the Civil Rights Act (1964), to the Marriage Equality Act (2015). These are important steps along the journey, and deserving of recognition and celebration. Nevertheless, we cannot merely rest on these achievements. We must continue pressing on toward a truly equitable society in which all diversity is embraced and all people are included regardless of differences in any dimension of their identity. Our influence may be limited to our own classrooms and neighborhoods, or we may someday find ourselves in positions of authority where we have greater power to enact our ideals more broadly. If we each do what is within our ability and in accordance with our values, we can look forward to a day when all people are free to live their potential without fear of discrimination and prejudice.

ONE LAST THOUGHT

Our classrooms are the proving ground for institutional efforts toward diversity, equity, and inclusion—if they fail with us, they cannot succeed on a larger scale. Our students' educational experiences are marked by the quality of their interactions with us, much more so than lectures we deliver, readings we assign, or exams we administer. All of the disciplinary expertise in the world is useless if an educator fails to make these connections or cannot establish a classroom climate that is conducive to learning.

Remember:

- Providing valuable feedback is among an instructor's most important responsibilities. The way you approach this task can inspire students to greater success or discourage them.
- Structure formal feedback around the principles of (1) recognize success, (2) suggest improvement, and (3) make a personal connection. You can remember this as "LBNT" as well.

Identify	Ideate
Why must we do all of these extra things as educators when they're not what we're used to? The point of this chapter is really about approaching our teaching from a learning-centric position. We don't only need to employ empathy when planning our curriculum and instruction, but in every interaction we have with our students.	How do we actually plan for being an excellent teacher? A large part of this task lies in anticipating common classroom situations and being prepared to address them as they arise. Part of this occurs through the classroom policies you establish in your syllabus, and part through how you choose to enforce them when students run afoul of your rules. If your first thought is for each student's individual learning needs, you should have fewer problems.
Iterate	Implement
When you teach, you seldom have a second opportunity to make things right with a student. However, if you learn from each interaction, you can continue to improve your practice as an educator and strive toward becoming the kind of instructor in whose classroom you'd have loved to be enrolled.	What can I do to become a better instructor? Make sure your syllabus is very clear in how you present your classroom policies. Make sure your policies tie into your course objectives and plan a lesson around each one so that your students understand them. When problems arise, choose to err on the side of the student rather than rigidly maintaining your hold on policy and procedure. Compassion is nearly always the best choice.

FIGURE 8.6 Chapter 8 Design Connection

- In every interaction with students, you teach them something, whether intentionally or unintentionally. They learn from your demeanor, the tone of your voice, your body language, and your email, as well as from your lectures and assignments. Make sure that what you're teaching in every interaction is what you want students to learn.

Notes

[1] Karia, A. (2015). *TED Talks Storytelling*. Self-published. http://AkashKaria.com

[2] Murphy, E., and Rodriguez-Manzanares, M. (January 2012). Rapport in distance education. *The International Review of Research in Open and Distributed Learning*, 13(1). www.irrodl.org/index.php/irrodl/article/view/1057/2076

[3] CAST. (2017). *Until learning has no limits*. www.cast.org/our-work/about-udl.html#.WJ0jS_JRI8I

[4] Adams, M. (1990). *The dead grandmother/exam syndrome and the potential downfall of American Society*. pages.ucsd.edu/~jlbroz/ . . . /DeadGrandmother.pdf. See also Patton, Stacey. (January 29, 2015). *Chronicle of Higher Education Vita*. https://chroniclevitae.com/news/886-dear-student-should-your-granny-die-before-the-midterm

[5] HailcarBarca. (February 9, 2013). Equality vs fairness, or, why empathy matters. *Daily Kos*. www.dailykos.com/story/2013/2/9/1185816/-Equality-vs-Fairness-or-Why-Empathy-Matters

[6] Burton, N. (2015). *Heaven and Hell: The Psychology of the Emotions*. Acheron Press. Printed by SRP Limited, Exeter, Devon: United Kingdom.

[7] Myers, S. (2009). Do your students care whether you care about them? *College Teaching*, 57(4), 205–210. Heldref Publications.

[8] Ibid.

[9] In the interest of full disclosure, this and the following quote are from my own RateMyProfessors.com page. www.ratemyprofessors.com/ShowRatings.jsp?tid=1829879

[10] In Myers (2009) from Richmond, V. P., Gorham, J., and McCrosky, J. C. (1987). The relationship between selected immediacy behaviors and cognitive learning. *Communication Yearbook*, 10, 547–590.

[11] Ibid.

[12] Witt, P. L., Wheeless, L. R., and Allen, M. (2004). A meta-analytical review of the relationship between teacher immediacy and student learning. *Communication Studies*, 71, 184–207.

[13] Myers (2009)

[14] Gallo, C. (May 31, 2014). The Maya Angelou quote that will radically improve your business. *Forbes*. www.forbes.com/sites/carminegallo/2014/05/31/the-maya-angelou-quote-that-will-radically-improve-your-business/#1eb6bb608d1a

[15] This phrase was popularized by Robert Havinghurst in his book *Human Development and Education* (1952), University of Michigan Press: Ann Arbor, MI, but existed prior even to the book's publication.

[16] Selingo, J. (2016). 2026 the decade ahead: The seismic shifts transforming the future of higher education. *Chronicle of Higher Education*.

[17] Jensen, E. (May 2013). How poverty affects classroom engagement. *Educational Leadership*, 70(8). www.ascd.org/publications/educational-leadership/may13/vol70/num08/How-Poverty-Affects-Classroom-Engagement.aspx

[18] Dweck, C. (September 22, 2015). Carol Dweck revisits the growth mindset. *Education Week*. www.edweek.org/ew/articles/2015/09/23/carol-dweck-revisits-the-growth-mindset.html

[19] Gasman, M. (2005, Fall). Teaching outside the classroom: Conversations on race and research. *Journal of Excellence in College and University Teaching*.

[20] Purdie, N., Milgate, G., and Bell, H. (2011). *Two Way Teaching and Learning: Toward Culturally Reflective and Relevant Education*. Australian Council for Educational Research. http://research.acer.edu.au/indigenous_education/38/

[21] Libby, K. (August 8, 2011). White savior complex. *By Their Strange Fruit: Christianity and Race*. http://bytheirstrangefruit.blogspot.com/2011/08/white-savior-complex.html

[22] Smith, D. L. (2011). *Less than human:Why we demean, enslave, and exterminate others*. www.npr.org/2011/03/29/134956180/criminals-see-their-victims-as-less-than-human

[23] Preface to the script of *The Forgotten Village* (1941) and the inspiration behind *The Grapes of Wrath* (1939). In George, S. (ed.) (2005). *The Moral Philosophy of John Steinbeck*. Scarecrow Press, Inc.: Lanham, MD, p. 112.

Chapter 9

Planning for Interdisciplinary Collaboration

CHAPTER SUMMARY

- Options for Collaborative Curriculum
- Potential Pitfalls
- Practical Solutions
- Proposal
- Impediments to Interdisciplinarity
- Flexibility and Resilience
- What We Can Accomplish

The shifting cultural emphasis toward teaming and collaboration in the 21st century workplace has begun to produce changes in higher education, including increased interest in interdisciplinary and collaborative teaching. Nevertheless, those seeking to implement these innovative approaches to teaching sometimes encounter unexpected challenges in organizational systems and institutional policies. A practical, common-sense approach focusing on establishing communication and developing a comprehensive plan of action helps overcome these problems, allowing partners to work within existing institutional structures for instructional delivery to meet their shared goals.[1]

The workplace outside of higher education has become increasingly collaborative. Job postings commonly require that candidates have the ability to work well on teams, corporations often refer to their employees as team members, and we speak of management or marketing teams. Even contexts dependent on individual accomplishment, such as accounting, organize employees in collaborative work groups. Nevertheless, the focus in academia remains on individual accomplishment. According to Crow and Dabars (2017):

> Entrenchment in discipline-based departments mirrors an academic culture that prizes individualism over teamwork and the discovery of specialized knowledge of problem-based collaboration. Our competitive culture values the individual over the group and because academia places greater value on the discovery of new knowledge by individual scientists, less prestige attaches to collaborative endeavors that target real-world problems. The same is true for team participation in projects that advance knowledge through assimilation, synthesis, implementation, and application. . . .[2]
>
> Disciplinary acculturation defines academic culture, just as the traditional correlation between disciplines and departments persists as the basis for academic organization. Such disciplinary partitioning represents one of the most critical impediments—or design limitations—to the further evolution of the American research university."[3]

Interdisciplinary approaches to teaching and learning help to surpass these limitations, beginning to bridge the gap between discipline-focused education and expectations that graduates will be prepared to become effective team members in the workplace. (For our purposes, "interdisciplinary" refers to any combination of disciplines, inclusive of all terms such as cross-disciplinary, transdisciplinary, and so on.) Harvard researcher Veronica Boix Mansilla explains:

> Interdisciplinary learning involves processes that operate in and across disciplines such as evidence-based reasoning, complex causal thinking, temporal and spatial representations, and critical argumentation. However, unique to interdisciplinary learning is the fact that these processes integrate information, data, techniques, tools, perspectives, concepts and/or theories from two or more disciplines, typically in order to craft products, explain phenomena, or solve problems, in ways that would have been unlikely through single disciplinary means.[4]

Collaborative and interdisciplinary curricula and pedagogies, therefore, provide opportunities to enhance student learning and to explore professional engagement beyond the bounds of a single academic field. Furthermore, studies such as Barbach, Washut, Heck, and Dahlbert's (2008) investigation of co-teaching report notably positive feedback from both faculty and students, a finding supported by evidence gathered in the Mellon Research Project (Mackh, 2015).

OPTIONS FOR COLLABORATIVE CURRICULUM

If you're interested in partnering with a colleague in a collaborative course, it's a good idea to become familiar with some of the varied options available. The list below is only a starting point. Collaborations are contingent upon many factors including the partners' disciplines, interests, and expertise, as well as institutional structures.

Co-teaching by faculty members from the same department or discipline is perhaps the least complicated approach to collaboration since they are each subject to the same norms and expectations. These partnerships usually involve individuals with distinct expertise, with each bringing something of value to the course they share, creating a richer learning experience for students than would be possible if either instructor were to teach the course alone.[5] However, sharing a course might mean that each person receives only half credit for teaching.

Linked courses represent another straightforward option. Here, a cohort of students enrolls in two courses, one taught by each of the partnering instructors. Course content draws upon the same set of themes and ideas, but approached from different disciplinary perspectives or featuring varied aspects of the central issue. Because each instructor continues to work within established disciplinary systems and expectations, this option presents few of the problems common to interdisciplinarity.[6]

Surveying the Landscape (2015) identified three main *interdisciplinary curricular configurations*. Potential partners from diverse disciplines who want to teach a course together may choose to work within any of these structures, depending on the relationship between their disciplines with regard to the central concept of the course.

- *Equal Partnership*: A co-taught, collaborative course partnering two professors from different learning areas. One example would be a Project Management and Creative Entrepreneurship course, taught by professors from both design and business, in which students would employ design-thinking methods to the creation of a product. The design professor would address the creative components, while the business professor would address topics like writing a business plan, sales and marketing techniques, and so on.
- *One Discipline Serves the Another*: A disciplinary course might incorporate content from a partnering discipline, such as a course in medical ethics where medical students study under a professor of philosophy, engaging in the most prevalent ethical issues involved in the practice of medicine.
- *Partnerships Between and Among Similar Disciplinary Areas*: The methods and approaches of many subdisciplines within the same field can be seen as sufficiently disparate to warrant classification as separate disciplines, so a

pairing of two or more of these diverse areas requires an interdisciplinary mindset because they are built upon different epistemologies. Pairings of sociology and social work, philosophy and psychology, or among different STEM fields could exemplify these kinds of collaborations.

POTENTIAL PITFALLS

Even the best of intentions can fail to produce a desired result if we're not prepared for the problems we might encounter along the way. Not only is higher education structured to favor individual achievement and disciplinary focus over collaboration and interdisciplinarity, but our training, experience, and work environments contain challenges we might overlook.

Unequal Expectations

Expectations between departments tend to be inherently asymmetrical, especially as these pertain to systems of instructional delivery.

> Disciplines began with the creation of rituals of certification and exclusion related to knowledge; in the more recent sense they are the product of university organization, and especially that part of university organization that joins research and teaching, knowledge production and reproduction, in the modern research university.
>
> (Turner, p. 9)[7]

In other words, our disciplinary configurations don't just shape our professional practices—they serve as exclusionary structures that make collaboration more difficult.

For example, disciplines may calculate contact hours and credit hours differently. Most lecture or seminar courses maintain a 1:1 relationship in which 1 hour in the classroom (1 contact hour) is equal to 1 credit hour of the course, so a course that meets for 3 clock hours per week is worth 3 credit hours. However, practice-based courses such as student teaching, clinical rounds, field work, or studio and performing arts worth 3 credit hours can meet for up to 6 clock hours per week. The instructor's contact hours with students are calculated at half the rate of a lecture-based course on the assumption that students will complete the majority of their work during class, whereas students in lecture courses complete their work on their own time. Laboratory courses, too, presume students will complete all of their work in the lab, so 1 credit hour may require up to 3 clock hours in the lab.[8] Those who want to establish a partnership between disciplines using different calculation methods encounter problems when attempting to schedule their course or determine appropriate contact hours for each partner.

209

Our systems for retention, promotion, and tenure also tend not to accommodate interdisciplinary or collaborative engagement very well, especially when it's difficult to discern which parts of a project can be credited to the person whose work is being considered. Furthermore, faculty members whose work diverges from standard expectations may meet with opposition from peers who prefer the status quo or are reluctant to embrace innovation.

Unequal Communication

Furthermore, Crow and Dabras cite differences in disciplinary communication as a significant barrier to collaboration.

> The maintenance of strict disciplinary boundaries undermines our impetus to initiate a conversation with those outside our own sphere of disciplinary expertise. . . . [No one has yet] developed a lingua franca to facilitate communication. . . . Because each discipline exercises its own vernacular, the impetus is lacking to cultivate 'interlanguages' intelligible to other disciplines—the pidgins or creoles that constitute the mutually comprehensible means of communication through which different subcultures negotiate trading zones.[9]

To establish a successful interdisciplinary teaching partnership, we must be willing to aside our previous assumptions about our partner's professional norms, and we must be equally transparent in our communications about our own practices, understandings, and expectations.

Unequal Resources and Requirements

Different learning areas demonstrate a markedly inequitable distribution of resources. Far more funding is available to STEM subjects than to the liberal arts, humanities, or the arts, and the same is often true of facilities and equipment. Other types of support vary greatly as well: Some colleges and universities enthusiastically promote collaboration, providing structural accommodations for co-taught or interdisciplinary courses. Other educational institutions, however, continue to maintain a traditional emphasis on individual teaching.

Furthermore, faculty and administrators tend to have different priorities. Administrators must keep the "big picture" in mind and must constantly remain aware of overarching issues such as budget, accreditation, institutional effectiveness, and student retention. Faculty members, on the other hand, might be more concerned with their particular department, career enhancement, professional reputations, or larger issues such as academic freedom.

Collaborations that don't appear to coincide with disciplinary norms, departmental practices, or administrative expectations, become quite difficult. The absence of precedent or tradition for such activities can problematize collaboration or discourage interested individuals from even making the attempt.

PRACTICAL SOLUTIONS

If you'd like to engage in co-teaching or interdisciplinary collaboration, knowing the challenges you might encounter and how your shared effort fits within your particular institutional context are each important. You and your partner also need to initiate an open dialogue about your project. Therefore, each of the following steps will increase the likelihood that you'll be able to achieve your goals.

1. An in-depth discussion of the partners' values and expectations for the collaboration
2. An assessment of institutional resources, support, and precedents
3. Creation of a detailed plan for the project or course

Let's look at each step more closely.

Values and Expectations

Establishing clear communication from the very start of a project is essential to any successful partnership. This is true even when both partners are from the same discipline, but it's all the more important when they come from widely different disciplinary cultures. General areas you should address include

- Vision for the course, its purpose, and scope
- Funding and budget ideas and concerns
- What you hope to gain from the collaboration
- Your availability and schedule, including other commitments
- Expectations for meetings and/or shared worktimes
- Deliverables each partner will expect from the other
- Anticipated challenges or impediments
- Expectations for student learning in the course
- Expectations for the distribution of disciplinary content between the partnering disciplines

Even though it might seem unnecessarily formal to begin your partnership in this manner, beginning with a formal discussion allows partners to acknowledge underlying issues that may derail the best of intentions. It can also facilitate a strategic understanding of one another's perspectives, expectations, and values.

Environmental Analysis

Beyond the partners' values and expectations, you should also systematically investigate the institutional structures and resources that might support or impede the course you and your partner are planning.

1. Have similar collaborations previously occurred at this institution? Elsewhere?
2. What institutional supports are available to us?
3. Which of our departments will be the home of our project?
4. To whom do we report?
5. What resources are available to us at present?
6. What can we expect from our departmental colleagues in the way of support, encouragement, or opposition?

Many other questions undoubtedly can and should be asked, but since each instance of collaboration will encompass a unique set of circumstances and involve participants with very different perspectives and expectations at different institutions, it's impossible to create an all-encompassing script appropriate for every circumstance. Instead, please take these questions as a starting point, priming the discussion between partners and leading naturally to a more complete development of a specific plan of action.

Collaborative Course Plan

Once the partners have established a mutual understanding of their values and expectations, the next step in planning a co-taught course is to create a comprehensive plan and syllabus, as we've discussed throughout the book. However, it begins with identifying key criteria related to the interdisciplinary nature of the collaboration.

- What we are trying to achieve through the proposed course?
- Why is an interdisciplinary approach valuable or necessary to achieve this goal?
- Which disciplines will be involved?
    - Why is each one important?
    - How will each make a substantive contribution?
    - How will each present a clearly distinct perspective and way of knowing?
    - What would be missing if any of the disciplines under consideration were not included?
- What level of expertise will be required of the instructor(s)?

- What are students expected to produce?
- How will the course lead students to engage in interdisciplinary thinking?

Successful interdisciplinary courses are goal oriented, bringing one or more learning areas together in order to address a central purpose that would not be possible through a single discipline. This purpose is the "big idea" that shapes the students' learning experience. A big idea can take several forms:

- *Developing Students' Interdisciplinary Skills and Knowledge*: Rather than an emphasis on teaching content-area knowledge, some courses' primary purpose is to equip students with the ability to think and work in interdisciplinary settings. In this case, the content is less important than the teaching methodology employed. Students are assessed on the growth of their understanding of interdisciplinary methods and their enhanced ability to embrace ways of thinking and knowing outside of their major area of study. Interdisciplinary courses for freshmen or sophomores usually fit this pattern.
- *Enhancing or Deepening Disciplinary Knowledge*: Incorporating content from a partnering discipline can lead students to a broader understanding of or greater skill in their chosen field. For example, a course for civil engineering students might engage with anthropology around solving the problem of reliable clean water in a remote community.
- *Community Engagement*: An interdisciplinary course could bring students from different learning areas together to contribute to the community, such as a partnership between kinesiology, special education, and landscape design to create a neighborhood playground suitable for special needs children.
- *Wicked Problem*: A course may involve a genuine and relevant problem or question for which there is as yet no clear solution. Examples include:
  - Social issues such as homelessness, poverty, domestic violence, or gender inequities.
  - Problems in the sciences such as climate change or the impact of technology on a natural resource such as oil pipelines, irrigation, or hydroelectric power.
  - Aspects of health and wellness like anorexia or obesity, physical fitness, or heart disease.

    Humanity is vexed with many such "wicked problems" in need of solutions, and any of these can serve as the driving force behind an interdisciplinary course.

Virtually any pairing or purpose is possible, but it should always be strategic, goal-driven, and demonstrate a need for each of the partnering fields. The course

213

under development need not necessarily be *about* the central topic (big idea); rather, the topic provides the unifying idea that brings cohesion to disparate learning areas and provides the purpose for engaging in interdisciplinary thinking. Each of the disciplines involved in the course should be important to consideration of the topic, and it should be evident that interdisciplinary study of the topic will provide greater insight and understanding than taking a monodisciplinary approach.

A course intended for first- or second-year students should account for the fact that these students are not prepared to engage in deep interdisciplinarity because they haven't yet formed a cognitive map of any particular discipline. Such a course should strive, instead, to introduce students to basic interdisciplinary thinking. Courses intended for third- or fourth-year undergraduates or graduate students could delve more deeply into interdisciplinarity because participants have begun to master one of the disciplines and are prepared to bring this knowledge to their engagement with the skills and knowledge of the partnering discipline(s). This would be required for highly technical pairings such as architecture and engineering, robotics and medicine, or computer science and cognitive/behavioral psychology.

Having determined the basic nature of the course, your next step is to work with your partner to create a detailed plan of instruction, fleshing out the course concept with a completed syllabus and all related documentation and materials, just as we've discussed in the preceding chapters. However, the outcomes and objectives must be compatible with all involved disciplines, and they should also include specific interdisciplinary learning goals such as:

- Enabling students to produce interdisciplinary work
- Ensuring that students learn how to critically synthesize and evaluate knowledge across disciplinary boundaries
- Leading students to understand the relationship of disciplinary knowledge to interdisciplinary inquiry

Courses involving students who have developed fluency in one discipline but are less familiar with the other need special consideration. Instructors should provide direct instruction in the academic discourse of the fields included in the course, especially key terms and ways of understanding the world. All students should receive direct instruction in methods of interdisciplinary inquiry, including specific structures and operations for synthesis, translation, accommodation, communication, and collaboration within the course. The course plan itself should demonstrate multiple perspectives and ways of knowing/understanding the central topic of the course.

Collaborative and interdisciplinary courses create valuable opportunities for students to develop higher-order thinking skills such as

- Metacognition: awareness of one's own thinking processes
- Procedural knowledge: analysis and application of two or more concepts
- Comprehension: the process by which individuals form new knowledge
- Creativity: divergent and convergent thinking to produce new ideas
- Insight: a sudden and unexpected solution to a problem
- Intelligence: multidimensional linguistic-verbal, logical-mathematical, spatial, musical, bodily-kinesthetic, interpersonal, intrapersonal abilities that influence one's approach to thinking and problem solving
- Problem solving: requires the synthesis or application of the other processes above
- Critical thinking: includes analysis, inference, interpretation, explanation, and self-regulation

Instructors should ensure that the syllabus clearly explains all requirements, especially assessment expectations and grading criteria. Students must know:

- What am I expected to do?
- Which skills do I need to do this?
- How am I expected to apply these skills?
- What will the instructor(s) deem to be high-quality work across both disciplines?
- To whom do I go with questions or concerns?
- How will my work will be assessed, and by whom?

A course with an equal emphasis on two disciplines should take into account that upper level, or graduate students will probably have an idea of the norms of one discipline but not the other. For example, biology majors know what good work in biology looks like. Biology students taking a co-taught course combining biology and sociology, such as an examination of the social impact of genetically modified organisms, would be unfamiliar with expectations for producing high-quality work in sociology. If students from both biology and sociology will enroll in the same section of the course, then both disciplines will require equal levels of exposition so that all students can be successful.

Partners should take care to balance the course between both disciplines. A pairing such as chemistry and graphic design in which students learn how to create digital models of chemical data should not be overtly skewed toward either discipline, taking care to avoid student perception of the course as either "too science-y" or "too arts-y," for example. The course's design should also include support systems for students who are hesitant to learn outside of the fields in which they're most conversant. Instructors must plan how to encourage students' willingness to venture into unfamiliar academic territory.

PROPOSAL

A well-designed plan of instruction is crucial for every course. New courses usually require administrative and committee approval before becoming reality, and courses that diverge from the norm require even more explanation than usual. A thorough proposal that includes all information needed to bring the course to life will have a greater chance of success:

- Budget, including possible supplementary funding through grants, donations, partnerships, or sponsorships
- Anticipated student enrollment
- Required materials and equipment
- Specific considerations for space in which to meet
- Technological requirements
- Community partners and guest speakers
- Transportation to field-based activities
- Displacement of standard teaching assignments
- Other factors specific to the given course

Both instructors usually want to receive full credit for their work, so their plan should demonstrate that both will actively teach for the entirety of each class period. With linked courses, this isn't a problem since each instructor teaches a regularly scheduled class alone. If the two instructors want to teach the same class at the same time, one option would be for each professor to prepare a 45-minute lesson for every class period and teach it twice, switching groups of students halfway through the class. This structure requires either two classrooms located in the same building or a space large enough to accommodate two groups that can also to meet jointly when desired. Alternatively, the two instructors may have to share a single teaching assignment, each receiving half credit unless enrollment numbers are sufficient to support a full section when cross-listed.

Not all interdisciplinary courses need special accommodations in terms of space to meet, materials, equipment, funding, or other resources. For those that do, however, it is important that you assess the availability of these things within your institution and inform your administrators of these factors in your proposal. A working knowledge of the applicable policies, procedures, or protocols necessary for you to launch the course within the existing organizational system is also helpful.

To take a course, students must be able to register for it. One way to accomplish this is cross-listing, whereby students from each disciplinary area register under separate course numbers and/or titles, but meet in the same place at the same time. Soliciting the cooperation of the registrar, departmental administrators, and others who must grant the necessary approvals makes this process much easier. You'll also need to generate positive publicity for the new course so that students know it exists and want to sign up. Finally, interested students must be able to fit the course into their schedules. If your interdisciplinary course meets at the same time as a course required for graduation in one of your targeted majors, students can't enroll no matter how interested they may be.

The Power of a Plan: Instead of asking, "How can we make this happen?" a well-developed plan and proposal allows faculty partners to approach their administrators proactively, saying, "This is how we want to make our course a reality. Here's what we've already worked out and this is what we need from you." A concrete plan will almost always have a greater likelihood of approval than a great idea accompanied by no plan at all, especially if that idea requires extraordinary effort by the administrator.

Since a collaborative or interdisciplinary course uses different instructional methods than usual, its assessment should also take some atypical factors into account, since we also want to know what our students learned about our interdisciplinary objectives.

- As we discussed in Chapter 4, formative evaluation can include a pre-course survey that assesses students' prior knowledge and attitudes. A student survey instrument utilizing open-ended questions could be completed as the first homework assignment of the course. The instructors would collect these responses and analyze them to determine students' misconceptions, knowledge deficits, and so on, adjusting the plan of instruction to address the findings. Questions could include
  – What is the purpose of this class?
  – How does each of the disciplinary areas contribute to this purpose?
  – What benefits would interdisciplinarity provide?
  – Why should we participate in interdisciplinary study?
  – How will an interdisciplinary approach contribute to the purpose of this class?
  – How will we actually do interdisciplinary work?

Repeating the survey at the end of the semester, then returning students' first papers and leading a side-by-side comparison allows everyone to see how much they have learned.

- Summative evaluation of interdisciplinary objectives can take place in an end-of-course assessment, asking students to respond to statements such as the following true/false items:
  – I learned to think in new ways.
  – I discovered new perspectives or ways of knowing.
  – I made connections between multiple disciplines.

217

- I used multiple disciplines to gain a deeper understanding of an issue.
- I understand what interdisciplinary inquiry is.
- I can conduct interdisciplinary inquiry.
- I can integrate, balance, and synthesize different perspectives.

These assessment mechanisms can become part of action research, which is a valuable professional tool for purposeful and continuous improvement of pedagogical practice. Many faculty members take to this approach quite naturally, but others might view the tasks of collecting data and implementing formative assessment to be challenging, unnecessary, or troublesome. However, bearing in mind that the goal is to achieve sustainability for our efforts, engaging in action research can yield a better educational product and help to ensure that the course will continue to be offered on a regular basis.

IMPEDIMENTS TO INTERDISCIPLINARITY

No matter how thoughtful and thorough our planning, institutional structures can subvert the best ideas and most laudable intentions. Some of the most significant impediments may come from our own colleagues and administrators, who may be wary of courses that they perceive as trivializing or diluting their subject area. If we hope to include these experts in our collaborations, we must be especially persuasive. Here, too, we see another benefit of developing a comprehensive proposal for an interdisciplinary course because you'll have well-thought-out arguments at the ready. Conversely, faculty members who are most interested in interdisciplinarity might not possess sufficient expertise in the partnering field to provide the depth of knowledge necessary to foster genuine learning, so choosing one's collaborators judiciously is important to the success of the course you'd like to teach.

Our departmental colleagues may raise objections to our planned course if they perceive it as having a negative impact either personally or professionally, even when these individuals are uninvolved in the course itself. For instance, if teaching the new course means that you are no longer available to teach a course for which you were formerly responsible, your administrator will have to shift this task into someone else's workload. Or faculty colleagues may simply oppose the very idea of interdisciplinarity on principle, preferring that the department maintain a traditional monodisciplinary approach in all of its curricular offerings. This is why it's important to garner the support of your departmental administrators because they can help you to minimize the potential for instigating resentment or fostering internal disagreements among your colleagues.

Teaching interdisciplinary courses may require special considerations during performance reviews or evaluation for retention, promotion, or tenure because educational systems aren't always equipped to handle professional activities that diverge from expected norms. If you and your partner have conducted an environment analysis, you can identify precedent that allows you to build your case and to suggest alternative means of assessment that your committee members may find useful.

FLEXIBILITY AND RESILIENCE

Everyone involved in a new venture must remain flexible, so our work isn't derailed by the first roadblock along the way. A comprehensive plan is a crucial first step, but it cannot be rigid, or a single challenge might put an end to the project. Rather, adopting a resilient outlook and being able to engage in creative problem solving when the unexpected inevitably occurs will help you to launch your interdisciplinary course successfully.

Innovation is rarely easy. For change to occur within tradition-bound institutions dependent upon longstanding policies and procedures, we must have an aptitude for perseverance and an advanced ability to take challenges in stride. Preparing for the challenge by taking a practical, deliberate, yet adaptable approach to your interdisciplinary or collaborative course will increase your chances of producing a high-quality educational product that has the potential be of significant benefit to a wide range of students.

WHAT WE CAN ACCOMPLISH

Collaboration is challenging, but it's also very rewarding. Those who have engaged in successful collaborations point to numerous intangible or unforeseen benefits, including the growth of professional relationships with colleagues whom they might not otherwise have had the opportunity to work, and the intrinsic rewards of working together toward a common goal. They report being energized by the excellent learning that took place during these courses and by students' positive feedback. Perhaps someday all of our institutions will have systems in place to accommodate interdisciplinary collaborations. But by operating within existing structures and beginning to collaborate before comprehensive transformation becomes a reality, we act as change agents in the evolution of higher education, one course at a time.

The phrase "the landscape of higher education" is a metaphor, invoking the concept of differing geographical features. All topography is not the same—that's why the world needs roads and bridges. Interdisciplinary curricula connect the uneven terrain between previously siloed disciplines. Our own collaborations' chances of success are strengthened by engaging in careful planning that takes potential pitfalls into account before they become insurmountable obstacles. This proactive and pragmatic approach to working within existing structures can increase our chances for success.

219

Identify $\longrightarrow$	Ideate
Why should you devote so much effort into your planning for interdisciplinary collaboration? When we work with colleagues across academic fields, we don't always take our essential differences in ontologies, epistemologies, and departmental norms into account. Taking a systematic and deliberate approach to planning for collaboration helps increase the likelihood that our partnerships will be successful and sustainable.	How can you begin to work toward collaborative relationships alongside colleagues with whom you don't usually work? The tools in this chapter can help to anticipate potential pitfalls that commonly derail our best intentions. Clear communication between partners that avoids assumptions based on our own disciplinary norms is essential, as is creating a comprehensive plan for the course we intend to teach together so that our administrators can more easily grant their approval to our proposal.
Iterate $\longleftarrow$	Implement
When we teach the course, we can take advantage of the opportunity it presents for action research that crosses established boundaries, not only working toward future refinement of the course, but enhancing our own professionalism and disciplinary accomplishment through our collaborative venture.	What else should we remember as we prepare to teach together? Balance between the partnering disciplines is crucial, as is flexibility and a willingness to remain open-minded. More than this, however, we must also be thorough in addressing technical aspects of our collaboration such as how the course will be listed, how credit hour/contact hour discrepancies will be reconciled, and a specific plan for how, where, and when the course will take place.

FIGURE 9.1 Chapter 9 Design Connection

Remember:

- Collaborations between colleagues from differing academic fields not only build professional relationships, but they also provide students with learning experiences that align with the inherent interdisciplinarity of the 21st century economy.
- The keys to successful collaboration between instructors from different disciplines are
  a. Transparency
  b. Clear communication
  c. Advance consideration of all details of the proposed course, including differences in the partnering faculty members' contact hours, credit hours, and professional obligations
  d. Development of a comprehensive plan for presentation to upper administration

220

Notes

[1] Much of this chapter is based on the research I conducted during the Mellon Research Project at the University of Michigan, a study of arts integration at research universities, during which I interviewed more than 900 individuals at over 40 institutions of higher learning, giving me an extraordinarily broad knowledge base regarding present practices in collaborative teaching across virtually all disciplinary combinations.

[2] Crow, M. M., and Dabars, W. (2017). Interdisciplinarity and the institutional context of knowledge in the American Research University. In R. Frodeman, J. T. Klein, and R.C.S. Pacheco (eds.), *The Oxford Handbook of Interdisciplinarity*, 2nd ed. Oxford: Oxford University Press, 475.

[3] Ibid., 472.

[4] Boix, M.V. (2017). Interdisciplinary learning: A cognitive-epistemological foundation. In R. Frodeman, J.T. Klein, and R.C.S. Pacheco (eds.), *The Oxford Handbook of Interdisciplinarity*, 2nd ed. Oxford: Oxford University Press, 263–264.

[5] Bachrach, N., Washut Heck, T., and Dahlberg, K. (March 2008). Co-teaching in higher education. *Journal of College Teaching & Learning*, 5(8), 9–16.

[6] For a thorough explanation of this approach, see Soven, M., Lehr, D., Naynaha, S., and Olson, W. (eds.) (2013). *Linked Courses for General Education and Integrative Learning: A Guide for Faculty and Administrators*. Sterling, VA: Stylus Publishing.

[7] Turner, S. (2017). Knowledge formations: An analytic framework. In R. Frodeman, J. Thompson Klein, and R.C.S. Pacheco (eds.), *The Oxford Handbook of Interdisciplinarity*, 2nd ed. Oxford: Oxford University Press, 9.

[8] U.S. Department of Education, International Affairs Office. (February 2008). *Structure of the U.S. Education System: Credit systems*. https://www2.ed.gov/about/offices/list/ous/international/usnei/us/credits.doc

[9] Crow and Dabras (2017), 482.

Chapter 10

Meeting 21st Century Challenges

Synthesis and Application

CHAPTER SUMMARY

- The Future of Higher Education
- Reflection
- Building Your Syllabus
- Your Turn: Build Your Syllabus

THE FUTURE OF HIGHER EDUCATION

The work of course planning comes to an end when we bring everything together in our syllabus. This must include departmental, college, or university requirements, but you'll also need to think through how to communicate your personal policies and expectations to your students. This offers an important opportunity to evaluate what we've planned thus far and to consider how we might reach beyond the norm to enhance our students' success and contribute to the future of higher education.

The world has changed dramatically, especially over the past decade, and further change is occurring with startling rapidity. Students face a workplace devoid of the security their parents or grandparents knew. It used to be reasonable to expect that a good education led to a well-paying job, and after 35 or 40 years of service, an adequate pension would secure a comfortable retirement. Instead, our students are more likely than ever to become independent contractors, to hold multiple jobs in their lifetimes, and to make half a dozen or more career changes before they reach retirement age. Furthermore, technological evolution may mean that the field in which they earn their degree could soon become obsolete, or their positions may be replaced by automation or outsourcing. Even more than the knowledge contained in our courses or a set of specific job-related skills, students need to learn how to be adaptable, how to continue learning throughout their lives, and how to cope with constant change.

The *Chronicle of Higher Education* published a report titled, "2026 the Decade Ahead: the Seismic Shifts Transforming the Future of Higher Education" (Selingo 2016), which is directly relevant to the concepts we've investigated. "Perhaps the biggest unknown in the decade ahead for higher education is an area that has remained largely unchanged for centuries: teaching and learning." This not only encompasses the growing prevalence of online learning, hybrid instruction, or proliferation of technology in the classroom. The structures of higher education itself are evolving, such as increasing interest in competency-based education, self-paced degree programs, digital badging, or the concept of a "university for life" in which students can enter and exit coursework at will as they work from introductory courses through graduate study.

These trends don't immediately affect us as individuals, but we should not ignore the changing reality around us. It is no longer enough to teach our subjects—we must teach our *students* and prepare them for the professional practice of our disciplines in a workplace that will not remain the same over their entire adult lives. To accomplish this goal, we need to address three key areas within every course we teach: the liberal arts, entrepreneurship, and career development, each tailored to the particular norms and practices of our academic disciplines.

Meeting this goal need not be a burden, nor should it be a disconnected "add-on" to your planned course. Your instruction can incorporate these areas naturally through examples, allusions, illustrations, and sharing your own experiences. We don't need to design an entire unit of study around "the liberal arts and [name of discipline]," or to remodel your entire course plan around the theme of entrepreneurship. Instead, these ideas should remain aspects of what you already teach, making overt connections as often as possible that tether your instruction to students' learning in the liberal arts, their potential entrepreneurial practice within your discipline, or their future careers.

The Liberal Arts

Businesses such as Cisco, IBM, and IDEO seek to hire graduates who possess the "21st Century Skills" of collaboration, teamwork, creativity, imagination, critical thinking, and problem solving in addition to disciplinary expertise acquired through focused study.[1] Both deep knowledge of a particular field or industry and broadly applicable cognitive, intrapersonal, and interpersonal skills are highly desirable in new hires. These are the very attributes that are taught in the liberal arts and humanities. Most universities have required students to take such coursework among their general education requirements for generations, based on an enduring belief in their value. According to Kathleen Haney of the University of Houston,

Training in the liberal arts produced a free and thoughtful person who could read anything written, understand anything spoken, and say whatever (s)he wanted to say. Liberal education aimed to produce persons who can think symbolically and continue to educate themselves when their university days were over. The liberally educated person was the emancipated human being who could possess his unique human nature fully.[2]

Similarly, Harvard University's 2013 study titled "Mapping the Future" examining the state of the humanities within the university contained a particularly apropos description of these fields' lasting value as providers of "transferable competencies" or "the tools to describe [human] experience, to evaluate it, to imagine it, and then to transform it."[3]

No academic discipline or professional field is completely devoid of the liberal arts and humanities because our disciplines are all essentially human.[4] To discover the ways that these fields affect your discipline, you might find it helpful to ask yourself the following questions to investigate the impact of these fields and consider how they might intersect with the content of the course you're developing. The more connections you can build, the more you enhance your students' understanding of your course content and their potential for career success.

History: Providing a historical context for your discipline and an explanation of its impact on our world helps students to comprehend your field, and therefore your course content, more effectively.

- How has your discipline been shaped by human history?
- How has its history affected human life?

Philosophy: Whether or not we actively study our disciplinary philosophies, they undergird our work nonetheless. Making the philosophical basis of your discipline explicit for students supports their acquisition of disciplinary knowledge, especially for those who lack prior knowledge in your field.

- What are the ontologies and epistemologies that define your discipline?
- How do these affect the ways in which practitioners in your discipline view the world and their impact upon it?

Literature/Media: The importance of understanding the types of literature and media common to your discipline is self-evident. It is also vital to know how your discipline is portrayed in literature and media, which helps you to identify underlying biases and to deconstruct them for your students.

- What tropes or stereotypes can we identify? (i.e., the absent-minded philosopher, the moody artist, the nerdy mathematician)

- How does this portrayal affect practitioners today?
- How has your discipline affected the world as expressed in literature or media?

Writing: Even students who are not majoring in your discipline can benefit from learning how to understand the written language of different professional arenas.

- What are the standards and practices for written communication in your field?
- How will you instruct your students in the forms of written communication expected?

Rhetoric: The ability to use spoken language effectively and to communicate ideas clearly is essential to all fields of human endeavor.

- How does this take place within the confines of your discipline?
- How should your students meet those expectations to demonstrate proficiency?

World Cultures and Languages: Students have historically been required to learn a language other than English in the belief that it broadens their perspective on the world as well as enhancing their understanding of their own language and culture. Introduction to this idea within a particular disciplinary context strengthens their learning by providing a fresh perspective and underscoring its real-world applicability. Understanding of the world around us is all the more important in an increasingly global society.

- With which other cultures and languages does your discipline primarily intersect?
- How has this affected your field? How is it likely to change moving into the 21st century?

Ethics and Religious Studies: Religion has a tremendous impact on human life, motivating our deepest passions and subsequent actions whether we associate ourselves with a particular set of beliefs or consider ourselves to be nonreligious, atheistic, or agnostic. Gaining a broad understanding of world religions helps students to become better global citizens, but this study also intersects with our particular disciplinary fields.

- What are the ethical standards of your discipline?
- How is your field affected by the religious beliefs of the individuals working in or served by this discipline?

225

Political Science: Aristotle famously said that "man is a political animal" because human beings are endowed with the power of speech and reasoning, having a sense of what is good and evil, just and unjust.[5] Building your students' knowledge of the ways in which government, legislation, or political activity affect your discipline will allow them to gain a deeper understanding.

- How has political activity manifested historically with regard to your discipline?
- How does it manifest contemporaneously?

Once you've answered each of the questions above, determine where you will incorporate each category into your course. Here are a few examples:

- One of your planned lectures can include additional content connecting to disciplinary ethics.
- A writing assignment could be revised to include an oral presentation giving students the opportunity to engage in the rhetoric of your discipline.
- Begin a class period with a short discussion about stereotypes surrounding your discipline as seen in some short clips you gather from literary or media sources.
- Ask students to find and read a current article about legislation or other political action and its impact on your discipline, then share a brief summary and reflection with the class.
- Require students to conduct case studies about the impact or action of your discipline in global settings, sharing their findings through a brief presentation.

None of these activities needs to be particularly time consuming unless you choose to make them so, but each aspect of the liberal arts should be overtly acknowledged at some point in the course to optimize our students' learning.

Entrepreneurship

The changing face of the workplace has fostered a growing "gig economy" where individuals move from one temporary work assignment (or gig) to another, rather than holding a single full-time position. A study by Intuit predicted that by 2020, 40% of American workers would be independent contractors,[6] and in some fields, this figure is 75% or even higher. This trend emphasizes the necessity of preparing students in all fields for the very real possibility that they will be self-employed at some point in their lives. Teaching entrepreneurial skills relevant to our disciplinary context acknowledges the changing landscape outside of the university and gives our students the tools they need to forge their own paths after graduation without having to settle for menial employment outside the fields in which they earned their degrees.

Much of entrepreneurship involves solving problems, so providing students with opportunities to engage in problem-based learning helps them to sharpen the skills necessary to meet workplace challenges. Furthermore, as we discussed in the previous chapters, students learn best when we move away from our traditional reliance on passive listening, reading, and writing and involve them in classroom experiences where they have to apply their learning to engaging problems, often by cooperating with their peers. Professional engagement in many fields is entirely about solving problems using teamwork: How can we bring more customers into our store? How can we raise money to put a new roof on our leaking facility? How can we make payroll when our funding was cut by the state legislature? Problem-based learning is not only more engaging for students, but better prepares them for whatever workplace they'll encounter, whether as an entrepreneur, an employee, or an administrator.

At its heart, entrepreneurship is about identifying opportunity and responding to it productively. Entrepreneurial efforts can be large or small, for-profit or nonprofit, limited in duration or ongoing. Ventures may be of benefit to only the entrepreneur or can serve a broad audience. If a campus acapella group holds a bake sale to raise money for a local food pantry, they engage in entrepreneurship just as much as students who invent the next Facebook or Snapchat and grow it to global proportions.

The stages of the entrepreneurial process are illustrated in Figure 10.1.

I am by no means suggesting that every course should teach students the entire entrepreneurial process. Most instructors are not entrepreneurs themselves and would be unqualified to incorporate this information as thoroughly or accurately as necessary to provide students with a high-quality educational experience.

Nevertheless, every academic area intersects with entrepreneurship on some level. Engaging in a bit of reflective assessment of your own field will help you

FIGURE 10.1 Entrepreneurial Process Flow Chart

to identify where such opportunities exist. Because this might not be an area with which you already possess a great deal of familiarity, some research might help you to answer the following questions. You could begin by looking at publications geared toward business such as Forbes.com, Inc.com, or Entrepreneur.com, searching their extensive databases for stories about entrepreneurial activity related to your academic area.

- Who are the leading entrepreneurs in your field?
- What are they doing?
- How can I find additional information about this topic?

After you've established this baseline understanding, evaluate the prevalence of entrepreneurial activity in your field:

- Do most practitioners have full-time jobs with a single employer for their entire careers?
- Are there opportunities to supplement one's income with entrepreneurial activities such as tutoring or consulting?
- Do most disciplinary practitioners work independently, making entrepreneurial skills a necessity for work in this field?

Even fields that can boast impressive employment statistics can also foster opportunities for entrepreneurship. Registered nurses, for example, experience only a 1.5% unemployment rate and earn an average median salary of $67,490,[7] yet entrepreneurial options still exist for visiting nurses, temporary or contract-based nurses, or nurses who choose to work in nontraditional areas of practice or wish to set their own schedules. Conversely, workers in the entertainment industry rarely hold permanent full-time positions, moving from one limited-term project to another. Clearly, this differs by field, so you'll need to investigate the opportunities for entrepreneurship that are most commonly associated with your discipline.

The following list is not exhaustive, but intended to stimulate your thinking as to how your field may intersect with opportunities for entrepreneurship.

- Independent research
  - A chemist participates in a limited-term study of the municipal water system, checking for hazardous materials that may be present in the city's drinking water
  - An anthropologist contracts with a government agency to study a historical site
  - An expert in world languages collaborates with an author who is writing a book about the impact of language on global commerce

- Teaching/tutoring
  - A high school English teacher tutors students after school to prepare them for the SAT
  - Members of a civic orchestra offer after-school music lessons to elementary students
  - A biologist works with a summer camp, helping to design curriculum to teach young children about the natural world
- Consulting
  - An accountant consults with a business to improve its financial efficiency
  - An engineer advises an architect who is designing a building for a hurricane-prone area
  - A historian works with a motion picture company that is producing a film set during the historical era in which the historian possesses expert knowledge, ensuring that the film's portrayal is accurate
- Development of business opportunities offering new products or services
  - A biochemist researches and develops an innovative line of haircare products[8]
  - A computer engineer develops a new gaming app for mobile devices
  - A fashion designer launches a product line featuring wearable technology
- Founding a social or nonprofit organization
  - A nurse launches an organization that provides affordable in-home health care for the elderly
  - A structural engineer designs a portable shelter that can inexpensively provide people living in refugee camps with greater safety and security than tents
  - A speech and language pathologist creates a game that helps parents of children with Autism Spectrum Disorders develop their language proficiency
- Freelance work
  - A sociologist is hired to study data gathered by a firm conducting political polls prior to an election
  - A photographer contracts with a social service agency to provide visual documentation of a persistent problem such as hunger, homelessness, or crime
  - A philosopher works with a large teaching hospital to assist the organization in developing a comprehensive policy statement regarding medical ethics

The next step is to incorporate this knowledge into the course you're teaching, determining natural points at which such discussion would be relevant and beneficial, enhancing students' learning of course content and stimulating their ideas about how they might approach future job prospects.

- Which of your planned lectures could include additional content about entrepreneurial activity in your field?
- Could you include an activity in which students brainstorm entrepreneurial ideas related to your subject?
- Could you invite a guest speaker to share their story of engaging in a successful entrepreneurial venture in your field?
- Could students conduct research into disciplinary entrepreneurship as part of a course requirement? Taking this a step further, could they actually engage in entrepreneurship within your discipline?

As we discussed earlier regarding the liberal arts, including entrepreneurship in your course need not dominate your teaching. Students should, however, be informed of all possibilities for future employment in your field, especially if this is the norm rather than an occasional exception.

Professional and Career Development

We continue to uphold a belief that earning a college degree is worthwhile for its own sake, preparing students to be intelligent, productive members of society. However, higher educational institutions at all levels are under pressure to link those degrees to students' future employment over and above the intrinsic value of earning an education. The financial return on investment for a college degree has grown significantly over the past 30 years. According to Selingo (2016), "in 1983, the college wage premium was 42 percent. Today, it surpasses 80 percent." In other words, a college graduate will likely earn 80% more over the course of a lifetime than someone who did not earn a degree. Such statistics are used to justify the substantial expense of a college education, especially as the cost of a degree has risen dramatically over the past 40 years. In 1975, tuition, room, and board at a public 4-year institution were just $7,833 per year (in adjusted 2015 dollars). By 2015, this number rose to $19,548 per year, or nearly $80,000 for a complete 4-year degree. At a private nonprofit institution this can top $43,000 per year, or more than $172,000 for a complete bachelor's degree.[9] When a middle-income family incurs debt equal to or greater than the mortgage on their home to send just one child to college, their motivation is probably the hope that it will allow their child to secure professional-level employment rather than a belief in the intrinsic value of the college experience.

Even though increasing numbers of students are entering higher education than in past generations, far fewer of them actually graduate or find positions in the field they studied.

Only a little more than 50 percent of American students who enter college leave with a bachelor's degree. Student success has been uneven, particularly among different socioeconomic groups that haven't traditionally attended college. Of those who do graduate, nearly 50 percent find themselves underemployed in jobs that don't require a degree.

(Selingo, 2016)

Think about this: If half of the students who enter college don't finish, and half of those who graduate are underemployed, that's only a 25% success rate—a statistic that should disturb everyone who works in higher education. The federal government instituted a data tool in 2015 to calculate the return on investment (ROI) of a college degree, called the College Scorecard. This and other rankings of higher educational institutions depend at least in part on graduates' attainment of gainful employment in the field in which they majored, featuring metrics comparing the cost of tuition to graduates' projected earnings.

Placing an economic premium on higher education frustrates and angers faculty and administrators, who continue to believe that a college education should be valued only for its own sake, since earning a degree doesn't just prepare a student for a career, but to be a better citizen and a better person. However, we ignore these external demands at our own peril, risking the future of our programs if we are unwilling to adjust our teaching to meet changing societal expectations. Why should a student choose to major in *any* field that does not offer evidence it will adequately prepare someone for a career? Whether or not we educators know that students' educational experiences in our classrooms are intrinsically valuable, it is difficult for students or parents to understand how they can be worth the expense when they cannot see how our course offerings will equip a student with the means to earn a living. Fields widely believed to lead to viable careers continue to grow, while those perceived as underperforming in this area diminished, especially as the result of increasing public criticism. For example, the governors of several states have been vocal opponents of the liberal arts.

- Florida Governor Rick Scott: "Do you want to use your tax money to educate more people who can't get jobs in anthropology? I don't."[10]
- North Carolina Governor Patrick McCrory: "I just instructed my staff yesterday to go ahead and develop legislation which would change the basic formula in how education money is given out to our universities and our community colleges. It's not based on butts in seats but on how many of those butts can get jobs."[11]
- Kentucky Governor Matt Bevin, (regarding his 2016 budget), "There will be more incentives to electrical engineers than French literature majors. There just will. All the people in the world that want to study

French literature can do so; they are just not going to be subsidized by the taxpayer."[12]

Governors in Texas, Wisconsin, and Illinois have also questioned the value of liberal arts and humanities at public colleges and universities, emphasizing an agenda of reduced state funding, lower tuition prices, increased vocational training, and performance-based pay for faculty members, tying state funding to students' job placement in "high-demand" fields, and increasing criticism of flagship institutions.[13] In particular, these politicians portray the liberal arts as a frivolous luxury that taxpayers should not be expected to support. Even former presidential candidate Senator Marco Rubio called for "more welders and fewer philosophers" in one of the Republican presidential debates leading up to the 2016 election,[14] further illustrating the disdain in which these fields are held because of this poor job placement record.

The most difficult pill for many educators to swallow in this regard is one of theory rather than practice: We believe that the learning taking place in our classrooms should be valued for itself alone, apart from potential applicability to a given career. Nevertheless, our students, their parents, and society at large no longer share this view. Regardless of our personal feelings, the focus of higher education today places greater emphasis on career preparation than the intrinsic value of knowledge. Therefore, we cannot only teach our students the theory and practices of a given academic discipline—we must also teach them *why* this learning is important and *how to apply it* in a practical setting. Students rarely grasp the intrinsic value of their learning intuitively, nor do they possess the ability to enact it in other settings unless we overtly teach them how to do so. This means we must adapt our instructional practices to provide our students with explicit instruction linking the theory of our disciplines to practical application of the transferable competencies we impart.

Value Proposition Design

To design an effective solution to the conundrum we face regarding the value of the education we offer to our students, we might look for inspiration to the idea of Value Proposition Design (see Figure 10.2).[15] Here, an entrepreneur builds a business model around three aspects of a customer profile: what customers are trying to achieve, the negative outcomes they face, and the positive outcomes they want. The Value Map addresses these aspects: a product or service that will help customers to achieve their goals, a means of alleviating a negative outcome, and a means of creating a positive outcome. We could re-envision this for higher education something like this, with the red sections on the left indicating parents' and students needs and expectations, and the blue sections on the right indicating what we can do as educators to address these important factors.

232

Graduates' career preparation	Includes preparation for the workplace in every course
Return on investment	Design educational experiences that meet students' needs and goals
Enjoying a fulfilling adult life	Emphasize the transferable competencies of a Liberal Arts Education

FIGURE 10.2 Value Proposition Design for Higher Education

Supporting students' career preparation and professional development must align with our program outcomes and course objectives along with our other teaching, assignments, and assessments. Of course, there is substantial merit in our disciplines for their own sake and for student learning in/through/with/about these disciplines, but we cannot ignore the fact that our students enrolled in our programs because they want a career they could not otherwise attain without the degree they are pursuing. If our teaching imparts no knowledge or skills that will be of demonstrable value to students after graduation, then we have done them a serious injustice. Courses designed for majors should feature the most intensive career connections, but even general education or elective courses can introduce students to these career fields or provide transferrable competencies that will benefit all students.

Practical Application

Beyond explicit connections to the liberal arts and entrepreneurship, additional opportunities exist in building connections to the professional workplace, especially for those students who major in our disciplines. Fortunately, many strategies can assist us in accomplishing this goal.

Establish industry partnerships: Building relationships with partners outside of higher education simultaneously serves many purposes. It allows students to gain experience in real-world settings, translating theory into practical engagement. It provides networking opportunities for students, potentially enhancing their career prospects. Industry partners might provide material resources or funding for classroom projects. Of all the institutions I've studied, MIT serves as the penultimate example of partnerships with industry, with corporate and nonprofit organizations aligned with programs, centers, institutes, and all manner of other organizational structures across the university. Students continuously relate their studies to real-world and professional contexts. I have used this strategy in my own teaching, albeit at a much smaller scale than MIT, forging partnerships with

233

local organizations so that my students can experience hands-on involvement in an authentic professional context.

To establish these productive relationships, only a few simple steps are necessary:

- Conduct an investigation into local businesses or organizations with which you might partner.
- Contact those organizations and begin discussions about establishing a working relationship that would be advantageous to both the organization and to your students. (I strongly recommend making a telephone call rather than sending an email. It's a more personal touch that tends to yield more positive results.)
- Examine the courses you teach and determine where assignments or projects could involve this partner organization.

The first time I taught my Marketing and Promotions course, the main project required students to select a nonprofit organization, conduct some online research, and design a hypothetical marketing strategy for the organization. The next semester, we partnered with a local nonprofit organization for which students designed and implemented a targeted social media marketing campaign. The organization experienced an upswing in their income and students mobilized their classroom learning within an authentic workplace setting, grounding the abstract and theoretical knowledge they gained in readings and lectures in practical experience. Furthermore, they forged relationships with individuals in this organization and gained workplace experience, beginning to build a professional network and deepening their understanding of the field.

Invite guest speakers: No matter how engaging a lecturer you are, guest speakers provide a breath of fresh air in a classroom. None of us can be an expert on everything our students need to learn. For instance, I might invite a social entrepreneur to explain her recent social media campaign that increased donations and gifts to her organization by 15% over the previous year's figures. Although students could have acquired the same information by reading a news release, hearing it directly from the person who was responsible for this improvement is a much more powerful learning experience.

- Seek out individuals who have stories to tell or experiences to share that would be applicable to the topics you're teaching and/or to students' overall learning related to both your course and their eventual professional engagement.
- Invite those speakers to come to your class. Here, too, I've found that a personal phone call is much more likely to garner good results than an email. We all know that people are busy and you might have to call more

than once, or you might leave a voicemail message and follow up with an email. The personal touch of the direct telephone call really does make a difference. Furthermore, you don't have to limit these invitations to potential speakers who live locally, although individuals who work for the organizations with which you've established partnerships are a great resource. Technology allows us to host virtual guests from nearly anywhere in the world.

- Guest speakers can enhance student learning beyond a single classroom. We might invite someone to present a talk to faculty and students from an entire department or program. These events can also extend to the whole university and the surrounding community. The most powerful example I've seen exists at USC in their Visions and Voices series. Not only do they attract a broad array of diverse and engaging lecturers, presenters, and performers, but students have the opportunity to interact directly with these guests following their presentations. Students from any major can partake in these events, bringing the university's core values to life and strengthening students' educational experience through exposure to inspiring content.

Connect theory and practice in your classroom: It's very difficult for students to retain an understanding of theory without a way to apply it to a real-life situation. Excellent educators maintain a firm connection to their professional discipline outside of an academic context and habitually connect the theoretical environment of the classroom to professional scenarios and examples. This is the purpose of tenured or tenure-track faculty members' obligation to engage in research or creative practice: to bring our ongoing professional engagement into our classrooms and share it with our students. It is also the rationale for hiring adjunct faculty who continue to work full time in a disciplinary setting, expecting that their professional expertise will inform their teaching. *All* of our research, creative practice, and professional engagement should inform our teaching, not exist separately from it.

Furthermore, everyone teaching in higher education has a responsibility to keep abreast of developments in our respective fields, making a habit of reading professional journals and remaining active contributors to our disciplines through membership in professional organizations and other forms of service.

Such ongoing professional engagement is as natural as breathing to many instructors, especially those who work in fields where knowledge changes quickly such as computer engineering, medicine and health sciences. However, faculty members in disciplines that experience less frequent change can find the same expectation to be a greater burden, particularly when their colleagues don't place a premium on continuous professional development. We tend to emulate the cultural norms already present in our workplace, so when our fellow instructors don't actively seek out current professional knowledge, it's likely that we will follow suit.

Unfortunately, I've visited departments where professional knowledge has remained virtually unchanged since senior faculty members earned their terminal degrees. Decades-old habit controls their professional practice and teaching. Worse, they subsequently communicate this outdated knowledge to their students, perpetuating a view that exists only within the narrow confines of their department. This was the very situation I encountered as a graduate student, inspiring the content of my doctoral dissertation as I sought to understand the cognitive dissonance between the theory and practice of the discipline in which I studied.

The same can be observed regarding our knowledge of effective teaching, where tradition can dominate pedagogical practice rather than actual knowledge of best practice. For example, I led a faculty development seminar at the request of a department chair who was concerned that her faculty were using antiquated pedagogical practices that did not align with established educational theory. When I introduced the idea of employing Bloom's Taxonomy of Knowledge to the task of writing course objectives, assignments, and assessments, faculty members from one of the two subdisciplines in attendance denied that Bloom was real and actually insisted that I had simply made it up myself. (Remember, Benjamin Bloom wrote his Taxonomy in the 1950s, but I delivered the presentation in 2014.) They also challenged the veracity of my citations of John Dewey, whose writings were published in the 1930s and remain influential to this day, as we saw in Chapter 2. Their practice had remained completely isolated from these theories, and they had no inkling that other approaches to teaching existed.

This group of professors adamantly resisted making changes to the theories and practices they had assimilated as the norm for their discipline, not only with regard to writing course objectives, but in their entire approach to teaching and learning. By clinging to their histories and traditions, they produced successive generations of scholars who also accepted these practices without question, perpetuating a vicious cycle. Not surprisingly, the subgroup of faculty members who voiced the most opposition to my presentation made no curricular changes, and enrollment in their courses continued to decline to the point that the department chair had to reduce the student credit hour requirement in these courses by 20%. The other subgroup, who were more amenable to making changes to their practice, saw a 70% increase in student credit hour production.

Fortunately, not every department is this extreme. When you are an active contributor to your discipline and you work to keep yourself informed of changing knowledge, you can link your professional engagement, research, or creative practice to your teaching, optimizing your students' learning. Many of us do this through the anecdotes and examples that we share during our lectures, linking stories of our professional experience, information found in our recent reading, new developments we've learned through conference attendance, or other activities that occur outside of our classrooms, all of which help our students connect theory to practice.

We can also accomplish this goal by designing course activities and assignments that utilize some of the teaching strategies from previous chapters, structured to engage students in the current developments or conversations taking place in our fields.

- Gather articles from recent issues of professional publications such as peer-reviewed journals and include them as part of your students' required readings and class discussions.
- Direct students to find an article from a recent issue of a professional publication and complete a short response paper about it.
- Require students to conduct case studies of authentic real-world instances related to your course content, either individually or as a small group, sharing their learning with their peers during class.
- Ask students to interview an industry professional about something you're teaching. (It's helpful to generate a list of individuals whom you know would be willing to assist your students in this task and to provide students with contact information.)

Cognitive neuroscience tells us that intelligence depends on the brain's ability to make connections and to "pull together several different kinds of processing, such as working memory."[16] Knowledge alone is not useful unless we connect it to something we already know. When you share stories of your own experience, students perceive it differently than the abstract theories or facts they gather from their textbook. Stories are personal, so they appeal to different parts of the brain. When students gain experience themselves, it also helps them to build these connections.

Our job as instructors is, of course, to cause our students to learn. This is a complex process governed by the building of connections, or associations, within the brain (emphasis added):

Human memory is fundamentally **associative**, meaning that a new piece of information is remembered better if it can be associated with previously acquired knowledge that is already firmly anchored in memory. The more **personally meaningful** the association, the more effective the encoding and consolidation.[17]

Other Practical Experience: In Chapter 7, we examined several strategies for engaged learning, including service learning, community-based learning, and other practical experiences such as externships, co-op, and volunteer work. These are

MEETING 21ST CENTURY CHALLENGES

not only beneficial for engaged learning, but they more firmly tie the abstract theory of the classroom to practice in the context of professional experience.

Whenever we link knowledge, information, and theory to practical examples and applications, our students simply learn more effectively. And when these connections directly support our students' career preparation, the results are even more powerful.

REFLECTION

Before we move on to the next section and finally build the syllabus for the course we've been planning throughout this book, let's take a moment to review and reflect on what we've accomplished. Many readers probably began this process thinking that they'd pick up a few handy tips on how to write better outcomes and objectives, or maybe learn how to create a better test. I hope that now you can look back and see that you're prepared to put together the best course you've ever taught and to approach your instruction from a position of greater knowledge and expertise.

- You have a more thorough understanding of the educational theories and philosophies underlying your work as an educator.
- You've formulated outcomes aligned with disciplinary standards that shape the educational experiences of the students in your program.
- You've written objectives that align your planned teaching with these outcomes.
- Each of your objectives is paired with an assessment mechanism such as an exam, project, paper or other means of determining whether your students have met your objectives.
- You have a comprehensive plan for your course, with plans for each module, week, and lesson. This plan includes:
  - Writing to learn and learning to write in your discipline
  - Strategies for engaged learning
  - Connections between your discipline and
    - The liberal arts as they are embodied within your academic field
    - Entrepreneurship
    - Career and professional preparation
  - Fostering diversity, equity, and inclusion
- You've acquired a deeper understanding of effective teaching and have considered how this knowledge will apply to the courses you teach.

BUILDING YOUR SYLLABUS

A syllabus is a utilitarian document, serving as both a roadmap of your course and an ongoing resource for your students. It sets out your expectations as an instructor, provides a schedule of assignments, and facilitates the smooth progression of the semester. Your syllabus may change over the duration of the course as your instruction evolves in response to students' needs or other factors. Nevertheless, it often carries the weight of a contract between the students and the instructor, defining what students can expect from you and making your requirements clear to your students.

University syllabi generally include a set of standard components:

Course Identification

- The names of the university and the program, department, department, college, and/or school in which the course is offered
- Course identifiers
  - Call number
  - Title
  - Term
  - Location and time classes will be held
  - Instructor information
    - Name and title
    - Office location[18]
    - Contact information (phone and email address)
    - Office hours
  - Course description (This can be copied from the Academic Catalog, but you may also include additional information if you wish.)
- Required Textbooks and Materials
  - Be specific—use a full citation formatted according to the style guide commonly used within your discipline, including the book's ISBN so that students can search for the book online to find the best price. Let students know if it is acceptable to use an earlier edition of the book, or if the specified edition is absolutely necessary.
  - Materials lists should provide information about where and how to purchase the items you require. You might include links or addresses and phone numbers of suggested vendors, such as an office supply store or the campus bookstore.

None of these items should pose a particular challenge to you as a course designer, but each of them is essential to include in a syllabus because they inform the student about vital information they need to begin the class.

Static Institutional Content

Every syllabus is subject to departmental, college, or university requirements. This usually involves information about such things as

- Disabilities services and/or accommodations for learners with special needs
- Definitions of academic misconduct (plagiarism, etc.) and stated penalties
- Disclaimers about course content or schedule changes
- General institutional policies regarding grading scales, missing or late work, or incomplete grades
- Available student services (libraries, writing center, or other forms of support), including contact information such as web links, physical addresses, phone numbers, or email addresses
- Depending on individual departmental policies, studio and laboratory courses may also include Health and Safety regulations and information about facility use and/or facility rules

Most course designers need to do a little bit of research to find the requirements in these areas. Of course, these will vary by institution, but the good news is that once they become part of your syllabus template, you don't have to keep recreating the verbiage unless the policies change. You should remember to cite the source from which you gathered the information, but most of the time a simple hyperlink to the policy's location on your institution's website will suffice since your syllabus isn't destined for publication in a peer-reviewed journal.

Classroom/Instructor Policies

As professional educators, each of us has a set of expectations for our students regarding their participation, attendance, late work, make-up work, extra credit, and so on. The syllabus is an ideal tool for communicating these policies to your students. It might take some time to commit these to print the first time, but once you've invested the time to do so, you can simply reproduce them on each subsequent syllabus. Furthermore, including written policies in your syllabus reduces potential conflict. When students violate your policy and run into a consequence, such as a point deduction on late work, they have little basis for argument when you can point to the policy statement on the syllabus, reminding them that they were fully informed of this policy on the first day of class and have had it in their possession ever since.

In order to think through these policies, you'll need to consider a number of important questions. Although some instructors combine these into a single classroom policy statement, it's best to break them into separate categories so that your students can access the information they're looking for more easily.

Attendance

- How many times may a student miss your class without penalty?
  - How should a student make up for a missed class?

- What are the college or university's policies about absence due to religious reasons or off-campus activities such as sporting events that might result in a student's absence? (Bear in mind that classroom policy cannot contradict university policy.)
- What is the penalty for exceeding the permitted number of missed classes?
- What constitutes an excused absence?
  - What proof or documentation do you require for an excused absence?
  - What must students do to make up this work? How long do they have to accomplish this?
- What is your policy about tardiness?
  - How many minutes late constitutes being tardy?
  - Do a certain number of tardies add up to an absence? If so, specify.

Participation and Appropriate Behavior

- What constitutes acceptable participation in your course? (Provide a detailed description of what you want your students to do, not just what you don't want them to do.)
- What student behaviors are unacceptable in your classroom?
  - Sleeping
  - Eating, drinking, gum-chewing
  - Use of personal electronics:
    - Texting
    - Audible phone ringers/vibrations/alert tones
    - Answering or making a phone call in class
    - Using an electronic device to access the Internet, play games, or engage in social media during class
    - Use of electronic devices to record your instruction
- What is the penalty for violating your behavior policy?
- What are your expectations for student behavior in a lab, studio, or shared workspace? Note: Many departments publish these guidelines: if so, you need only copy them into the syllabus. However, if your policies differ, you must provide an explanation.
  - Use of shared resources
  - Cleaning up after yourself
  - Removal of personal items or completed projects
  - Safety procedures
  - Hours the workspace is available
  - Whether or not it is permissible for students to bring friends who are not enrolled in the class into the workspace

241

- Civility in the classroom: What are your expectations for interpersonal communication? What are the consequences for violations?
  - Use of profanity
  - Derogatory language
  - Negativity
  - Personal criticism

Student Work Policies

This is likely to be one of the most important portions of your syllabus because it is where you establish your expectations for how you will, and will not, accept your students' work on their assignments and assessments. As we've emphasized throughout this book, every classroom policy should exist to support student learning, not just to make your own job easier. If you cannot articulate a cogent rationale for establishing the policy, you should think twice before instituting it. You should also provide direct instruction in explanation of these policies so that students can connect your expectations to standards of professionalism in your discipline. Admittedly, some classroom policies are truly for our own convenience as instructors, but students deserve at least an explanation of this fact. For instance, asking students to format their documents according to a consistent set of criteria makes them much easier to grade, which is to the students' advantage since we are then able to provide more timely evaluation of their work. It also prepares students to meet external expectations, which is something they're likely to encounter in virtually any workplace.

- Document Formatting
  - Which style guide do you require students to use for written work, if any?
  - What are your expectations document formatting?
    - Margins, font, spacing
    - Acceptable document types (.doc,. docx,. pdf, etc.)
    - Unacceptable document types (make a list)
  - Do you require printed copies or electronic submittals?
  - Are handwritten or manually typed documents acceptable?
- Assignment Submission
  - How must students submit their work to you?
    - Printed copies, in class only
    - Posted to the class web page (include hyperlink to the submission area on the site)
    - Emailed to you (include hyperlink to your email address)
    - If the assignment involves multiple components that will be submitted electronically, do you want a zipped (compressed) folder or posted as separate files?

- Late Work
  - What is your standard policy for the time when students must submit their work?
    - This should be very specific and clearly stated on the syllabus. Ex: "All work must be posted to our course website by 11:59 p.m. EST on the stated due date."
  - Will you accept students' work early?
  - What is the penalty you will impose for late work?
  - What mitigating circumstances will you allow as exceptions to this policy? Examples include:
    - Death of an immediate family member (parent, sibling, child)
    - Military deployment
    - Serious medical or mental health emergency requiring the attention of a health care professional (self, parent, or child)
    - Natural disaster or weather catastrophe (earthquake, tornado, tsunami, hurricane, flood)
  - Will you require documentation of these mitigating circumstances before you waive the point deduction? If so, please specify.
- Make-Up Work
  - Will you allow students to make up for a class period from which they were absent?
  - Provide a clear explanation of your expectations and your rationale for them.
  - For example, if you will allow students to complete an alternative assignment to make up for a missed class period, you'll need to explain exactly what the student must do to meet this requirement such as: "With prior approval by the instructor, students may make up for a missed class period by completing a 3-page précis about an article from one of the following peer-reviewed journals [insert journal titles]."

As we discussed in Chapter 8, students may face personal hardships that can make it difficult for them to submit their work on time, and these don't always fall into the standard categories we allow. In these situations, you'll need to use your best judgment, but I believe it's best to err on the side of the student unless enforcing the penalty is the best lesson the student could learn.

Outcomes, Objectives, Assignments, Assessments, Grades, and Schedules

The most challenging part of syllabus development is formulating the content of your course, but since we've already worked through these essential elements, placing them on the syllabus should now be fairly easy: Simply copy and paste the tables you created into your working document. This makes it very clear to students exactly why they're being asked to do what you require, when they must do it, and how you will evaluate their work.

Take a moment to answer the following questions as you build these elements into your syllabus.

1. Does every outcome align with my knowledge of the professional norms and standards of my discipline and with the requirements of my program, department, college, or school?
2. Does every objective align with my outcomes?
3. Is every objective paired with an appropriate assessment?
4. Have I planned for instruction related to everything that students could do (or fail to do) that may affect their grade in this course and linked these to an objective?
5. Is every activity that carries a point value or grade clearly indicated on the course schedule? Have I included written expectations, due dates, and evaluation criteria for each of these activities?
6. Do the point values for assignments and the planned grading schema align mathematically?
7. Does the course schedule take the institution's academic calendar and my personal schedule into account? (i.e., I need to cancel class during Week 4 because I'll be traveling out of state to present at a professional conference.)
8. Have I made every effort to structure the course in a way that promotes diversity, equity, and inclusion?
9. Have I built writing into the course, as appropriate to my academic field?
10. Have I included connections between my academic discipline and the course's content with the liberal arts, entrepreneurship, and preparation for professional practice?

Student Resources

The last part of a syllabus contains resources students might need during their time in your classroom. These can include:

- Copies of important classroom handouts
- Departmental procedures, policies, or requirements (e.g., safety guidelines for labs or studios; open hours for work areas)
- Specific directions for course assignments
- Guidelines or resources for discussion or critique

- Grading criteria such as rubrics or checklists
- A course bibliography or list of additional recommended readings
- Lists of links to required or recommended websites

When you ensure that all of the materials your students will need are ready to go before the first day of class, you begin teaching from a position of preparedness rather than having to scramble to meet emerging student needs. It also spares you from the aggravation of answering repetitious questions, incessantly reminding students about basic information, or endlessly providing them with duplicate copies of forms you want them to have. If your course has many such resources, you can post them to a course website or your institution's Learning Management System, directing students to this site through a hyperlink in the syllabus.

Presentation and Formatting

The way you organize your syllabus is entirely your choice, subject to external expectations. However, certain conventions can make the syllabus easier for students to read, understand, and use. Consider utilizing the following options rather than writing lengthy narrative paragraphs:

- Select a clear and legible font style and size.
- Use at least 1.15 line spacing and 1-inch margins.
- Utilize outline formatting, bullet points, tables, or charts rather than blocks of text
- Include:
  - Page numbers
  - Page breaks between different sections
  - Headers or titles for each section
  - Graphics, pictures, borders, highlighting, and/or colorful fonts (Suggestion: Many instructors use their school colors and official logo.)
  - Hyperlinks

Finally, it's very important to proofread and edit your syllabus thoroughly. Make sure that all of the dates are correct and that you've tested your hyperlinks. Your students and administrators will notice every misplaced punctuation mark or spelling error, which makes you look unprofessional.

All of the essential information for your course must appear on the syllabus, providing concrete evidence of your expectations.

In my work as a program consultant, one of the first things I do is to request copies of all of the instructors' syllabi. When the dates on these documents are 3 or more years in the past, they are full of spelling and grammatical errors, or the formatting is chaotic and difficult to navigate, it speaks volumes about the caliber of the program as a whole. The worse the syllabi, the more work will be necessary to enact program improvement. The better the syllabi, the stronger the program and the more professional the faculty, as well.

YOUR TURN: BUILD YOUR SYLLABUS

We now come to the very last step in course development—compiling all of the information and materials we've created in the previous chapters, shaping them into a comprehensive syllabus for your course.

If you've been using the tables provided in this book to format your outcomes, objectives, assignments, grading, and course schedule, it will be a simple matter to copy and paste these into your syllabus draft.

Identify	Ideate
Why should we look beyond the primary content of the course we're planning to incorporate 21st century connections to the liberal arts, entrepreneurship, and professional practice? Parents, students, and even our society at large expect more from higher education than ever before. We must uphold the value of the education we offer to students by making overt connections between our classrooms and students' eventual engagement in the professional sector.	How can we mobilize the transferable competencies of the liberal arts as they apply to our disciplines, inform students about entrepreneurial options for professional practice, and prepare them for successful engagement in the workplace they'll face after they graduate? None of these requirements is as daunting as they may seem. Look over your weekly plans and find points at which you can insert additional content into your lectures, modify planned assignments, or include practical experience that helps students to build crucial connections between theory and practice.
Iterate	Implement
When you plan your course and design your syllabus, you prepare yourself for success as an educator. Each time you teach the course, revise your syllabus to ensure that what you've learned as you taught the course in the preceding semester improves the next semester's teaching.	What you choose to include and exclude from your course has a considerable impact upon the educational experience you deliver to your students. You're not diverting your attention away from the content you need to teach when you develop a comprehensive plan that facilitates student connections—you're preparing them to mobilize their learning beyond the walls of your classroom. All of these choices are reflected in your syllabus, which is your best preparation for excellent teaching.

FIGURE 10.3 Chapter 10 Design Connection

Remember:

- Higher education is no longer the same as it was in previous decades. More is expected of us as educators than ever before. When we plan our courses with the future of our profession in mind, we not only help to ensure that our students receive the best possible educational experience that it is within our power to deliver, but to uphold the continuing value of our disciplines.
- Incorporating 21st century connections to career preparation, entrepreneurial opportunities, and to the intersections between the liberal arts and disciplinary practice equips students with transferable competencies that help to facilitate their success after graduation.
- Your syllabus must be as comprehensive as possible, including each of the areas we've discussed in this book. The better your prior planning, the more effective your instruction.

Notes

[1] Selingo, J. (2016). 2026 the decade ahead: The seismic shifts transforming the future of higher education. *Chronicle of Higher Education*.

[2] Haney, K. (August 15, 1998). The liberal arts and the end of education. *Paideia Project, Online*. Twentieth World Congress of Philosophy, Boston, MA. www.bu.edu/wcp/Papers/Educ/EducHane.htm

[3] Ireland, C. (June 6, 2013). Mapping the future. *Harvard Gazette*. http://news.harvard.edu/gazette/story/2013/06/mapping-the-future/

[4] Determining a comprehensive list of disciplines encompassed by terms such as *liberal arts* or *humanities* is problematic because each institution organizes them somewhat differently. The fields above are those often included among such designations but are not intended to be definitive.

[5] Aristotle. (date unknown). *Politics*, Book 1, section 1253a. Retrieved from the Tufts University Perseus Digital Library, Gregory R. Crane (ed.). www.perseus.tufts.edu/hopper/text?doc=Perseus%3Atext%3A1999.01.0058%3Abook%3D1%3Asection%3D1253a

[6] Rouse, M. (2016). What is the gig economy? *TechTarget*. http://whatis.techtarget.com/definition/gig-economy

[7] *Registered Nurse*. (2016). Best jobs: U.S. News rankings. http://money.usnews.com/careers/best-jobs/registered-nurse

[8] Krause, R. (February 23, 2017). This single dad created a Frizz-fighting product for the sweetest reason. *Refinery29.com*. www.refinery29.com/2017/02/142390/frizzy-hair-treatment-lubricity-father-daughter-story

[9] College Board. *Trends in higher education. Trends in college pricing. Complete list of figures and tables*. https://trends.collegeboard.org/college-pricing/figures-tables/list

[10] Birch, B. A. (October 12, 2011). Florida's Gov. Scott: We don't need more anthropologists. *Education News*. www.educationnews.org/higher-education/floridas-gov-scott-we-dont-need-more-anthropologists/

[11] Kiley, K. (January 30, 2013). Another liberal arts critic. *Inside Higher Ed*. www.insidehighered.com/news/2013/01/30/north-carolina-governor-joins-chorus-republicans-critical-liberal-arts

[12] Beam, A. (January 26, 2016). Kentucky Gov. Matt Bevin wants state colleges and universities to produce more electrical engineers and less French literature scholars. *U.S. News*. www.usnews.com/news/us/articles/2016-01-29/in-kentucky-a-push-for-engineers-over-french-lit-scholars

[13] Kiley, K. (January 30, 2013). Another liberal arts critic. *Inside Higher Ed*. www.insidehighered.com/news/2013/01/30/north-carolina-governor-joins-chorus-republicans-critical-liberal-arts

[14] Rappeport, A. (November 11, 2015). Philosophers (and welders) react to Marco Rubio debate comments. *New York Times*. www.nytimes.com/politics/first-draft/2015/11/11/philosophers-and-welders-react-to-marco-rubios-debate-comments/

[15] Osterwalder, A., Pigneur, Y., Bernarda, G., Smith, A., and Papadakos, T. (2014). *Value Proposition Design*. New York: Wiley.

[16] Gläscher, J., Rudrauf, D., Colom, R., Paul, L. K., Tranel, D., Damasio, H., and Adolphs, R. (February 22, 2010). The distributed neural system for general intelligence revealed by lesion mapping. *Proceedings of the National Academy of Sciences*. doi:10.1073/pnas.0910397107. www.sciencedaily.com/releases/2010/02/100222161843.htm

[17] Maslin, L. (2010). *The human memory: Memory encoding*. www.human-memory.net/processes_encoding.html

[18] If you only teach online, you may not have a physical office on campus. Students should be informed of this fact on the syllabus. Sometimes an adjunct or term-faculty member does not have an office, either. Students should likewise be informed of this fact and given specific information about how and when to contact the instructor.

Chapter 11

Becoming the Educator You Want to Be

CHAPTER SUMMARY

- Growth and Change
- Intention and Invitation
- Focus on the Positive
- Turn Theory Into Practice
- Persevere
- Have Faith

Being an outstanding researcher, noted scholar, or renowned practitioner doesn't automatically make someone an excellent educator. Like any other skill, teaching requires knowledge, practice, and a certain amount of aptitude.

Qualitative aspects of teaching are difficult to define. Educators can learn how plan for effective instruction, how to create a syllabus, or even how to write a quiz, but demonstrating empathy and compassion to students, and nurturing their curiosity and creativity even though they might take students in directions contrary to departmental norms are closely linked to our personalities as well as to our knowledge of best practices in teaching.

Faculty members occupy a highly coveted professional position—just think of the tens of thousands of new graduates every year who would do almost *anything* to have your job—and we wield enormous power over our students' learning and eventual career success. Although the ideas presented in this book might run contrary to your previous experience with teaching, implementing these instructional methods will make you a more accomplished educator and improve your students' experience in your classroom.

The longer you've been teaching, the more difficult you might find making substantive changes to your teaching practice to be. It's easy to become comfortable with the way we've done things, to rely on lessons and assignments we know to be tried and true. Change, on the other hand, is hard.

If you go into this adventure with your eyes wide open, expecting to be uncomfortable and understanding that you might sometimes be frustrated, you'll be better prepared to face the inevitable challenges that accompany any new initiative. However, you'll come to see the benefits of beginning with the end in mind as you implement these improvements to your teaching practice, and of keeping the big picture of ensuring your students' success in the forefront of every educational effort. You'll also contribute to the growth of your program, department, college, school, or university through the excellence of your teaching, which directly supports its institutional mission, vision, and values.

The purpose of this book has been to lead you gently through the daunting territory of curriculum planning, but it's no substitute for the personalized assistance you might need later on. Fortunately, there are many resources available. First, nearly all colleges and universities offer a Center for Teaching and Learning, Office of Faculty Development, or similar resource. Many of these are outstanding, staffed with helpful, knowledgeable people who are happy to assist you in this task. Next, if you're feeling good about the course you've designed using this book and don't think you need any extra help, you might still consider asking your administrator or a colleague to proofread and troubleshoot your syllabus with you. It's much better to find your typos and errors before you publish the document than to have your students point your mistakes out to you. Finally, your colleagues in the College of Education (or similar academic unit) might also be a good resource, since they possess a wealth of professional knowledge in pedagogical tasks such as lesson planning and curriculum development.

As we approach the end of our journey together, I'd like to leave you with a few additional words of inspiration.

GROWTH AND CHANGE

Change is hard. Growth, on the other hand, is built into nature, proceeding according to a mathematical formula known as the "Golden Section" or the "Fibonacci Sequence." We see this pattern in snail shells, the arrangement of seeds in the head of a sunflower, and even the swirls of hair on our own bodies. It's present across virtually all fields of human endeavor: mathematics, biology, philosophy, music, dance, theater, and art, among others. Even the galaxies reflect this powerful rhythm. The formula begins with zero, each new number then taking the number before a step farther, expanding ever more quickly with each successive step.[1]

$0 + 1 = 1$
$1 + 1 = 2$
$2 + 1 = 3$
$3 + 2 = 5$
$5 + 3 = 8$
$8 + 5 = 13$
$13 + 8 = 21$
$21 + 13 = 34$
$34 + 21 = 55$
$55 + 34 = 89$
$89 + 55 = 144$
And on it goes.

I find this sequence to be tremendously inspiring. We all start at zero, but when we take action—when we choose to move forward—each step we take builds on the one before; gaining momentum the farther we go. Imagine for a moment that you're about to begin a bike ride: You start from a standstill—that's zero. You need to expend extra strength and effort to begin to move the bicycle forward. Nevertheless, as you continue to pedal, each motion of your legs yields increasing kinetic energy, making your progress faster, more efficient, and more productive.

When you're stopped, inertia demands that you remain still. Your beginning efforts seem to go nowhere, and you wonder if you've made any progress at all (0, 1, 2, 3, 5). But if you press on, inertia quickly becomes your ally, carrying you forward even if you stop pedaling for a time (89, 144, 233, 377).

Change demands a deliberate act of will, but growth occurs in all living things. Right now, today, you might not be ready to change what you do as an educator. But you can *grow* even if you don't think you can change. You can take that first step. You can choose to act.

Growth and change exist in a paradoxical relationship, especially in higher education. We want to grow in our research or creative practice, to advance in rank, to increase our enrollment or expand our programs. If someone mentions change, however, it triggers our defenses. We dig in our heels and cling to our histories and traditions with all our might. Like growth, such paradox is a part of life. When we give to others, we receive benefits in return. When we lose one thing, we find something else. To become wise, we must first recognize our own lack of knowledge. The most exalted leaders are sometimes revealed to have feet of clay, while the most humble servants can rise to positions of power. No matter where you are in your personal journey, the capacity for growth resides within you—the power is yours to act, or not.

INTENTION AND INVITATION

Beyond our valuable professional contributions to knowledge and culture, the impact we have on our students can be even more profound. Over the duration of a typical career in the professorate, we might teach for 30 or more years. If we maintain a typical teaching load, we'll teach 5 courses per year, or 150 courses all told. For the sake of argument, let's say each of those courses has 20 students enrolled, bringing our tally to *3,000 students* whose lives we will affect in one way or another. If any of those 3,000 students moves on to a teaching position, this impact might increase exponentially. How do you want these students to remember you? As someone who encouraged them, inspired them, and set them on the path to a fulfilling career? Or as someone who didn't have time for them, was condescending and cold, or was more concerned with strict adherence to the policies on the syllabus than with the quality of their learning?

We communicate through more than our planned instruction. Everyday mannerisms such as our habitual tone of voice, word choice, and body language send a message to our students, whether we're aware of it or not. The same is true of both our deliberate and inadvertent approaches to pedagogical practice. We constantly invite or disinvite our students to learn, both intentionally and unintentionally. William Purkey (1991, 2015) categorizes these instructor behaviors as shown in Figure 11.1.[2]

Intentionally Disinviting
- Deliberately discouraging, verbally demeaning
- Too busy to take the time to assist students
- Focused on students' and colleagues' perceived shortcomings
- Actively seeking to harm, oppress, or discriminate against others

Unintentionally Disinviting
- Well-meaning, but condescending
- Focused on policies and procedures
- Oblivious to the feelings of others
- Rigidity: unwillingness to extend empathy or to make exceptions to stated policies

Unintentionally Inviting
- Well-liked
- Reasonably effective
- Inconsistent and uncertain when making decisions
- Able to explain what they do as teachers but not why they do it; unaware of the reasons behind success or failure

Intentionally Inviting
- Optimistic, respectful, trustworthy
- Affirming, while also guiding students
- Fluency in teaching to the point where it seems natural or effortless
- Focus on students and colleagues as whole people rather than merely the aspects we see in our classrooms and offices

FIGURE 11.1 Intention and Invitation

Purkey's ideas closely mirror several of the underlying premises of this book, with some additional advice we would all be wise to remember.

- Treat all persons respectfully and encourage them to reach for high aspirations; oppose discrimination or oppression in all its forms.
- Engage in continuous professional development; never allow ourselves to remain stale and static in our work as educators.
- Build relationships such as spending time with colleagues socially; practice politeness; celebrate our students' and colleagues' successes; develop appropriate rapport with students.
- Allow ourselves sufficient rest, exercise, and recreation that fuel our abilities to live our lives more fully.

The pace of life in the 21st century is increasingly hectic. We're beleaguered with duties and responsibilities, and we never have enough time to do everything we think we must do, which makes slowing down to have coffee with a colleague or to engage in personal recreation seem like a frivolous waste of our precious time. Perhaps it's a remnant of our Puritan heritage that we place a greater value on hard work and personal achievement than on the actual quality of our lives as a whole. Yes, we should devote the same level of professional energy and curiosity to our teaching as we do to our research and creative practice. Teaching should never take a backseat to our other professional obligations. Nevertheless, we cannot allow either activity to subvert what's truly important in life: Our relationships with others and treating ourselves with the same care and respect that we would show to someone whom we value.

FOCUS ON THE POSITIVE

From Norman Vincent Peale's *The Power of Positive Thinking* (1952)[3] to Shawn Achor's *The Happiness Advantage* (2010), psychologists have explored the powerful impact of our thoughts on our quality of life. Achor delivered one of the most-watched TED Talks in the organization's history,[4] explaining that our deeply held belief that hard work leads to success, and success then makes us happy, is fundamentally wrong. Rather, happiness fuels success by making us more creative, increasing our motivation, and enhancing our productivity.

Our mindset powerfully shapes our reality. If we focus on what's good in our lives, we see our lives as good. If we devote more attention to what's wrong, we then think everything is bad. Of course, each of us experiences both good and bad in our lives. In every class we teach, some of our actions as instructors will turn out wonderfully. A lecture really hits the mark with our students, they surpass our expectations on an assignment or exam, or they give us outstanding end-of-course evaluations. Naturally, the reverse is also true. We'll deliver a lecture that

253

falls flat, students turn in terrible assignments that make us think nobody listened to a word of our instructions, or they say and do things we find to be unbelievably infuriating. If we choose to focus on the annoyances, disappointments, or just general stress of teaching, then we can't be effective instructors. Instead, we should focus our minds on the positive aspects of our jobs, allowing us to become the kind of inspiring, motivational, and positive role models that our students will remember throughout their lives. Think back to your own experiences as a student: Did you learn best in the classrooms of sour, grouchy professors? Or were your best learning experiences in the classrooms of professors who conveyed infectious optimism?

TURN THEORY INTO PRACTICE

Our ability to enact the goals we set for ourselves depends greatly upon our level of motivation. Human nature dictates that we'll usually take the path of least resistance unless we have strong reasons to do otherwise. How many of us spend New Year's Eve making well-intentioned resolutions that we fail to keep for even a few weeks? We know intellectually that we should eat more healthfully, exercise daily, go to bed earlier, and any number of other worthy goals. Until we establish these intentions as habits, however, they're nearly impossible to sustain. The same is true of our professional lives. We might resolve to become better educators, but we're not always able to put these worthy intentions into practice

The secret is to break our goals into manageable portions. Acclaimed author Stephen King said, "*Write* a page a *day*—only *300 words*—and in a *year, you have written* a novel." Similarly, there's an old adage that suggests, "How do you eat an elephant? One bite at a time." If we want to transform our curriculum and instruction, we can't expect to jump directly to the end of the process—we only need to complete one task at a time. Try just one of the suggestions in this book during the next course you teach. Work just one new strategy for engaged learning into each week of your plans. Try adding one new assignment, writing one new exam, or implementing any given suggestion or strategy each week. If you make continuous improvement a habit, you'll eventually become the outstanding instructor you intend to be.

PERSEVERE

Becoming as accomplished an educator as you are within your field of disciplinary expertise is no easy task, requiring a significant outlay of your valuable time and attention. It's not something that comes naturally to most of us. C. S. Lewis wrote,

> As long as you notice, and have to count, the steps, you are not yet dancing but only learning to dance. A good shoe is a shoe you don't notice. Good

reading becomes possible when you need not consciously think about eyes, or light, or print, or spelling.[5]

Although Lewis was speaking of another subject, his remarks are quite appropriate to good teaching. When we observe a highly skilled teacher, we don't notice the syllabus, the schedule of assignments, or the instructional technologies used in a lecture. Our attention turns, instead, to the students' rapt attention to the lesson, the excellence of the students' coursework, and their achievements after graduation.

HAVE FAITH

At present, most of us are still counting the steps and learning this dance. Our work together will help you through this process. But just as our instruction in every class must begin with the end in mind by structuring all that we do around our outcomes and objectives, so too must our approach to professional pedagogical practice. As educators, our specific goal is to equip students to achieve competence in our academic disciplines. *That* is the end we must always bear in mind.

Each of us possesses the power to become a better instructor today than we were yesterday, and we can be better tomorrow than we are today. Every day

Identify ⟶	Ideate Identify
Why should we decide to grow as educators? We strive to improve in our research or creative practice, so our teaching deserves an equal share of our professional energies.	How can we become better educators? Every journey begins with just one step. Each time we implement a new best practice, we continue along this path.
Identify Iterate	⟵ Identify Implement
When we teach, we have an advantage over many other professions because every semester, every new course, is a chance to begin again. We learn from our successes and failures as educators and constantly apply this knowledge to each successive teaching experience. The design mindset of continuous iteration is well known to educators who shun the natural tendency to simply repeat the same approach ad infinitum. Rather, we engage in repeated iteration so that we keep our growth spiral going.	What can I do to get started? Choose one area from among all of those we've discussed. Given our philosophy of "backwards design," it might be best to start with your outcomes and objectives, since these drive all of our course-planning tasks. Once those are completed, think about how you'll assess your students' learning. By following the sequence of actions in this book, you'll eventually become a more skillful educator than you were before you began.

FIGURE 11.2 Chapter 11 Design Connection

presents a fresh opportunity to apply what we've learned to engage in the continuous professional improvement that leads us step by step toward achieving greater excellence. By making the choice to employ a growth mindset to our work as educators, just as much as we seek to grow and improve in other areas of our professional lives, we will eventually become the outstanding educators we hope to be.

Remember:

- The tendency to remain stale and static is strong, but we can combat this law of physics by embracing the equally strong mandate to grow.
- Positivity, perseverance, and faith in our own potential for growth will ensure that we are able to meet our goals.
- Each of us can become a more skillful educator than we were before—it is merely up to us to act upon this knowledge.

Notes

[1] Parveen, N. (n.d.). *Fibonacci in nature.* University of Georgia, Department of Mathematics. http://jwilson.coe.uga.edu/emat6680/parveen/fib_nature.htm

[2] Purkey, W. (February 1991). *What is invitational education and how does it work?* Presentation at the International Conference on Self-Esteem, Santa Clara, CA. ERIC Number: ED334488; see also Purkey, W. W., and Novak, J. M. (2015). *An introduction to invitational theory.* The International Alliance for Invitational Education. www.invitationaleducation. net/

[3] Peale, N. V. (1952). *The Power of Positive Thinking.* New York: Fawcett Crest.

[4] Achor, S. (2010). *The Happiness Advantage: The Seven Principles of Positive Psychology That Fuel Success and Performance at Work.* New York: Crown Business. See also *TEDxBloomington— Shawn Achor—The happiness advantage: Linking positive brains to performance.* (June 30, 2011). www.youtube.com/watch?v=GXy__kBVq1M

[5] Lewis, C. S. (1963, 2004). *Letters to Malcolm: Chiefly on Prayer.* Orlando, FL: Harcourt, Inc., p. 2.

Epilogue

In the final hours of editing this book for publication, I received a new report from the *Chronicle of Higher Education* titled, "What Graduates Need to Succeed: Colleges and Employers Weigh In" (2017).[1] It contains all sorts of interesting facts and figures about the skills and competencies employers think students should possess upon graduation, identifying a notable gap between how colleges and universities judge their performance in preparing students for graduation and how industry, writ-large, judges our graduates' career readiness. Of course, all of this is fascinating, but the real point is this study confirms the assertions I've made throughout this book.

We must rethink our curriculum and instruction. Pedagogical practices dependent on unstudied, deficiently designed, static standards of the past are increasingly irrelevant to today's students. In addition to the disciplinary depth and breadth we provide, our students emphatically need new skills and competencies to be competitive in today's job market. Furthermore, design thinking, systems thinking, effective communication, entrepreneurship, creativity, collaboration, and critical thinking are not only essential to our students' education, but these skills and competencies are essential for all of us in higher education. Among other things, this book is dedicated to that holistic proposition.

With every good wish,

Bruce M. Mackh, PhD

Note

[1] Bourbon, J. (2017). What graduates need to succeed: Colleges and employers weigh in. Maguire Associates, sponsored by Workday. *The Chronicle of Higher Education*. http://iris.nyit.edu/~shartman/graduates.pdf

Index

Note: Page numbers in *italics* denote references to Figures.

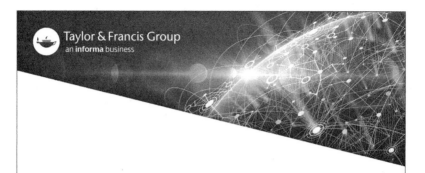